Malise Ruthven, described by the *Guardian* as 'one of today's most perceptive observers and historians of religion', is internationally recognised for his work on Muslim thought and theology, fundamentalism, the social impact of religion and migration and the nexus between contemporary politics and belief. His many books include *The Divine Supermarket: Travels in Search of the Soul of America* (Tauris Parke Paperbacks, 2012) and *Mormonism: An Introduction* (I.B.Tauris, forthcoming).

'Malise Ruthven is the leading British authority on modern Islam. His books are essential for understanding what is going on in the Middle East today, and *Encounters with Islam* is an ideal entrée to his thinking on some vital issues.' – **Robert Irwin**

'There is no better guide to analysing and explaining the West's long engagement with Islam than Malise Ruthven. Accessible and – even more importantly – brilliantly judicious, his latest book is ever careful in this most treacherous of territories filled as it is with myth and fear. Here is a magisterial overview to help us understand these recent years of violent confrontation and stubborn misunderstanding. We have much to be grateful for in Ruthven's wise insights.' – **Madeleine Bunting, the Guardian**

'Malise Ruthven has spent a lifetime studying Islam: as a cultural force, its role in politics, its place in international relations, and its place in ordinary people's lives. No one has been more consistent and persistent in trying to understand the wider forces which have shaped Islam's role and presence in the modern world; and fewer still have been so successful in educating the rest of us. It is therefore with great pleasure that I hold a copy of Malise's *Encounters with Islam* in my hand: he is as readable and instructive as ever!' – **Anoush Ehteshami, Nasser Al-Sabah Professor of International Relations, Durham University**

'Over the last decade Malise Ruthven has consolidated his position as one of our most consistently stimulating and sophisticated writers on contemporary religion in general and Islam in particular. The essays here are as wide-ranging, versatile and intellectually curious as they are well-written, witty and constantly surprising. In a crowded field Ruthven remains way ahead of the pack.' – **William Dalrymple**

MALISE RUTHVEN

ENCOUNTERS WITH ISLAM

ON RELIGION, POLITICS AND MODERNITY

I.B. TAURIS

LONDON · NEW YORK

Published in 2012 by I.B.Tauris & Co. Ltd
6 Salem Road, London W2 4BU
175 Fifth Avenue, New York NY 10010
www.ibtauris.com

Distributed in the United States and Canada Exclusively by Palgrave Macmillan
175 Fifth Avenue, New York NY 10010

Library of Modern Religion: 24

ISBN   978 1 78076 023 0 (HB)
          978 1 78076 024 7 (PB)

A full CIP record for this book is available from the British Library
A full CIP record is available from the Library of Congress

Library of Congress Catalog Card Number: available

Designed and typeset by 4word Ltd, Bristol
Printed and bound by TJ International Ltd, Padstow, Cornwall

Contents

Introduction

There may be a corner of Purgatory, unremarked by Dante, where those of us who have worked in journalism and the media will be required to review a lifetime's hack-work and to confess our intellectual sins before being admitted to Paradise. In preparing reviews and articles for this book – the product of some 30 years' observation and commentary on Islam and the Middle East – I have striven to pre-empt the recording angel by weeding out banalities and fits of intemperance before he (or she, or it) gets to see it, and confronts me with some horribly embarrassing copy.

As a scriptwriter at the BBC World Service, I was required to make programmes and write commentaries on a wide variety of topics – domestic politics, economic and industrial issues, even theatre and the arts – as well as Arab and Islamic questions. I am aware of how wonderfully approaching deadlines – symbolised by the hands of the synchronised clocks that still surface, unmelted, in my dreams – serve to concentrate the mind, forcing words into consciousness, on to the page and from there into the microphone. But I also recognise that the demands of the media are ephemeral, and that true comprehension is not to be found on the spotlit surface of events, but rather in the deeper human structures and configurations that we think of as cultures. For a writer, radio has its virtues. The greatest of these is the imperative of clarity, based on a simple, technological fact: while a reader can re-read a sentence on the page of a book or newspaper, the listener doesn't get a second chance. But radio also has its drawbacks: the medium is by definition transient – 'in one ear, and out the other' as the saying goes.

In my case, the search for clarity of phrasing – however imperfectly realised – has been matched by a quest for understanding. When it comes to Islam and the Middle East, this cannot be achieved without some heavy intellectual spadework: a knowledge, however inadequate, of its languages; a grasp of its history and its anthropologies; a recognition that religious experiences and identities are meaningful for some people; and a sufficient awareness of one's own culture to be able to make meaningful correspondences between different cultural systems, so that terms and concepts that seem alien are not entirely 'lost in translation'.

In approaching the Islamic world, my preliminary spadework was not the mandatory university course, but rather a spell of living alongside the Huwaitat Bedouin in southern Jordan during my 'gap year' before attending university, and a year of Arabic study at the Foreign Office-funded Middle East Centre for Arab Studies (MECAS) at Shemlan, in Lebanon, after I had graduated from Cambridge (in English Literature). MECAS, where the Foreign Office trained its Arabists, was widely known as 'the spy school'. The locals assumed that the place, set in the splendid hills overlooking Beirut airport, was some kind of James Bond establishment, where we learned the black arts of seduction, cryptology and murder (if only…). I recall an uncomfortable conversation with a taxi driver who took me to downtown Beirut, half an hour's drive from Shemlan:

'You're at the spy school, madrasat-al jassousiyya,' he said.

'Nonsense,' I replied, 'It's just a place where they teach you Arabic.'

'OK,' he said, 'What about Kim Filibee and Georgie Blake?'

The cabbie was well-informed. Before his defection to the Soviet Union, the spy Kim Philby, who had worked as a correspondent in Beirut, had close associations with the school. George Blake, who fled to the USSR in 1966 after escaping from Wormwood Scrubs Prison, where he was serving a 42-year sentence for espionage, had actually been picked up at MECAS by Special Branch detectives.

'Wrong team,' I tried to explain. 'Both were working for the other side.'

My sojourns in Jordan and Lebanon were informative, but only the beginning of a quest for understanding. Arabic and other Muslim languages may help, but they are not sufficient for embracing the phenomenology of Islam, or the rich mosaic of Muslim ideas and societies, in an increasingly complex, globalised world. As I suggest in my critique of Bernard Lewis (see page 24) the textual knowledge or 'coal-face scholarship' of which he is such a distinguished example can actually be misleading, unless it is accompanied by a certain empathy and the intellectual humility that comes with a willingness to learn from non-textual human sources (including those conveyed by the social scientists and anthropologists whom Lewis clearly disparages).

'Why Islam?' I used to be asked. 'Are you a Muslim?' a BBC colleague queried, evidently bemused at the thought that anyone outside the Islamic faith community could find the Islamic world interesting or exhibit some knowledge about it. It may be the case that expertise on aspects of Christianity – New Testament scholarship, for example – is largely restricted to believers or professionals who belong to the faith, but the fact remains that Christianity in a wider sense, as a dominant belief system that leaves vast residues in literature, art, architecture and music, remains a pervasive presence in our Western culture. Islam (by contrast) is configured in most Western peoples' minds as 'other'. (The American historian, Richard Bulliet, addresses this issue in one of the books reviewed in these pages.) Because our (Western) culture is received without question, absorbed, as it were, by osmosis, the idea that a monumental statue, or classical portico, or even a nude centrefold spread from a girlie magazine may appear 'Christian' to the non-occidental, simply never occurs to us.

In the West, when we use words such as Christianity or Christian, the assumption may be that we are talking mainly about matters relating to people of faith, a presupposition that is reflected in our use of words such as Islam and Islamic. As a consequence, it becomes all too easy to confuse cultural engagement with belief and belonging. There is a world 'out there' comprising approximately a fifth of humanity and its variegated cultures, which is informed in some cases by Islamic beliefs and practices, but is not necessarily religious.

The great American historian, Marshall Hodgson (1922–68), whose three-volume masterwork, *The Venture of Islam: Conscience and History in a World Civilization*, published posthumously in 1974, has been a major influence on my thinking, tried to address this problem by distinguishing between phenomena he described as Islamic (pertaining to the religion) and those he described as Islamicate (deriving from regions where Muslims were culturally dominant, but not necessarily based on religion). Thus poetry celebrating wine can be described as Islamicate, but not Islamic.

Hodgson's terminology – he was a great coiner of new terms, which he hoped would avoid the generally Eurocentric bias infecting the study of Islam – has never really caught on, except in some academic circles, but the distinction remains an important one. It informs many of the books – and my essays about them – that feature in the following pages. For example, in critiquing Christopher Caldwell's account of the threat posed by Muslim immigrants in Europe (see page 187), I suggest that he makes assumptions about Muslims as believers that may be exaggerated. Virtually everyone living in Western countries celebrates Christmas, yet only a minority go to church – and a significant part of that minority may be once-a-year attendees who have only a vestigial connection with Christian beliefs. The same applies, a fortiori, to attendance at weddings and funerals. Muslims who observe Ramadan or the big religious festivals may be conforming, like regular Christmas-observers, to long entrenched social patterns. The suggestion that such observance implies strenuously held religious beliefs is clearly overdrawn.

None of this means, of course, that there are no dangers posed by Islamic radicalism, or that Islamic belief systems are somehow innocent of atrocities committed using Islamic references. The following pages include extensive review articles written in the wake of the 11 September 2001 attacks on New York and Washington, DC. A more detailed expression of my thoughts will be found in *A Fury for God: The Islamist Attack on America* (Granta Books, 2002/3) The point to make here is that Islamic labels can serve to mobilise and legitimise. They form an extensive part of the political repertory. 'Islam' – to express this crudely – serves as a kind of 'branding', an argument made, in a different context, by Carl Ernst in his critique of a Pakistan High Court judgment, where 'Islam' is compared to Coca-Cola (see page 7). My argument, in *A Fury for God*, is that the ideology needs to be distinguished from the labels used to 'brand' it. This has an important bearing on discussion about the much abused term 'Islamo-fascism' which I have been accused of coining.

I plead guilty to having used the term, in an article in *The Independent* newspaper in 1990, in a glancing reference to the authoritarian regimes that are now being challenged by protestors throughout the Arab region. I doubt if I was the first person to use this term, though I did not consciously borrow it from anyone else. It has stuck to me (like the proverbial albatross) because internet search engines largely stop at 1990, when 'wiki-history', as it were, began. Usages prior to that time are lost in the dust of libraries.

There may be parallels between today's Islamists and 1930s fascists but, I would argue, the differences are more compelling. Fascist movements require organisation, discipline, a unified leadership and a monopoly over the ideology. It may be the case that some Islamic movements – such as the Egyptian Muslim Brotherhood – exhibit the first three qualities, but I would argue that sustaining a monopoly over the ideology – in this case, the interpretation of Islam, is an impossibility. The discourses of Islam, like those of other religions, are too rich and varied to allow themselves to be welded into a single doctrinal system. The dangers facing Muslim societies at the present time come from anarchy, on one side, and a restored authoritarian rule on the other. 'Islam' is not the danger – but neither is it the solution.

Saint Jacques de Néhou, France

Part One

A Clash of Civilisations?

On the face of it, the attacks on New York and Washington, DC on 11 September 2001 (termed subsequently '9/11') seemed to vindicate the thesis originating with the influential Princeton scholar, Bernard Lewis, and popularised by the Harvard political scientist, Samuel Huntington, that a 'clash of civilisations' was looming between 'Islam' and 'the West'. Without rejecting Huntington completely, I found his position simplistic. There may be conflicts of values between what might broadly be called Western and Islamic cultures, particularly over issues such as gender roles and sexual display, while there are numerous disputes over land and resources between Muslims and non-Muslims in many parts of the world, where 'defending Islam' can become a rallying point. But it is wrong, I believe, to subsume a wide variety of conflicts involving different ethnicities and competing value systems into a single headline-grabbing 'clash of civilisations' comparable to the Cold War standoff between the West and the Soviet Union.

All the review essays in Part 1 of this book address the 'clash of civilisations' thesis, and ensuing debates about Islam from different perspectives. While anthropologist, Jack Goody, and historian, Richard Bulliet, reveal the commonalities between Islamic and Western cultures and civilisations, Carl Ernst exposes the complicity between the Western media and some Islamic authorities in fostering images of bigotry and intolerance at the expense of the 'squeezed middle' of Islam comprising more nuanced, tolerant and mystical interpretations of the faith. Tariq Ramadan, the controversial Swiss-born Muslim professor, whose grandfather, Hasan al-Banna, founded the Muslim Brotherhood, argues against the ghettoisation of Muslims living in Western countries, urging them, rather, to become models of responsible citizenship. Bruce Lawrence, an expert on the militancies that cross religious boundaries, finds evidence to support Ramadan's position in the professional attainments and business success of South-Asian-born immigrants – many, if not the majority, of them Muslim – now living in the United States. On a related but highly controversial theme, my review of Fred Donner's pioneering book about Islamic origins aimed to inform sophisticated American readers that, contrary to the received accounts of Muhammad's career that dominate the textbooks, revisionist versions exist. These have suggestive affinities with the 'higher criticism' of the Bible that troubles conservative Protestant believers, in the same way as their Muslim counterparts are unhappy. Before writing this review I searched in vain for John Wansbrough's name in the New York Review of Books' electronic database. It seems extraordinary that the scholar whose path-breaking textual studies launched an impassioned debate about Islamic origins in the 1970s was so little known in the country of his birth.

The essay Politics and the Prophet, published in 1996, features anthropologist Michael Gilsenan's superb account of the patriarchal culture in a Lebanese Muslim village – a book that dents the Huntington thesis, since, far from being specific to Islam, the values of masculine honour it describes could equally be found in Sicily or the Balkans. The passages covering a new publishing venture – the Oxford Encyclopedia of the Modern Islamic World – and the late Fred Halliday's essay on the 'myth of confrontation' challenge the Huntington thesis more directly. In a brilliant formulation, Halliday exposes the unspoken intellectual complicity between 'Huntingtonians' and militant 'Islamists'. Complicity of a more menacing kind completes this section, with a review of A Brutal Friendship: The West and the Arab Elite, in which Said Aburish, a foremost Arab journalist, shows how the Western arms industry, abetted by greedy oil consumers, keeps the gerontocratic Al Saudi dynasty in power, along with other Arab dictatorships now threatened by the uprisings of the 'Arab Spring'.

1

Muamalat: Islamic Obligations at Home and Abroad

Since 11 September 2001, barely a day has passed without stories about 'Islam' – the religion of about one-fifth of humanity, as noted earlier – appearing in the media. The terrorists who hijacked four American airliners and flew them into the World Trade Center in New York, and the Pentagon near Washington, DC, killing some 3,000 people, not only unleashed a 'War on Terrorism' by the United States and its allies, but also led to the removal of two Muslim governments, in Afghanistan and Iraq. They raised the profile of 'Islam' throughout the world as a subject for analysis and discussion. The debates, in newspaper columns and broadcasting studios, in cafés, bars and homes, have been heated and passionate. Questions that were previously discussed only in the rarefied atmosphere of academic conferences or graduate seminars have entered the mainstream of public consciousness. What is the 'Law of *Jihad*'? How is it that a 'religion of peace' subscribed to by millions of ordinary, decent believers can become an ideology of hatred for an angry minority? Why has 'Islam' since the fall of communism become so freighted with passionate intensity?

Such questions are no longer 'academic', but of vital concern to all the peoples of this planet. That 'Islam', or some variation of it – whether distorted, perverted, corrupted or hijacked by extremists – has become a force to be reckoned with, or at least a label attached to a phenomenon with menacing potentialities, is undeniable. Numerous atrocities have been attributed to and claimed by extremists, both before and since 9/11, causing mayhem and carnage in many of the world's cities and tourist destinations: Nairobi, Dar es Salaam, Mombasa, Riyadh, Casablanca, Bali, Moscow, Tunisia, Jakarta, Mumbai, Istanbul, London, Madrid: the list grows longer, and the casualties mount. The responses of governments and the consequences of these responses for international peace and security should be enough to convince anyone that extremist manifestations of Islam are setting the agenda for discourse and action in the twenty-first century.

Muslims living in the West, and in the growing areas of the Muslim world that come within the West's electronic footprint, understandably resent the negative exposure that comes with the increasing concerns of outsiders. Islam, it is said, is a pacific religion of peace: the word Islam, an Arabic verbal noun meaning submission (to God) is etymologically related to the word salam, meaning peace. Westerners who have accused Islam of being a violent religion, it is said, misunderstand its pacific nature. Attaching the label 'Muslim' or 'Islamic' to acts of terrorism is a gross distortion: when Timothy McVeigh blew up the US Federal Building in Oklahoma City, killing 168 people, the worst atrocity committed on American soil before 9/11, he was not described as being 'Christian' despite his links to a fundamentalist, white supremacist church. In the view of many of Islam's adherents, 'Westerners' who have abandoned their own faith, or are blinkered by religious prejudice, do not 'understand' Islam, their views are distorted by a hostile media, their attitudes are prejudiced by Islamophobia – the equivalent of anti-Semitism being applied to Muslims rather than Jews.

All four of the books under review are seeking to address the negative images of Islam and Muslims since 9/11, and to balance news reports of terrorist atrocities by citing or advocating positive examples of Muslim creativity, adaptability and commitment to social change. In his broad-ranging survey of Islam in Europe, Jack Goody argued that, while Islam is often regarded as 'other', it is in fact intrinsic to the religious tradition of Western monotheism found in both Judaism and Christianity. Instead of regarding Islam as an alien socio-cultural tradition, Europeans should recognise it as an integral part of their past. Long before Muslims from Turkey, Pakistan and North Africa became indispensable to the labour forces of Germany, Britain and France, they were transforming the agriculture of Sicily and Andalusia, introducing commodities, such as paper, to Europe, and transmitting many of the ideas of philosophy, mathematics and the sciences that made possible the rise of modern Europe. While many of the examples cited by Goody are well known, at a time when American neo-conservatives are attempting to impose their own questionable version of 'democracy' on the Middle East by the use of military force, it is good to be reminded that the idea of Islam as 'other' once contained a positive charge: when Enlightenment philosophers such as Montesquieu and Voltaire looked to the East in order to burnish their critiques of absolutism at home. Sir Adolphus Slade, who served in the Ottoman navy during the 1820s, marvelled that the Ottoman subject, from the lowliest of origins 'might aspire without presumption to the rank of pasha', and concluded that 'the Osmanley has enjoyed by custom some of the dearest privileges of free men, for which Christian nations have so long struggled'.

As an anthropologist, Goody takes his readers into areas often ignored by writers schooled in the discourse of 'Islam versus the West'. Rather than simply condemning the destruction of the Bamiyan Buddhas by the Taliban as the typically barbaric act of Islamic fundamentalist fanatics, he contextualises this egregious act of vandalism within the broader traditions of iconoclasm to be found in the West Asian monotheisms as well as in Buddhism itself during its earliest phase. 'Doing away with the image ... resolves or avoids the whole problem of the material manifestation of the spiritual, and more specifically of humans creating gods rather than gods creating humans.' Goody suggests that, while trade, intermarriage and the processes of cultural exchange have been sources of innovation and creativity, religion as such has often been balefully divisive: there was more harmony between Europeans and Arabs than between Christians and Muslims. During the Spanish Reconquista, 'poets on either side were largely spared. We hear of the killing of Arabs learned in religious law, but not of those who were more learned in secular accomplishments'. Goody's is a wide-ranging and somewhat eclectic overview, containing flashes of insight into unfamiliar corners of history. A surprising omission is that, in examining Islamic and European societies, he avoids discussing the crucial area of kinship, the subject he addressed so revealingly in his indispensable 1983 essay, *The Development of the Family and Marriage in Europe*.

Writing in the United States in the aftermath of 9/11, when Islamophobia was rife in university campuses and state legislatures, Carl Ernst confronts the negative stereotyping of Islam much more directly:

> *No respectable authorities defend anti-Semitism anymore, and there is a widespread consensus that insulting statements and stereotypes about Jews are both factually incorrect and morally reprehensible, whether in reference to physical appearance or behavior. Yet at the same time, it is commonly accepted among educated people that Islam is a religion that by definition oppresses women and encourages violence.*

While sharing Goody's view that negative views of Islam are partly the result of a spin-off from the Arab–Israeli conflict, Ernst attributes the entrenched pro-Israeli attitudes of most Americans as much to Protestantism as to the lobbying activities of American Jews. Israeli authorities have found it expedient to encourage Christian fundamentalists who believe in biblical prophesies predicting the destruction of Muslim monuments in Jerusalem and the coming of the Messiah, 'despite the demise of Judaism envisioned in these apocalyptic scenarios'. In the face of media treatment of conflicts which suggest that violence is in some way inherent in the Muslim faith, Ernst points out, 'we do not hear any similar accusations about intrinsic violence in Christianity or European culture' or what it was about Christianity that motivated the world conquests of the nineteenth century, or such recent atrocities as the massacre of 6,000 Bosnian Muslims by Orthodox Serbs. Like the late Edward Said, Ernst sees the media, with its addiction to sound-bites and adversarial confrontations, as being largely to blame for such distortions: 'When a religious extremist tells a television reporter that Islam requires holy war against the infidel West, this prescriptive minority view ... suddenly acquires an authority from the media that it could never attain within its own social context.' According to Ernst, the exclusivist zeal of the Islamist radicals is abetted by the Protestant filter through which most Americans view the Islamic world: the self-taught Salafiyya reformists who abjure traditional scholarship are the mirror images of the fire-breathing missionaries and fundamentalists who dominate many Protestant denominations, driving the world towards the 'clash of civilisations' embarked on by the neo-conservatives in Iraq.

In seeking to restore a sense of proportion and balance to the image of Islam for his Western readers, Ernst gives proper weight to the layers of mystical humanism, philosophical speculation and hermeneutical flexibility that are no less a part of the Islamic tradition than the legacies of conquest and militancy. He also points out that intolerance and bigotry are far from being the exclusive prerogative of the Western media. An example of Islamic bigotry he cites at some length would be comical, were not its implications so pernicious. The Ahmadiyya sect, a wholly peaceful movement dedicated to the proseletysing of Islam, is active in many countries. The sect is persecuted in Pakistan because of government rulings denying the Ahmadis the right to call themselves Muslims. If they do so they are liable to criminal charges, including imprisonment. On most matters of ritual and belief, the Ahmadis are orthodox. They differ from other Muslims – or are alleged to differ, because the claims and counter-claims in this area are ambiguous and contested – over the question of the 'finality' of Muhammad's prophethood, believing that their founder Murza Ghulam Ahmed (d. 1908) might have had prophetic powers, or a prophetic status, on a par with that of Muhammad. On the basis of such claims, the Pakistani courts have legally deprived the Ahmadis of the right to call themselves Muslims on the grounds that certain religious terms (such as 'mosque', the 'call to prayer' and the 'profession of faith') are peculiar to 'Islam' as defined by legislation enacted with the specific purpose of excluding the Ahmadis. In its 1993 majority ruling, the Supreme Court of Pakistan made a curious analogy with the law on trademarks and copyrights. For the Pakistani judges, 'Islam' is in effect a product, like Coca-Cola. Since Islam is the state religion of Pakistan, the courts have the right – the duty even – to protect its 'logo' (as well as its spiritual recipes) from being pirated by 'imposters'. As Ernst observes:

> The implications of this decision are breathtaking. Not only is a religion being defined as a commodity or piece of property, which the judge actually compared to Coca-Cola, but also the courts – not the religious communities – are entitled to decide what is essential to any religion. Moreover in this decision the limits of Islam are being defined in relation to a modern sectarian group.

A similar outlook of narrow intolerance has been inculcated into students in Saudi Arabia, who were told in lesson after lesson that a good Muslim living among foreigners 'must feel deeply inside hatred for them, their religion and everything they represent' (The New York Times, 24 November 2003). The Saudi government, sensitive to the charge that it allowed its religious leaders to foster a climate of anti-Western hatred (as well as hatred of other Muslims, especially Shi'a, who do not share the tenets of Wahhabism) only recently excised this passage from its 10th grade text books. Fifteen of the 19 suicide hijackers of 9/11 were Saudi citizens.

The climate of intolerance that generates violence is fully addressed by Tariq Ramadan in his ambitiously titled Western Muslims and the Future of Islam. A grandson of Hasan al-Banna, founder of the Muslim Brotherhood, Ramadan has become something of a cult figure among European Muslims, who attend his public lectures in droves. His latest book is nothing less than a comprehensive rethink of the Islamic tradition to accommodate the realities facing European Muslims and, by extension, their counterparts in the North American diaspora. Ramadan's approach is systematic and uncompromising. Adopting the classical methodology or approach to the sources forged by the religious scholars during the formative era of Islam, he makes a fundamental distinction between the religious duties of Muslims and their social and political obligations. While the former (including prayers, fasting during Ramadan, payments to charity, and the once-in-a-lifetime performance of the pilgrimage to Mecca) are non-negotiable, all other duties derived from the Qur'an and the corpus of Islamic law are contingent on the wider socio-political environment.

Ramadan's book appears to be addressed to Muslim rather than to non-Muslim readers. His writing is prescriptive rather than analytical. Muslims, he informs us, must avoid things that are forbidden under Islamic law, but permitted under Western legislation, such as alcohol, soft drugs, interest derived from financial dealings, and extramarital sexual relations. In the area of muamalat (social obligations), according to his analysis of the divine text of the Qur'an,

> almost never allows itself, alone, to lay down a universal principle. It is the human being that derives both absolute and relative principles, as appropriate, from the Text and from the reality of the context in which it was revealed.

On the basis of his methodology, Ramadan takes his grandfather's Salafist followers to task for encouraging Muslims living in the West to develop a ghetto mentality; for example, by adopting dress codes that set them apart from their host societies. Instead, they should strive to engage with the majority communities by setting a good example and influencing public policies that reflect Islamic values. While he is stronger on the principles than the details (there is no discussion, for example, about a distinctively Muslim approach to questions that vex other religious communities, such as abortion, homosexuality and the artificial prolongation of human life) he marks out the political territory he sees as appropriate. If Muslims living in Western countries 'are truly with God their life must bear witness to a permanent engagement and infinite self-giving in the cause of social justice, the well-being of humankind, ecology and solidarity in all its manifestations'. If this sounds rather vague, if not ambiguous, he is more specific when stating that 'to work for a multinational that plunders the planet, or in an armaments industry that produces death, or for banks that fuel a murderous economic order is not "to say nothing"'. He concludes that Islam is definitely opposed ideologically to the neo-liberal capitalist policies currently in the ascendant, and that Muslims living in 'the system's head' have a greater responsibility than their co-religionists in the poorer parts of the globe to propose solutions. For Ramadan, a Swiss citizen, toleration of Muslims is no longer in question: their agenda must be to win respect: 'Western Muslims are at home, and should not only say so but feel so. There is no longer a place of origin from which they are exiled or distanced.'

Ramadan's prescriptive neo-orthodoxy may raise the hackles of both traditionalists and separatists and militants who share (with their fundamentalist Christian and Jewish counterparts) the apocalyptic dream of 'restoring' the good society under the rule of God. For the moderate majority, however, it offers a middle way between radicalism and traditionalism, with a powerful emphasis on social commitment and (within limits) local patriotism. Muslims are commanded, he says, to submit to the laws of their countries of residence 'in the name of the tacit moral agreement' that already supports their presence. At the same time, 'they are not allowed to fight or kill for money, land or power, and they should absolutely avoid being implicated in a colonial or oppressive war'. Fine-tuning the space between these rubrics, evidently written before the current war in Iraq, is left to a reference note, where it is explained that Islamic scholars offered American Muslim citizens contrary opinions about the lawfulness of fighting their co-religionists in Afghanistan. Ramadan concludes, somewhat lamely, that in such a situation of conflicting loyalties, the choice must be left to the individual, an argument that undermines his advocacy of a common Muslim group identity.

In contrast to Ramadan, Bruce Lawrence offers no prescriptions for American Muslims and other Asian immigrants, including Sikhs and Hindus, who come under his scrutiny. His purpose is ethnographic and anthropological: to see how Muslims and others are faring in the American dream, to chart their progress up the ladders that are taking many of them into positions of privilege and success. The South-Asian-born immigrants to the US currently enjoy the highest household incomes of any immigrant group, with almost 50 per cent of breadwinners occupying professional or managerial positions, including 35,000 doctors. The Hart Celler Act, passed in 1965 at the height of the Vietnam War, led to a substantial increase in Asian immigration to the United States, with the Asian origin population amounting to more than 7 million, or 3 per cent of the population, by 1980. In addition to African-American Muslims there are now at least 700,000 Muslims of mainly South Asian origin, a similar number of Buddhists, around 1 million Hindus and 100,000 Sikhs. The figures are not huge, compared with the numbers of what might be called Judao-Christians (a classification that includes some 3 million Mormons and perhaps 30 million Christian evangelicals who pay as much attention to the Old Testament as to the New, plus 6 million Jews), but they add significantly to the country's religious diversity. In charting a course through this variegated and complex religious landscape, Lawrence superimposes his own sophisticated co-ordinates on the two great maps of American spirituality drawn by de Tocqueville in the 1820s and Will Herberg in the 1950s. Both of these master cartographers recognised that the culture of Protestantism determined the nature of American religious life: de Tocqueville, a Catholic, saw how his New World co-religionists behaved more like Protestants than did Old World Catholics. Herberg, a Jew, saw how America's Jewish communities had been changed into a triple-identity grid labelled 'Protestant–Catholic–Jew'. Lawrence notes that American Jews have more in common with Protestants than they have with European Jews. Building on this groundwork he adds the crucially unacknowledged dimension of race. Since the 1950s, he suggests, Herberg's triple identity has morphed into Progressive Patriotic Protestantism (PPP), a 'religious reflex' or 'civic virtue' writ large in civil society that is 'Protestant even when the creed is Catholic or Mormon or Jewish'. Above all, though few observers care to mention this, PPP is 'white', a legacy of those nineteenth-century waves of immigrants from Ireland, Italy and other parts of Europe who became identified with previous waves of Protestant settlers, defining themselves as white in order to maintain their social distance from the indigenous Native Americans and the descendants of African slaves. Until 1970, Asian Americans were classified as 'white' on US census forms. Since then 'Asian' has become a separate category, 'compelling Asians to think of themselves as distinct from both Anglo and African Americans, while framing in their own minds a new value preference that is at once racially and class based'. Lawrence takes issue with scholars who suggest that Muslims on the path to Americanisation will become assimilated to PPP, losing the 'sharp Muslim edge' to their culture, though he cites some evidence that would support this view, such as the fact that only 2 per cent of 'Irangelinos' (the 100,000-strong community of Iranians in Los Angeles) are religiously observant. The persistence of the fault-line dividing Asian Muslims from African-American Muslims is likely to prevent such smoothing of boundaries. Bruce concludes his thought-provoking essay with a powerful critique of multiculturalist approaches that ignore divergences within religious traditions and the competing identities that face their adherents, while concealing the hegemonic hand of PPP. In the aftermath of 9/11 it has become essential

> to maintain the space between church (temple/mosque) and state. The frequent invocations of 'In God We Trust' or 'God Bless America' carry the message that only faith can sustain genuine patriotism; yet the implicit message is that only those with the 'right' faith can fight those enemies who have targeted us because of their 'wrong' faith. Wrapping religion in the flag not only undermines a polyvalent patriotism, it also makes the God of all humankind and all history into a partisan for one group and its political/strategic objectives.

Published in *The Times Literary Supplement*, 6 August 2004.

The books reviewed were:

Carl Ernst (2004) *Following Muhammad: Rethinking Islam in the Contemporary World.* Chapel Hill, NC: University of North Carolina Press.

Jack Goody (2004) *Islam in Europe*. Cambridge, UK: Polity Press.

Bruce B. Lawrence (2002) *New Faiths, Old Fears: Muslims and Other Asian Immigrants in American Religious Life*. New York: Columbia University Press.

Tariq Ramadan (2004) *Western Muslims and the Future of Islam.* Oxford, UK: Oxford University Press.

2

An Unnecessary Clash

Since the 1950s, when the full horrors of the Nazi atrocities were revealed and Europeans on both sides of the Atlantic were made aware of the ghastly consequences wrought by centuries of anti-Semitism, it has been customary to talk of Judao-Christian civilisation. A demonstration of solidarity, perhaps, or, as Richard Bulliet puts it in this stimulating essay, 'the expression of a new feeling of inclusiveness towards Jews, and of a universal Christian repudiation of Nazi barbarism'. Setting aside the irony of linking in a single term two faith communities that have been at spiritual loggerheads for the better part of two millennia, the term has sound historical justification:

> *Common scriptural roots, shared theological concerns, continuous interaction at a societal level, and mutual contributions to what in modern times has become a common pool of thought and feeling give the Euro-American Christian and Jewish communities solid grounds for declaring their civilisational solidarity.*

Adopting the same criteria, a case can be made for regarding Islam as integral to the same broad tradition – as part of what has come to be known, for want of a better term, as Western civilisation. According to the 'clash of civilisations' hypothesis popularised by Samuel Huntington, Bernard Lewis and others, the Judao-Christian West has always been and always will be at odds with Islam. According to the Islamic–Christian model proposed by Bulliet, Islam and the West are historical twins whose resemblance did not cease when their paths diverged. The problem today is that 'neither sibling seems capable of seeing itself or its twin in a comprehensive and balanced fashion'

Taking the role of a disinterested outsider, Bulliet points out that the 'scriptural and doctrinal linkages between Judaism and Christianity are no closer than those between Judaism and Islam, or between Christianity and Islam'. Muslim thinkers contributed decisively to the movement of ideas that would crystallise in the modern West. At least 14 of today's 34 European states were at one time or another wholly or partially under Muslim rule for a century or more – a political engagement as substantial as any governing relations between Christian rulers and their Jewish subjects.

Yet how different are the assumptions governing the prevailing discourses about Islam, whether among clergy, in the academy, in the media or policy circles, especially in the United States! When the Reverend Bailey Smith, one-time President of the Southern Baptist Convention, proclaimed that 'God does not hear the prayer of the Jew', the chorus of protest was deafening, reflecting the sea-change in attitudes that has converted the overwhelming majority of US evangelicals into the most ardent supporters of the Jewish state. By contrast, the White House's favourite preacher, the Reverend Franklin Graham (son of superstar crusader Billy Graham) has stated, without incurring even the mildest official protest, that the God of Islam is not the same God as the God of the Judao-Christian faith: 'It is a different God and I believe [Islam] is a very evil and wicked religion.'

Fundamentalist preachers such as Jerry Falwell and Pat Robertson, extracting Qur'anic phrases out of their original historical context, denounced Islam as a religion of violence ('Mohamed was a terrorist'). Threatened with lawsuits and under pressure from state legislators, the University of North Carolina at Chapel Hill had to backtrack on a proposal to make Michael Sells' translation of passages from the Qur'an a mandatory text for first-year students.

To regard such attitudes as understandable, if not excusable, in the rage and confusion that followed the attacks on New York and Washington in September 2001, misses an essential point. In the eyes of many Americans (including some academics with influence over policy) the violence that destroyed the Twin Towers is normative or fundamental to the religion, rather than the outcome of a particular political-ideological construction incorporating some religious symbols. Such an assumption, as Bulliet's analysis makes clear, long pre-dates the atrocities of 9/11. It is predicated on the notion of Islam as alien or 'other', a construction that necessarily denies the history of trade and cultural exchanges between the central Muslim lands and Christian Europe that prevailed over many centuries. Timothy McVeigh, executed for the 1998 Oklahoma City bombing, is rarely if ever described as a Christian or Protestant terrorist, despite his links to a fundamentalist Protestant church proclaiming a white supremacist theology. While occasional public gestures are made towards 'moderate' Muslims, Osama bin Laden and his associates are perceived in the wider US culture as authentic or representative exponents of their faith.

In the eyes of many Muslims, the suspension of civil liberties under the US Patriot Act, the scandalous violations of international law in the gulag of Guantanamo Bay, ostensibly aimed at combating terrorism, are in reality expressions of Islamophobia, a new style anti-Semitism that is scarcely less menacing than the old. Bulliet does not exaggerate its dangers: 'The potential for tragedy in our current zeal for seeing Islam as a malevolent Other should make us wary of easy formulations that can cleave our national societies into adversarial camps.' The basis of the prejudice that would deny the inclusion of Islam as an integral part of modern civilisation lies, he argues, in a 'historical master-narrative rooted in fourteen centuries of fear and polemic', along with the current conviction held by many Westerners (and fuelled by the writings of scholars such as Lewis, Huntington and Daniel Pipes) that something has gone 'wrong' with Islam and its history. We

> do not include Islam in our civilisation club because we are heirs to a Christian construction of history that is deliberately exclusive … Shifting Western portrayals of Islam over the centuries make it clear that reasons for disliking Islam have been constructed as rationales for a preexisting and ongoing animosity and not vice versa.

In the master-narratives of European history, Bulliet concludes, precedence is given to 'violent conflict over cultural borrowing'. His assertion could be fleshed out with numerous examples from European literature. As the Cambridge scholar, Tim Winter, has observed, the founding epics of many European nations, including *The Lusiads*, *El Cid*, *La Chanson de Roland* and epics of St Louis, and Serbia's *The Mountain Wreath*, are all celebrations of the triumph of Christianity over Islam.

To stress the commonalities between Islamic and Christian worlds is not to deny significant points of divergence, however. Bulliet's argument that the sum of these differences is no greater than those that exist between the different versions of Christianity or Islam (indeed, it is customary to refer to Mormonism as a branch of Christianity, though the relationship it bears to its parent tradition is in no way closer than that between Christianity and Judaism). The most persuasive part of Bulliet's essay is his account of the processes of acculturation in Europe and Western Asia, and the divergent paths taken by the religious specialists in their relations with the state. Christian missionising paved the way for Islamic governance, and later conversion, in many of the lands that were heirs to the Graeco-Roman imperium. Popular antinomian movements challenged the consensus of orthodoxy in both traditions. (Indeed, though Bulliet does not mention this, a comparison of heresiological literature turns up some virtually identical cultic groups, such as the primitive Adamites, said to have practised ritual nudity and free love, who appeared in tenth-century Bahrain and fifteenth-century Germany.) But whereas in the West the Church relied on the state to enforce conformity, Islam lacked a mechanism for doctrinal enforcement comparable to the Catholic Inquisition. The latter actually empowered secular rulers by imposing religious conformity (a practice persisted in by Protestant rulers after the Reformation). Lacking the institutional weight of their Christian counterparts, the *ulama* (Islamic legal scholars) had of necessity to come to terms with religious diversity, inveighing against it rhetorically while remaining vulnerable to the vagaries of power in a precarious political world.

The consequences were far-reaching and enduring. Unlike Western princes, the sultans and amirs who succeeded to caliphal power were unable to wrest the law from its religious guardians. Whereas, in the West, 'the kings bested the priests' in judicial matters, the *ulama*, as upholders of the *Shari'a* (divine law), retained their role as guarantors of justice. 'For Muslims,' says Bulliet (in a sentence that ought to replace 'They Hate Our Freedoms' on the Oval Office wall), 'the converse of tyranny is not liberty but justice … When a Muslim community feels threatened, looking to religious leaders for help is an ingrained characteristic of Islamic political culture.' The resistance of the *ulama* to efforts by reforming autocrats, such as Mehmet Ali in Egypt and the Ottoman Sultan Abdul Hamit II, to curtail their autonomy and short-circuit the divine law is not explicable only in terms of their innate conservatism or group self-interest – though these factors were undoubtedly present. Their opposition to reform was in part a manifestation of their time-honoured opposition to tyranny: '*Ulama*, basing themselves in traditional Islamic political theory, predicted that rulers freed from the bonds of the *Shari'a* would seek absolute power, and (the rulers) regularly lived up to that expectation.' Such rulers, Bulliet usefully points out, were inspired as much by their Western peers as by their own autocratic instincts. Abdul Hamit II's suspension of the Ottoman parliament fell in line with similar steps by rulers Otto von Bismarck, Napoleon III and Nicholas II. The emasculation of the *ulama* in the interests of modernisation consolidated the Muslim autocracies without conferring on the new rulers the religious legitimacy that sultans and emirs had received from the *ulama* in the past.

In the post-colonial era, when intellectual prestige in Muslim lands has gravitated towards people with technical training in fields such as engineering and medicine, the crisis of Islamic religious authority has deepened. Many of the militant activists engaged in the modern Islamist movements (including the engineer Osama bin Laden, the paediatrician Ayman al-Zawahiri and the architect-planner Mohamed Atta) are the products of a secular education system that lacks the rounded and comprehensive Islamic perspective inculcated in the traditional religious academies.

The final part of Bulliet's essay is devoted to a critique of the modernisation theories of Daniel Lerner, Manfred Halpern and other social scientists he regards as having exercised a baleful influence on Middle East studies and the US government policies flowing from them. Too often, he says, Americans have looked for friends among the Westernised suit-wearing anglophone elites – 'people like us' – rather than listening to the men wearing beards or, indeed, the women in veils. (Bulliet is amused by the zeal with which his fellow Americans now urge Muslim women to uncover their hair, after a century during which puritan missionaries campaigned to persuade non-European women to cover their breasts.) His comparisons are always thought-provoking, if sometimes eclectic. The esoteric field of quantitative onomastics is invoked to chart, in comparative surveys of children's names, trends towards secularisation in colonial Massachusetts and modern Turkey. Other anthropologically significant factors – such as the prevalence cousin-marriage in central Muslim lands, contrasting with Church-directed outmarriage in Western Europe – are overlooked, as is any consideration of the contrasting geographical milieus of Western Europe and the Middle East, which had an important bearing on differences in the relations between government, religion and civil society. Well known to specialists, there are issues that deserve wider discussion in the US policy community than they have hitherto received: how many lives could have been saved – American as well as Iraqi – if the US Defense Department had focused on the clan networks surrounding Saddam Hussein instead of disbanding the Iraqi army and top echelons of the Baath party, the only Iraqi agencies capable of preventing chaos? Despite the range of its subject matter, it is not clear whether this book is aimed at Bulliet's fellow-specialists or at the larger interested public. This is a pity, because it deserves the widest possible readership, addressing as it does with wit and insight one of the most freighted issues of our time

Published in *The Times Literary Supplement*, 29 July 2005.

The book reviewed was:

Richard W. Bulliet (2004) *The Case for Islamic–Christian Civilization.* New York: Columbia University Press.

3

The Birth of Islam: A Different View

What do we know of Muhammad? Can we even be sure that such a historical personage existed? For the vast majority of believing Muslims, the question simply does not arise. The Prophet lived in Arabia from the time of his birth in approximately CE 570 until his death in CE 632, during which time he received and transmitted the revelations from God contained in the Qur'an, while forging the warring tribes of that region into an all-powerful movement under the banner of Islam.

Building on this formidable religious and political achievement, his immediate successors, the Rightly Guided Caliphs, led the triumphant tribes beyond the bounds of Arabia, inflicting almost simultaneous defeats on the two most powerful Near Eastern empires, the Persian Sassanids, who collapsed completely, and the Byzantines, who lost two of their richest provinces – Syria–Palestine and Egypt. Despite having reservations about the reliability of the oral traditions underpinning the Muslim narrative, most Western scholars have tended to accept its basic premises. There *was* such a person as Muhammad, and it is his utterances – divinely dictated or otherwise – that make up the 114 'suras', or chapters, of the Qur'an. According to the generally accepted Muslim account, the holy text acquired its present form under the Caliph Uthman, Muhammad's son-in-law and the third of his successors as leader of the Islamic community; he reigned from CE 644 to 656.

There are, however, a number of sceptics, mainly in Western universities, who question the Muslim narrative. Even when accepting that the text of the Qur'an represents the authentic utterances of Muhammad, they have cast doubt on the details of the Prophet's life, as recorded in the oral literature known as *Hadiths* ('traditions' or reports) passed down by the generations following his death. Many of these details, based on stories conveyed through 'chains of transmission' of varying reliability, were intended to elucidate the meaning of Qur'anic passages by reference to 'occasions of revelation' in the life of the Prophet.

The earliest written biography of Muhammad, by Ibn Hisham, who died in CE 833, contains parts of the missing work of an earlier scholar, Ibn Ishaq, who lived from about CE 707 to 767. The dating of Ibn Hisham's work, composed nearly two centuries after the Prophet's death, may be contrasted with that of St Mark's gospel, considered by most New Testament scholars to be the earliest of the three synoptic gospels and to have been written some four decades after the death of Jesus. The story of Jesus has long been subjected to the rigours of formal criticism, with scholars such as Rudolph Bultmann claiming that almost nothing can be known about his life or personality, as distinct from the 'message of the early Christian community, which for the most part the Church freely attributed to Jesus'. Yet despite widespread recognition of the unreliability of oral traditions, most scholars have tended to accept the Muslim narrative.

A startling exception to this record of scholarly complacency appeared with two landmark studies by the American linguist, John Wansbrough (1928–2002), who taught at the School of Oriental and African Studies (SOAS) in London. In *Qur'anic Studies* (1977) and *The Sectarian Milieu* (1978) Wansbrough trawled through a substantial body of the earliest manuscript sources and concluded that 'Islam' may not have arisen in western Arabia, as the traditional narrative holds, but in a 'sectarian milieu' of Christians, Jews and monotheistic Arabs in the same lands of the Fertile Crescent (modern Israel–Palestine, Jordan, Syria and Iraq) that saw the emergence of Rabbinical Judaism and Christianity. 'Both the quantity and quality of source materials,' he cautiously suggested, 'would seem to support the proposition that the elaboration of Islam was not contemporary with but posterior to the Arab occupation of the Fertile Crescent and beyond.' Far from being finalised under the Caliph Uthman, the text of the Qur'an as we now have it, in Wansbrough's view, may have emerged over some two centuries in the course of religious polemics with the older traditions of Judaism and Christianity.

Wansbrough was careful to avoid drawing firm historical conclusions from his studies: his method was strictly textual and literary. But two young scholars influenced by him, Patricia Crone and Michael Cook, endeavoured to put historical flesh on the bones of his literary analysis in their highly speculative and controversial book *Hagarism*. Setting aside the Islamic accounts, they examined a number of the earliest non-Muslim sources dealing with the Arab invasion, with a view to constructing an alternative version of Islamic origins. On the basis of what they admitted was rather thin evidence, they hypothesised that the original Islam was a messianic movement of Jewish refugees from Palestine who went to the Arabian desert and joined forces with Arab tribesmen to recover the Holy Land.

The messianic union of Jews and Arabs was short-lived, and afterward the Arabs – known in these sources as Hagarenes, from the Arabic Muhajirun, or emigrants – contrived to preserve their distinctive identity by adopting Samaritan scriptural positions (rejecting prophetic writings outside the Pentateuch) and moving towards a position equidistant between Judaism and Christianity. For Crone and Cook, Muhammad emerges as an Arabian Moses recapitulating the Mosaic themes of exile and the dispensing of laws received from God on a holy mountain.

The Crone–Cook theory has been generally rejected, and Patricia Crone has since refined her views, accepting that Muhammad definitely existed as a historical personage, and that most of the Qur'an is a record of his utterances. Andrew Rippin, a Canadian scholar and leading Wansbrough disciple, argues that while Cook and Crone draw attention successfully to the problems involved in the study of Islam, they have not been able to get beyond the limitations inherent in the sources, for they are all of questionable historical authenticity and, more important, all are treatises based in polemic.

Nevertheless, while Wansbrough's studies are far from being conclusive, they do address some of the difficulties facing the traditional view of Islamic origins, including the fragmentary and allusive character of the Qur'anic discourse – with its assumption of prior knowledge of many of the stories to which it alludes – as well as some archaeological and numismatic issues, such as the fact that the Qibla (direction of prayer) in some of the earliest mosques points not toward Mecca but to a shrine much further north, and the appearance of Christian and other figurative images on coinage with Arab inscriptions. (The consensus of modern scholarship, however, attributes the wrong orientation of early Qiblas to simple miscalculation.)

One of the most contentious theories, originally advanced by the Protestant theologian Günter Lüling, and elaborated more recently by the pseudonymous scholar Christoph Luxenberg, suggests that the Qur'an may have originated in the strophic hymns of Aramaic-speaking Christianised tribes. These may have been adapted by Muhammad, or projected retrospectively on to him, after the original messianic movement collapsed. Volker Popp, a numismatist working in Germany, argues – with Luxenberg – that the name Muhammad, which appears on coins and on the interior of the Dome of the Rock in Jerusalem (alongside some of the earliest written examples of Qur'anic texts, dating from the CE 690s), may in fact refer to Jesus: the word 'muhammad' can be read as a passive participle meaning the 'praised' or 'chosen one', raising the possibility that the original Arab conquerors might have been Arian Christians opposed to Byzantine rule. Readers interested in exploring these issues will find articles by Popp,

Luxenberg and other sceptical scholars in *The Hidden Origins of Islam: New Research into Its Early History*, edited by Karl-Heinz Ohlig and Gerd R. Puin.

It may be a long time before revisionist theories gain the acceptance that higher criticism has obtained in the field of biblical studies, not least because of differences between the perspectives of 'early Qur'an' theorists such as Lüling, Popp and Luxenberg, including Wansbrough's former student, John Burton, who regards the whole Qur'an as contemporaneous with Muhammad, and 'late Qur'an' theorists who follow Wansbrough in suggesting that some, if not most, of the material was compiled after Muhammad's death. Nevertheless, the seeds of doubt about the version adopted by nearly all Muslim and most Western scholars have been firmly planted. The green shoots of scepticism concerning Islam's account of its own origins are unlikely to disappear.

Fred Donner's new book, *Muhammad and the Believers*, is written in an accessible style and is mercifully free from the daunting obscurities, scholarly allusions and technical apparatus that make Wansbrough's books almost impenetrable. Aimed at a much broader readership of students and interested observers than Wansbrough's work, its approach might be labelled 'Revisionism Lite'. Unlike the more radical sceptics, Donner accepts the main outlines of the traditional Muslim narrative while questioning many of its details. So, after providing an exemplary résumé of the orthodox story, he acknowledges that 'the vast ocean of traditional accounts ... contains so many contradictions and so much dubious storytelling that many historians have become reluctant to accept any of it at face value'. He insists, however, that rejecting everything in the conventional accounts would be going too far and would involve 'as uncritical an approach as unquestioning acceptance of everything in the traditional accounts. The truth,' he argues quite sensibly, 'must lie somewhere in between.'

To the student of religious history, Donner's middle path is likely to seem plausible, not least because it replicates the gradual process of separation between parent and daughter religions that scholars such as Geza Vermes see as having occurred between Judaism and Christianity. One problem it poses, however, is that Donner rejects the theories of the 'late Qur'an' revisionists. If the text had not acquired its final form during Muhammad's lifetime and in the decades immediately after he died, he says, we would be surely aware of this; yet 'meticulous study of the text by generations of scholars has failed to turn up any plausible hint of anachronistic references'. He argues that such anachronisms would certainly be the case if the text had crystallised later.

Donner argues that the Qur'an is not only free from such anachronisms, but that its style and vocabulary reflect its origins in western Arabia in the last part of the sixth century CE and the first part of the seventh. His acceptance of an early 'Muhammadan' Qur'an allows him to use it, cautiously, as a source for Muhammad's life and the earliest Muslim community. He points out that many more of its messages are addressed to 'Believers' than to 'Muslims': the word 'Believers' occurs almost a thousand times, compared with fewer than 75 instances of 'Muslim'. The terms are not interchangeable: 'islam' and 'muslim' refer to submission or surrender, as in the case of the Bedouin tribes who are said to have submitted to Muhammad in Arabia: 'Belief obviously means something different (and better) than "submission" (islam), and so we cannot simply equate the Believer with the Muslim, though some Muslims may qualify as Believers.'

By factoring in some of the themes and insights selectively culled from the same stockpile of sources deployed by more radical revisionists, Donner concludes that the original movement that came to be known as 'Islam' was actually an ecumenical pietistic movement.

Readers bemused by Donner's argument – and sharing Crone's impression that he might be 'arguing for incompatible positions' – will find relief in *Faith and Power*, the latest offering by Bernard Lewis, the prolific Princeton Orientalist born in 1916, whose pathbreaking first book, *The Origins of Ismailism*, appeared in 1940. Lewis is the best-known Middle East specialist in America, if not in the whole Western world. While making only passing references to debates about Islamic origins, he espouses the traditionalist view wholeheartedly.

Lauded by the neo-conservatives, he was the recipient in 2007 of the American Enterprise Institute's prestigious Irving Kristol Award. An unapologetic foreign policy hawk, his best-selling book, *What Went Wrong? The Clash Between Islam and Modernity in the Middle East* (2002), was already in proof form when the 9/11 attacks took place; and while he explained in his Preface that the book did not deal with the attacks themselves, it clearly struck a chord with readers in the aftershock of those dreadful events. As Lewis explained, his book was related to the attacks, 'examining not what happened and what followed, but what went before – the longer sequence and larger pattern of events, ideas, and attitudes that preceded and in some measure produced them'. Within a year of its appearance, Amazon.com was listing it as one of the world's most popular books – and near the top of the poll in several American states and campuses, number 13 in Denmark and number 19 in Italy.

While disclaiming that 'Islam' as such was responsible for the attacks on America, Lewis' analysis focused on the failure of Muslims to adapt their religious tradition to present requirements, unlike their age-old Christian rivals, who embraced modernity in its entirety. Lewis lent the enormous prestige he had acquired over many decades to the US invasion of Iraq, the most disastrous Western intervention in the region since the Suez Crisis of 1956. On 19 September, eight days after the attacks on New York and Washington, DC, he was invited by Richard Perle to address the US Defense Policy Board, which Perle then headed. Lewis and his friend, the prominent Iraqi exile Ahmad Chalabi, reportedly argued for a military takeover of Iraq in order to prevent worse terrorist attacks in the future.

In his latest book, consisting mainly of recycled articles and lectures produced over the decade of the 2000s, Lewis dwells on the themes that feature prominently in his more recent publications – the 'clash of civilisations' between seemingly incompatible entities known as 'Islam' and 'the West', and the all-embracing totalitarian temptations of Islam manifested by the failure of Muslim societies to produce vibrant democratic institutions. Here, Lewis' 'Islam' is conflated with the Arab–Muslim world: there is no recognition that functioning democracies and successful industrial economies have established themselves in Malaysia and Indonesia, two of the most populous Muslim countries. Islam, Lewis tells his audiences, is not just a religion, but rather a 'complete system of identity, loyalty, and authority' that provides Muslims with the most appealing and convincing answer to their problems. Unlike Jesus, who distinguished between the duties owed to God and to Caesar, Muhammad established a state. In Islam 'there was no need for a church since the establishment, so to speak, of a community and polity in the lifetime of the founder, who ruled as both prophet and sovereign'.

In certain respects, Lewis' analysis of Islam, unencumbered by doubts about origins, issues of ethnicity, the impact of climate and geography, or the dynamic changes effected by modern education, industrialisation and urbanisation, mirrors the views of fundamentalists such as Osama bin Laden. Lewis, while finding bin Laden's actions abhorrent, admires the Saudi dissident for his command of classical Arabic, writing that he 'is very articulate, very lucid, and I think on the whole very honest in the way he explains things'.

Rooted in the classical Orientalist tradition of scholarship based on the study of written texts, as distinct from the anthropological observation of actual human behaviour, Lewis arrives at the sorts of judgement that – when enacted into policy – have led to disaster in Iraq and possibly also in Afghanistan. He takes textual knowledge at face value, without probing beneath the surface, risking generalisations that would be difficult to defend, for example, in the case of India and Sub-Saharan Africa, where Islam takes on the colouring of numerous local traditions. Lewis' disdain for the social sciences, and his reliance on textual knowledge derived from classical texts as well as newspapers or government propaganda, can mislead. Thus, in stating baldly that two Middle East countries, Iraq and Syria, 'went all the way in adopting and applying the continental European model of the totalitarian dictatorship', he takes their own propaganda at face value, seeming to take no account of studies – such as that of the distinguished Dutch scholar and diplomat, Nikolaos van Dam – that demonstrate how an East-European-style party organisation can be infiltrated and taken over by a sectarian kinship group (in the case of Syria by the Alawite minority).

In some cases, however, even Lewis' textual knowledge may be flawed by his failure, or perhaps his refusal, to take into account written materials that do not fit his preconceptions or his firm pro-Israeli commitment. Thus, in stating that Baathism involved the 'adaptation of Nazi ideas and methods to the Middle Eastern situation' (a favourite neo-conservative theme), he ignores crucial texts by Michel Aflaq, co-founder of the Baath party, expressing admiration for the 'solid conviction that informs ... the Jewish people with courage and a spirit of sacrifice', as well as Aflaq's efforts to eliminate from the party's constitution the 'stupid ideas' he associated with Nazism.

Lewis' insights are sometimes penetrating, but frustratingly he often displays his penchant for the telling anecdote and aphoristic generalisation at the expense of analytical coherence. Thus, in a powerful passage on democracy in the Middle East, he makes a telling point (rarely noted by other commentators) about its distinctive political culture:

> What is entirely lacking in the Middle Eastern political tradition is representation and what goes with it – the idea that people elect others to represent them, that these others meet in some sort of corporate body, and that that corporate body deliberates, conducts discussions, and, most important of all, reaches decisions that have binding force ... In Roman law and in most of the European systems derived from it or influenced by it, there is such a thing as a legal person, a corporation, an abstraction that nevertheless functions as a legal person.

I have suggested in my *Islam in the World* (2006) that this absence, derived from a feature of the Islamic *Shari'a* law, which has no concept of legal personality, goes to the heart of the 'democratic deficit' of many Middle East polities, where family, tribe, coterie or sect tends to subvert the authority of public institutions at the expense of civil society. Under these conditions, real power almost invariably accrues to the armed forces, whose command and control systems and institutional boundaries are determined by the exigencies of military logic rather than by structures responsive to the ebb and flow of political ideas and social needs. In the long term, the participants in mass demonstrations that brought down the Mubarak regime in Egypt, while responsible for a hugely impressive expression of public feeling, will need to overcome the inertia of military governance – with its networks of properties and other vested interests – in a country where the institutions of civil society have been weakened by decades of top-down, kleptocratic rule by the mukhabarat ('intelligence') state.

If, as Lewis rightly argues, democratic representation is rooted in institutional structures and forms of accountability that are absent from many Muslim and Middle Eastern societies, how can he have blandly endorsed a policy driven by the belief that successful, functioning democracies could be imposed using outside force? Tunisia and Egypt, and probably other countries in the region, are demonstrating that it is internal forces facilitated by information technologies outside the control of the mukhabarat state that are setting the democratic agenda. The Islamist threat – which the regimes used to blackmail Western governments into supporting them – has so far been conspicuously absent. The battle cry 'Islam Is the Solution' was not to be heard in Cairo's Tahrir Square.

At its heart, the 'clash of civilisations' thesis originally promulgated by Lewis, and popularised by Samuel Huntington, rests on shaky intellectual foundations. Would the more modest scholars who wrestle critically with the obscure and controversial origins of one of the world's great religions have dared to produce such a facile generalisation? Is there perhaps a connection between the serene dogmatism of Lewis' approach, with its tendency to accept the 'traditional' view of Islamic origins, and his failure to scrutinise the propositions put forward by the advocates of intervention, whether these be other hawkish scholars, administration officials or prominent exiles? Lewis is an always entertaining and highly readable commentator on the Muslim world, but for all his brilliance, his judgements are sometimes flawed, and dangerously so in the case of America's adventure in Iraq.

Published in *The New York Review of Books*, 7 April 2011.

The books reviewed were:

Fred M. Donner (2010) *Muhammad and the Believers: At the Origins of Islam.* Cambridge, MA: Belknap Press of Harvard University Press.

Bernard Lewis (2010) *Faith and Power: Religion and Politics in the Middle East.* Oxford, UK: Oxford University Press.

4

Politics and the Prophet

For too long, Islamic studies have existed in an academic ghetto, which reinforced the essentialist view shared by the Islamologues that Islam was in some way 'different' from the West. A more fruitful approach is taken by Michael Gilsenan in *Lords of the Lebanese Marches*, based on field work he conducted in a Sunni Muslim rural area of North Lebanon during the early 1970s, before the recent civil war. This beautifully written book describes the culture of masculinity in its multiple refractions through violence and narrative, joking and play, a world where status and power are organised vertically, where big landowners use the small landowners as their strong-arm men to control the sharecroppers and labourers at the bottom of the social hierarchy and to compete for supremacy with their rival lords. Sharaf, 'the honour of person and family, which is particularly identified with control of women's sexuality, is crucial to the public, social identity of men'. The sharaf of the mighty is linked with the destruction of the sharaf of others: great lords gain honour by ritually humiliating subordinates, whom they force to transgress their own codes of honour. Not surprisingly, life at the bottom is brutish and insecure. The poorest women and their children must undertake work that others regard as shameful. They are powerless to resist sexual exploitation or abuse by their masters. It is not so much these actions themselves, as the stories to which they give rise and which give them meaning, that interest Gilsenan: 'Men struggle to reproduce, memorialise and guarantee narratives of being and place in the world against the ruptures, absences and arbitrariness that continuously subvert them.'

The story of the rape of a 13-year-old peasant girl by a landlord's son before the helpless eyes of her parents, who were compelled to watch by the rapist's armed bodyguards, becomes 'a metaphor of rule. Rape stands not only for a whole "backward" agrarian set of relations constructed on violence, but by extension, for relations of power and property within the modern state'. Maleness and brute strength are at the centre of these narratives. A quarrel over a prostitute rapidly acquires a heroic dimension, becoming a 'narrative of status, honour, blood and violent revenge'.

In the public recital of the conflict, which leads to several murders, the original motive and setting are suppressed because the squabble was 'culturally loaded with negative value and no setting for serious confrontation between men of honour'. Humour and the art of ridiculing one's social inferiors confirm the social pecking order. Greater than the threat of being murdered (a common occurrence in these pages) are the shame and danger of 'being taken to demonstrate publicly, not a proper concern for sharaf, but the discrepancy between the proper assertion of capacity and empty pretension'. This applies to modern trades and occupations as much as to traditional ones. A chauffeur-mechanic, for example,

> *had to be able to talk, knowledgeably, about the machines and swap stories. He was expected to know what kind of tractor was good for what job, the costs and capacities of all the new models, and to talk with assurance and eventually some connoisseurship about any car on the street. Most important, he had to know the limits of his own competence. It was no use affecting a skill one did not possess, since one could so easily be exposed as a fool.*

Islam is conspicuous by its absence. Though the society Gilsenan describes is a Muslim one, the patriarchal themes he uncovers and celebrates – the obsession with gender and status, the assertion of power through violence – are to be found in many non-Muslim Mediterranean societies, as well as others further afield, and this calls into question the widely held view that Islamic texts or values can of themselves be held responsible for types of behaviour that underpin male supremacism.

The *Oxford Encyclopedia of the Modern Islamic World* includes articles on feminism and Muslim counter-feminism, which suggests that many of these values are now being challenged. So, too, is the narrow association, in Western minds, of Islam and terrorism, though this is no easy matter: the suspicion that the God of Abraham delights in sacrificial blood and human carnage is not entirely groundless. In the most intractable of all conflicts, between Israelis and Palestinians, the brave and painful efforts of human peacemakers are being unravelled systematically by the God who feeds his chosen agents contradictory messages. Baruch Goldstein, who was responsible for the massacre of Arab worshippers in Hebron in 1994, is, like the late Yitzhak Rabin's assassin, a martyr for those Jews who believe that the divine manifests itself in real estate. The suicide bombers of Hamas take things a stage further in their identification of territory with the sacred, wrapping themselves in explosives and fusing martyrdom with murder. Secularists have many crimes to answer for in this century, but the return of

God to the public domain heralds blood, not brotherhood. While Muslims and the scholars who come to their defence argue that the actions of Hamas are unrepresentative, that terrorism emanates from Ireland, Sri Lanka, the Basque region, even Oklahoma (where revolutionary anarchism meets Christian eschatology), some of the mud, or Semtex, inevitably sticks.

To guard against stereotyping and name-calling, accurate information about Islam has never been more urgently required in the West. What does 'Islam' actually say about terrorism, holy war or suicide? In denouncing extremism, should we use 'our' language – the language of liberal democracy – or 'theirs', the language of the Qur'an? Journalists and politicians are asked to frame questions or take positions on 'Islamic' matters. This is not easy; until very recently Islamic studies was confined to a relatively small number of specialists.

There is undoubtedly, as John Esposito, editor of the *Oxford Encyclopedia*, states in his Preface, a need for an 'easily accessible major reference work' in which students, journalists and political analysts can find 'readily available and succinct information on contemporary Muslim politics and societies'. The principal academic reference work, *The Encyclopedia of Islam*, is still incomplete and relies largely on traditional Orientalist scholarship in classical and medieval texts. This new encyclopedia therefore fills an important gap; it does not shy away from such controversial issues as terrorism, holy war, human rights and the status of women. Commenting on the limited nature of the wars conducted by the Prophet of Islam, in *Unfolding Islam*, P. J. Stewart writes: 'If Islamic rules were followed today, much of modern warfare would be impossible, and terrorism would be unthinkable. There would be no attacks on civilians, no retaliation against innocent parties, no taking hostage of non-combatants, no incendiary devices.' He adds, rather lamely, that 'many Muslims have failed to respect these limitations'. His book, based on a reading of the original Arabic sources, offers no explanation as to why some contemporary Muslims have deviated so far from these original principles, beyond arguing that Western governments are largely to blame. They have failed to accept Muslim nation states as equal partners, or to give the reformists who inherited power 'adequate help to lift their economies out of poverty', leaving the masses to turn to revolutionary 'theo-politics' (a term he prefers to 'Islamism' or 'fundamentalism'). He has little to say about the systemic corruption of contemporary Muslim governments, the failure of public institutions, or the repression and absence of human rights in a region that must rank with China in its hostility to intellectual freedom and democratic government.

In his article on *Jihad* in the *Oxford Encyclopedia*, Rudolph Peters points to the ambiguity of the Qur'anic verses on warfare: 'It is not clear whether the Qur'an allows fighting the unbelievers only as a defence against aggression or under all circumstances.' The classical commentators, however, generally endorsed the view that war was the permanent condition of the relationship between Muslims and non-Muslims, emphasised by the division of the world between the *Dar al-Islam* (the sphere of submission) and *Dar al-Harb* (the sphere of war) with an intermediate category, *Dar al-Aman* (the sphere of truce), gradually developing as more complex models of international relations became necessary. There are plenty of Prophetic precedents for the peaceful resolution of conflicts, notably Muhammad's bloodless 'conquest' of Mecca in CE 630 (a feat consciously emulated by Ibn Saud, Arabia's modern unifier, in 1924). The trouble lies not with the original models, but with the mentality of those who resurrect them without regard to historical contingencies or the 15 centuries of refinement by Islam's rabbinical class, the *ulama*. Several of the contributing editors to this *Encyclopedia* address this issue, notably Shahrough Akhavi in his biographical entry on Sayyid Qutb, the Egyptian ideologue executed by Nasser in 1966 and the lodestar of today's Islamic militants. Akhavi shows how Qutb constantly refers to Islam's primary texts, the Qur'an and *Hadith* (Prophetic Traditions) ahistorically, while reinterpreting them in such a way as to claim Islamic origins for concepts such as democracy and social justice largely derived from unacknowledged Western intellectual sources. In a similar vein, Dale Eickelman attributes the new Islamist movements to the rise of mass education and the decline of the *ulama*. The results are tragically obvious in Algeria, where religious autodidacts, rejecting the body of traditional scholarship, have murdered innocent people in the name of Islamic rectitude.

Editorially, the *Oxford Encyclopedia* claims to balance the social science orientation of much Western scholarship on Islam and the more faith-oriented and 'essentialist' approach of an increasing number of Muslim scholars now writing in Western languages. Many of the former, alert to the infiltration of Western political discourse into the modernist Islamic movements, make a distinction between political Islam, or Islamism, and the popular religiosity on which this style of politics feeds. The lines between them, however, are not easily drawn. As Esposito points out in his overview of Islam, the re-emergence of political Islam has been accompanied by a revival of religious observance at a private level: 'The indices of an Islamic reawakening in personal life are: increased attendance at mosque and to prayer and fasting, a proliferation of religious publications, audio and videotapes, greater emphasis on Islamic dress and values, and the revitalisation of Sufism.' Among the factors contributing to the Islamic revival, says Esposito, were rapid urbanisation and migration to the big cities. Loss of village life, with its extended family networks underpinned by traditional values, was accompanied by the shock of modern urban life with its Westernised cultures and customs. Many people, 'swept along in a sea of alienation and marginalisation, found an anchor ... in their religion'.

In *Islam and the Myth of Confrontation*, Fred Halliday attributes the appeal of Islamist movements in the Middle East to the crisis of the post-colonial state – in particular, its inability to meet the economic and cultural aspirations of its people. The movement in Iran 'has an Islamic ideological character, yet it cannot be explained by Islam any more than an abstracted Christianity can explain the peasant movements of Germany in the early 16th century, or the Solidarnosc movement of the Seventies in Poland'. Where does this leave the 'modern Islamic world'? If Halliday is right and Islamist movements in different parts of the globe really have local and particular causes, can such an entity be said to exist at all? Even if it is thought to be a convenient label to pin on a variety of religio-political cultures to which approximately a fifth of humankind belongs, can a significant part of these cultures really be said to constitute a 'threat' to the West?

For many Muslims, 'the West' (a construct as hard to pin down and describe as the 'modern Islamic world' itself) is still the enemy or rival, and the same underlying perception, of two competing cultural and religious systems with fully developed alternative world views, informs many of the *Oxford Encyclopedia*'s contributions. As Halliday points out with admirable lucidity, this is one aspect of the myth of confrontation recently popularised by Samuel Huntington of Harvard University. Yet, for Halliday, the idea that Islamic and Western 'civilisations' are on a collision course is in reality a reflection of conflicts within the Islamic world.

Halliday writes:

> The myth of confrontation is sustained from two apparently contradictory sides – from the camp of those, mainly in the West, seeking to turn the Muslim world into another enemy, and from those within the Islamic countries who advocate confrontation with the non-Muslim, and particularly Western, world.

Even if the present governments fighting Islamist terror in North Africa and the Middle East were to fall tomorrow, the revolutionary alternatives would not pose a serious challenge to the West. There is no single Islamic order. No particular form of government is deducible from Islam's holy texts any more than it is from Christianity's. Spanish fascism relied on Roman Catholicism for its ideological legitimacy; but Catholic thinkers could equally have relied on Catholic tradition to uphold democracy.

The variety of Muslim approaches to politics is documented in many of the *Oxford Encyclopedia*'s articles. Shahrough Akhavi, following Sami Zubaida, points out that the founders of the schools of Islamic law (madhabs) in the eighth and ninth centuries CE did not contest the separation of the spheres of religion and state by the ruling caliphs of those times. Modern Muslim governments that have imported institutional and legal structures from the West are not necessarily departing from precedents established centuries ago. Today's Islamists, who recognise the contribution of the great legists to the very identity of Islam, are nevertheless implicitly criticising these same legists when they declare the rulers of contemporary Muslim states to be infidels.

Is one to conclude from this that there are no characteristics that distinguish the world of Islam from the rest of the modern world? On matters relating to the status of women, it is arguable that Muslims are committed to forms of segregation that differ widely from 'Western' notions of equality. Some of these forms are retained symbolically through the custom of veiling, even when economic conditions dictate that women participate in the workforce. Male–female separation in public has become one of the Islamist shibboleths, and in this respect Muslim practice differs from the social conservatism governing male–female relations in, say, India or Japan. The significance of such symbolic forms, however, is questionable. Is the 'veiled' Malaysian female aeronautical engineer treated better or worse than her Japanese counterpart? And would any difference in the treatment she receives be attributable to religious factors?

In his chapter on human rights, Halliday rejects the thesis that 'Islamic' and 'Western' ideas of human rights might be incompatible: Islam is a 'varied, multivocal system' and the 'actual record of human societies, contemporary and historical, shows a great variety in the degree to which the state has, by universal standards, violated the rights of its subjects'. But, as Halliday himself points out, there remain some key Islamic texts that are not easily discounted. These include the testamentary inferiority of women (whose evidence is only worth half that of a man in certain legal proceedings); the inferior status of non-Muslims (formally protected if Jews or Christians, but denied full equality in marriage, for example); and the fate of apostates (subject to legal disabilities or punishable by death for their 'treason'). Ann Elizabeth Mayer, in her *Encyclopedia* article on human rights, explains how the Organisation of the Islamic Conference – the world's leading international Islamic body – has introduced 'Islamic' qualifications into its Declaration on Human Rights in Islam, reducing protection for these very categories and in effect admitting that there is indeed a conflict between *Shari'a* law and international human rights theory, which does not permit religious criteria to override rights.

In his historical survey of the Middle East and North Africa, Peter von Sivers links the rise of the modern Islamist movement with the decline of the Sufi – or mystical – orders, which developed in the twelfth and thirteenth centuries. The inward and ascetic aspects of the main orders – and of the body of Sufi verse in Persian, Turkish and Urdu – have for several centuries aroused the suspicions of reformist and modernist Islam. Von Sivers believes that, without a revival of mysticism allowing for a degree of pluralism in society, the Islamists will never be able to accommodate all faithful Muslims. Sufism, the 'vision of union and oneness' described by another contributor, William Chittick, is the heart and soul of Islam. If 'the understanding of the inner domains of Islamic experience is lost ... nothing is left but legal nit-picking and theological bickering'.

At present, the Islamic reformists and 'theo-politicals' are locked in a debate that deliberately excludes Sufism. Yet, for P. J. Stewart, who believes that Islam may well become the world's majority religion, its future must lie in a rejuvenated mystical orientation where depth of religious feeling can be yoked to metaphorical understandings of the Qur'an and to the Prophet's traditions. There are signs that this is already happening. Islamism has been checked, if not defeated, in Central Asia, where Muslim populations benefiting from the universal literacy bequeathed by the Soviets are turning to Sufism rather than political Islam. Despite the clamour of media-grabbing organisations, such as Hizbul Tahrir and its offshoot Al-Muhajiroun, one of the fastest growing Islamic movements in the West (and worldwide) is the pietistic Tablighi Jamaat, a strictly non-political organisation whose spiritual roots lie in the reformed Sufism of the Naqshabandi order in India.

If the future of Islam lies with Sufism, despite temporary appearances to the contrary, the future of Islamology looks much less certain. In his article on methodologies in Islamic Studies, Mohammed Arkoun, the Algerian-born Professor of Islamic Thought at the Sorbonne, berates the lack of caution of Orientalist scholarship in 'overgeneralisation of the data concerning Islam'. His criticisms appear to be directed at Western writers, but on the evidence of this *Encyclopedia*, it also applies to those Muslim writers (too numerous to list) who promote what are essentially doctrinal positions based on a partisan and ahistorical interpretation of texts:

> *The academic discourse on 'Islamic studies' has still to proffer explanation as to how so many diverse fields, theories, cultural spheres, disciplines, and concepts came to be associated with a single word 'Islam' and why the discussion remains so*

> *one-dimensional where Islam is concerned. In contrast, the study of Western society is characterised by careful scrutiny, attention to precise detail, meticulous distinctions, and theory-building. Indeed, the study of Western cultures continues to develop along such lines and to move in a different direction altogether from the unfortunate approach adopted in the area of 'Islam' and the so-called 'Arab world'.*

Islamic studies, Arkoun insists, is the last bastion of Western hegemonic reason inherited from the Enlightenment, an ideological discourse whose counterpart is the single-party nation state that monopolises power in developing countries while denouncing Western 'imperialism' and 'neo-colonialism'. The popular response to this is an 'Islam' that has become a 'collective phantasm, unrealistic and preoccupied with a romanticised past'. This, says Arkoun, is a new historical force requiring analysis and interpretation, using the tools of social psychology and cultural anthropology. But this is not 'Islam' as such. There are few social or political realities that can be attributed to the faith itself.

Published in *London Review of Books*, 1 August 1996.

The books reviewed were:

John L. Esposito (ed.) (1995) *The Oxford Encyclopedia of the Modern Islamic World.* Oxford, UK: Oxford University Press.

Michael Gilsenan (1996) *Lords of the Lebanese Marches: Violence and Narrative in an Arab Society.* London: I.B.Tauris.

Fred Halliday (1996) *Islam and the Myth of Confrontation: Religion and Politics in the Middle East.* London: I.B.Tauris.

P. J. Stewart (1994) *Unfolding Islam.* Reading, UK: Garnet Publishing.

5

Our Deputy Sheriffs in the Middle East

Last month [September 1997] saw the massacre of 200 innocent people in the Algiers suburb of Bentalha, but British newspaper headlines were taken up with more exotic matters: the sentences facing two British nurses apparently convicted of murdering a third at a hospital complex in Saudi Arabia. Executions and floggings are routine in the wealthy desert kingdom: a version, Aziz al-Azmeh suggests in one of the best essays yet written on Saudi Arabia, of the 'bread and circuses' principle favoured by the Romans. Until now, however, the victims of these popular spectacles have either been Saudi nationals or expatriate workers from poor countries such as Sri Lanka or the Philippines. The much more menacing situation in Algeria would have barely merited a mention had it not been for the fact that the latest massacre – the third in as many weeks – took place near the centre of Algiers, too close to the international communications networks to be ignored.

Both events, however, represent public relations disasters for their governments. Saudi Arabia, while holding executions and floggings in public to demonstrate to its own subjects that its legal system fully conforms to Islamic law, prefers to conceal the practical consequences of that system from the outside world, to which its suave and highly-educated Bedouin princes like to present the image of a uniquely harmonious blend of modernity and tradition. In Algeria, the government-controlled media studiously avoid drawing attention to the escalating chain of massacres, which are believed to have cost 100,000 lives since the war between the government and the Islamists began in 1992. On the night of this latest horror, the state television was showing coverage of the funeral of Diana, Princess of Wales. Both governments seek to present themselves as stable, civilised and modern, not only because such is the custom of governments everywhere, but because they depend on Western support. The Saudi regime, as shown with devastating clarity in 1991, is utterly dependent on Western military power. Like the other oil-rich sheikhdoms, it spends billions of petrodollars on highly sophisticated equipment, which it lacks the manpower, training or expertise to use itself. The tag of 'medieval barbarism' cuts to the quick.

The government of President Zeroual in Algeria, military in all but name, is sustained diplomatically and to some extent militarily by France. It was France which, fearful of a 'fundamentalist' regime on its doorstep, supported the Army's decision to go against the will of the Algerian people, who voted in favour of the now banned Islamic Salvation Front in the first round of the elections of 1991. It is important for the Algerian generals to show the French government that they are in control of the country while demonstrating that their enemies, the Islamists, are beyond the pale of civilisation: hence the allegations of connivance, if not complicity, by the security forces in some of the worst atrocities.

Said Aburish is a persistent and informed critic of virtually all of today's Arab governments, and the events of September [1997] should provide plenty of grist to his mill. His previous book was entitled *The Rise, Corruption and Coming Fall of the House of Saud*. In his latest, which covers the Middle East but not Algeria, he pulls no punches. 'Reporters,' he writes, 'know King Fahd to be lazy, corrupt, ignorant and a drunk, but little is written about these things and he is still the West's man.' He goes on to say that Prince Sultan, the Saudi defence minister, is one of the Kingdom's biggest 'skimmers', making billions out of arms contracts; King Hussein of Jordan is a playboy who protected his hashish-smuggling uncle, the Sharif Nasser, and misappropriated CIA funds for his personal use. Camille Chamoun, the former Lebanese President and the man largely responsible for launching the civil war in 1975, 'dazzled Westerners with his wit and charm' but was really 'nothing but a skirt-chasing, narrow-minded tribal chief who saw nothing wrong in lying, stealing and murder'. Aburish's judgements of the Western actors who did so much to shape the region's history after the defeat of the Ottoman Empire are just as jaundiced and, arguably, superficial: Gertrude Bell, Oriental Secretary in Mesopotamia, who had a crucial hand in the creation of modern Iraq, was 'an example of the empty socialite managing to misjudge everything in her way and creating havoc in her aftermath'; St John Philby, the friend and supporter of Ibn Saud and father of Kim, was an 'upstart contrarian ... bent on creating noise'.

What rankles is the absence of a broader historical and geopolitical analysis in which the actions of these individuals might be evaluated. True, British and French imperial interests were decisive in shaping the modern Middle East; and given the industrial West's appetite for cheap oil, it is hardly surprising that Western interests still play an important part in sustaining current regimes, despite endemic corruption, a generally poor record on human rights and the absence of real democracy. The export of armaments far in excess of the external defence requirements of the autocratic regimes of Arabia and the Gulf, initiated quite cynically as a way of recycling petrodollars, raises important moral and humanitarian issues. Britain and the United States armed Saddam Hussein to the hilt, with devastating consequences for Kuwait, and later for the Kurds and Shi'a of southern Iraq. Then UK Foreign Secretary Robin Cook's backtracking on the fate of the British nurses, after his indignant outburst to the effect that a sentence of 500 lashes has no place in a modern society, was not only inspired by the thought that shouting at Saudis is an unreliable way to persuade their monarch to exercise his prerogative of clemency; it was also intended to reassure the arms industry, on which thousands of British jobs depend. There is a significant irony in the fact that what has become one of Britain's most successful export industries was assiduously featherbedded in the years of free-market Thatcherism, injected with government money and provided with lavish credit guarantees underpinned by the taxpayer.

Aburish writes:

> For 70 years the West has used its position as the primary arms supplier in the Middle East to provide its deputy sheriffs with the ability to kill their enemies. They have used this ability to create phoney states, to maintain them against popular forces, to enforce Western designs to divide Palestine, to pressure unfriendly regimes into co-operating with them, to make money and corrupt leaders who became more dependent on them, and to sponsor minorities to stay in power and uprisings against unfriendly regimes or groups.

He supplies a wealth of detail to support his argument, including evidence of CIA involvement in the overthrow in 1963 of the Iraqi leader General Kassem, an honourable and genuinely popular figure, and of the Agency's machinations in the run-up to the 1967 Arab–Israeli war (which led to the Israeli takeover of the West Bank). He sees the venality of some of the actors, and the opportunism of others, as sufficient explanation for the Arab world's failure to realise the promise of independence and freedom that was held out after the First and Second World Wars.

That promise was embodied in the only hero of his book, Gamal Abdel Nasser – the one leader who came 'very close to breaking the back of the abusive pro-West Arab establishment'. To Aburish, Nasser was

> *the only man who represented Arab dreams, complexes and foibles against Western hegemony. His quarrels with the West can be judged as an expression of the complex relationship between the Arabs and the West. The core of this relationship was an intrinsic desire on his part to be understood and respected and a consequent desire to be left alone and free. In this, he was the average Arab. And to this day the average Arab wants nothing more than a recognition of his or her rights against Western strategic interests and commitment to special interest groups.*

But Nasser, and the hope he represented, was deliberately destroyed by Western support for his rival in the Arab world, King Faisal of Saudi Arabia. Had it not been for the West's support for Saudi Arabia and Saudi support for the monarchists in Yemen, Aburish argues, 200,000 of Nasser's best troops would not have been tied up in Yemen in 1967 when they could have been deployed against the Israelis.

There is much to be commended in the detail of this fascinating book. Its underlying theme of Western cunning and hegemonic control exercised through corrupt rulers and greedy arms merchants is not without its attractions. But again, on the broader themes, Aburish sometimes sounds naïve and unacceptably partisan in an old-fashioned Arab nationalist way. In the light of the present struggle in Turkey can we really be expected to believe that 'the Kurdish rebellions of 1948, '56, '67 and '75, like the present one, have had little to do with Kurdish aspirations and more to do with Iraq's unwillingness to follow a pro-West line'? Taking a similarly conspiratorial view, he suggests that General Kassem's decision to go his own way after overthrowing the Iraqi monarchy in 1958 rather than join Nasser's United Arab Republic – 'the point at which', he believes, 'the Nasser movement lost its momentum and Nasser his chance to control the whole of the Arab Middle East' – was influenced by the secret support he secured from Britain's ambassador, Sir Michael Wright, in exchange for a promise not to join the UAR. Only Arab sources are cited for this interesting claim: according to Aburish, the relevant documents are not yet available [in 1997] at the Public Record Office. It is hard to believe that an Arab superstate comprising Iraq, Egypt and Syria would have been any more viable than the union between Egypt and Syria, which collapsed in 1961 when the Syrians seceded. Despite the rhetoric of Arabism, and that of the pan-Islamism into which it has recently been subsumed, the economic, religious and ethnic differences between the countries making up the Middle East have always been irreconcilable and will remain so, regardless of the machinations of the West. The territorial divisions agreed between the Great Powers after the First World War may be arbitrary, but in the modern world, territorial units are meshed into an international system and it is the primary interest of the elites controlling those units to weld them into states using whatever force is necessary and the best available ideological tools. The ideological nuances distinguishing 'regional' Syrian Baathism from 'national' Iraqi Baathism sustain the competing power structures of Syria and Iraq, just as the ideology of Wahhabism (a sectarian version of Islam distinguished by xenophobia, misogyny and intolerance) sustains the power of the Saudi dynasty. The elites Aburish so despises are not puppets: they are willing and active partners in a bilateral process that helps to keep them in power. If, as Aburish implies, 'obsolete monarchies', 'special interest groups' and military regimes continue to govern undemocratically, without genuine popular mandates, that is because (as he rightly points out) institutions which reflect the will of the people and protect their rights have yet to be created.

Unfortunately, Aburish fails to address the deeper reasons for the democratic deficit in Middle Eastern societies – the product of history, and to a considerable extent of Islamic law itself. The sociologist, Bryan Turner, refers to a 'cluster of absences' in Islamic history: no concept of liberty, no autonomous corporate institutions and assemblies, no 'city', no self-confident middle class. Many of the institutions through which popular power is channelled in Western societies originated in the Church, the paradigm for the corporate bodies through which power is now routinised and mediated in impersonal ways. *Shari'a*, by contrast, remains uncompromisingly personal and unmediated – with the consequence that the public interest, in the form of city, state or any other institution standing between the individual and God, suffers from a lack of legitimacy. As Aburish points out, popular demands for representation throughout the Arab world are currently couched, not in the universal language of human rights, but in Islamist terms which most Westerners find incomprehensible, even repulsive. However, the absence of a democratic tradition in Islamic history should not automatically lead to the conclusion that Islam and democracy are incompatible, or that Islamists should be denied the right to stand in elections (as they are in Egypt and Algeria) on the grounds that once having come to power by democratic means, they will necessarily suppress democracy. Democrats of any political stripe deserve all the support they can get – even when they adopt the language of Islam. The only valid test for a democrat is a willingness to stand for election and to abide by a fair result. The alleged threat that Islamists pose to pro-Western and spuriously pro-democratic regimes is not a reason to supply those regimes with weapons of torture and internal suppression.

Published in *London Review of Books*, 16 October 1997.

The book reviewed was:

Said Aburish (1997) *A Brutal Friendship: The West and the Arab Elite.* London: Victor Gollancz.

Part **Two**

Faith, Power and Terror

Even before the attacks on New York and Washington, DC, on 11 September 2001, 'Islamic terrorism' was a highly-charged topic. Public opinion in the West, driven by television images of bearded militants, has tended to identify suicide missions with Islamic fanaticism, with young acolytes lured into sacrificing themselves, and others, by the prospect of Paradise with the infinite pleasures it offers. In the case of the Iran–Iraq war, the Hezbollah campaign in Lebanon and the campaigns against Israel by Hamas and Islamic Jihad, there was some truth in this picture: before undertaking suicide missions, the militants prepared videos in which the themes of sacrifice, martyrdom and Paradise loomed large. It would be a mistake, however, to over-emphasise the religious factor. A significant number of suicide missions have been undertaken by non-religious operatives, including the Marxist-oriented Tamil Tigers in Sri Lanka and the Syrian Socialist Nationalist Party in Southern Lebanon – the latter producing 13 'martyrs' during the 1980s, half of them women. Secular-oriented Palestinian groups such as the al-Aqsa brigade and the Popular Front for the Liberation of Palestine have also undertaken suicide missions. In general, the tactic spread because of its perceived efficacy, rather than its supposed religious inspiration.

The use of violence directed at non-combatants has historic roots in the Middle East but is far from being exclusive to one confession. Arguably the first modern act of political terrorism in the region was the bombing in July 1946 of the King David Hotel in Jerusalem by Irgun Zvi Leumi under the leadership of Menachem Begin; and the assassinations of Lord Moyne, the British Minister Resident, and Count Bernadotte, the UN mediator, by Jewish extremists long preceded that of Anwar Sadat by their Muslim counterparts. The massacres of Palestinians in the refugee camps of Sabra and Shatila in Lebanon, in September 1982, connived at if not actively encouraged by the Israeli Army, and the Israeli bombings of other Palestinian camps in Lebanon, cost many more non-combatant lives than atrocities committed by Palestinians.

At the same time it would be wrong to deny that there can be a religious dimension to modern terrorism and it is not just related to the VIP treatment that martyrs expect in Paradise. What might be called the 'ideologisation' or 'reification' of religious narrative is a phenomenon of our time, with militants seeking justification for their actions in the scriptures as well as in ideological tracts. God assisted Joshua in the slaughter of the Canaanities – a lesson not lost on Dr Baruch Goldstein, the American-born physician who massacred 29 Muslim worshippers at the Tomb of the Patriarchs in Hebron in February 1994. Muhammad expelled or massacred the Jewish tribes of Medina and waged jihad against the Meccan polytheists. Though his campaigns might have been moderate by the standards of the day, the precedents remain, enshrined in the Qur'an and still usable by those modern Islamist ideologues who push aside centuries of qualifying scholarship with a dismissive sweep of the hand.

This section looks at terrorism and counter-terrorism, including al-Qaeda and US President George W. Bush's ill-conceived response to its attacks in the 'war on terror' through the writings of notable experts, including Richard English, a specialist in the Ulster conflict; Peter Bergen, noted television journalist and security expert; and Marc Sageman, a former CIA operations director. Explorations of the Islamic factor in conflicts that include terrorism are provided by historians Michael Bonner and John Kelsay, while the former Dutch MP Ayaan Hirsi Ali and dissenting Catholic theologian Hans Küng offer broader theological perspectives. The section concludes with a piece on the Lockerbie affair – the worst terrorist atrocity to have taken place in Britain. Doubts about its true perpetrators persist, despite the fall of the Qaddafi regime in 2011.

6

Does Terrorism Work?

Does terrorism work? For years, scholars and military experts have been debating this question with a view to formulating the appropriate responses of governments. The answers are both complex and ambiguous. There are indeed some instances where a presumed terrorist act has produced the result intended by its perpetrators: in October 1983, for example, a suicide truck-bomb launched by Hezbollah killed 241 US marines, soldiers and civilians who were part of a multinational force sent to Beirut in the wake of the Israeli invasion in June 1982. The attack persuaded the Reagan administration to withdraw its forces from Lebanon the following year. A question of definition, however, immediately arises: should the Beirut truck-bombing even be described as a 'terrorist attack'? The US Code prepared by the House of Representatives defines terrorism as 'premeditated, politically motivated violence perpetrated against non-combatant targets by subnational groups or clandestine agents'. Though some civilians died (an example, it could be argued, of 'collateral damage') the overwhelming majority of the victims were military personnel. Can uniformed soldiers ever be described as 'non-combatants'? The same issue arises in the case of the attack on the USS *Cole* in Aden in October 2000, in which 17 American sailors were killed. By contrast, a terrorist act that fully fits the US model – the Madrid railway bombings in 2004, which deliberately targeted civilians two days before a general election – could be said to have 'worked' in that it tipped Spain's electoral balance towards withdrawal of Spanish troops from Iraq.

In the main, however, terrorist activity seems more likely to conform to the law of unintended consequences than to the idea of a military or quasi-military option with long-term and clearly defined strategic aims. Instead of achieving its ultimate goal of a British withdrawal from Ulster, the Provisional IRA – as its leading historian Richard English explains in this book – merely succeeded in triggering a loyalist backlash. Furthermore, during the early phase of the Troubles in Ireland the organisation may have failed in its most plausible rationale of protecting the Catholic community:

> *The Provos had emerged partly because of a perceived need to protect Catholic communities from violent attack. Could they, in fact, do this? Largely, the answer has to be that they could not ... IRA violence could at times prompt increased rather than diminished likelihood of murderous loyalist assault on Catholic victims. And while Gerry Adams has argued that by 1972 the Provisional IRA had 'created a defensive force of unprecedented effectiveness' this is a view which conflicts with the evidence.*

Yet there is a further twist in the logic of events set in motion by IRA violence and the responses it engendered from British and loyalist forces. While the loyalist response contradicted republican aims by ensuring the continuing British military presence, it also persuaded Sinn Fein–the IRA to move from violence towards participatory constitutional politics – a shift that was sealed by the 1998 Good Friday Agreement. English opens his essay with the striking image of Gerry Adams and Martin McGuinness – two still-serving members of the IRA's ruling Army Council – skateboarding with Tony Blair's children in the garden of 10 Downing Street in the summer of 1999. Only 15 years earlier, in October 1984, an IRA bomb came close to killing Prime Minister Margaret Thatcher and half her cabinet at Brighton's Grand Hotel.

English devotes a chapter to exploring various definitions of terrorism, a task of more than semantic interest. Definitions matter because they bear legislative weight. Labelling someone or something as a terrorist has real world consequences, with far-reaching implications for political representation and funding – the boycotting of the Palestinian Hamas movement, which is grudgingly moving towards de facto acceptance (if not de jure recognition) of Israel is an obvious example. By labelling Hamas a 'terrorist' organisation, the United States and the European Union have imposed unnecessary suffering on the people of Gaza. Yet terrorism is a slippery term, with more than a hundred definitions regularly used in the literature. Some definitions are so broad that they lose any meaningful distinction between legitimate and non-legitimate use of violence. According to one version: 'Terrorism is the intentional generation of massive fear by human beings for the purpose of securing or maintaining control over other human beings.' Clearly the 'shock and awe' tactics used by coalition forces in Iraq in 2003 – not to mention Hiroshima and Nagasaki in 1945, or the Israeli onslaught on Gaza in 2008–9 – could fall under such a catch-all definition, depriving the term of any meaningful distinction from war itself. As English questions: 'Is the ETA, Hamas or IRA bomb more literally, centrally and actually defined as relying on "terror" than are, say, US bombings in some of America's own wars during the past seventy years?' Yet a narrow term that limits the 'T-word' to non-state actors also makes for difficulties, since many terrorist atrocities are funded or otherwise sponsored by states, or people with access to state resources.

After emerging from the semantic maze of terrorist definitions, English comes up with his own definition:

> *Terrorism involves heterogeneous violence used or threatened with a political aim; it can involve a variety of acts, of targets and of actors; it possesses an important psychological dimension, producing terror or fear among a directly threatened group and also a wider implied audience in the hope of maximising political communication and achievement; it embodies the exerting and implementing of power, and the attempted redressing of power relations; it represents a subspecies of warfare, and as such it can form part of a wider campaign of violent and non-violent attempts at political leverage.*

This is not exactly a crisp definition, but it is pragmatic and realistic, and recognises above all that wherever it is practised, terrorism, like war, has a historical dimension. Being a mode of combat or 'subspecies of war' it cannot be extrapolated from its context. Eric Hobsbawm – cited by English – has argued that President Bush's 'war on terror' was an absurdity: 'Except as a metaphor, there can be no such thing as a "war against terror" or against terrorism, only against particular political actors who use what is a tactic, not a programme.'

In English's view, the most serious danger posed by terrorists is their capacity to 'provoke ill-judged, extravagant, and counter-productive state responses' rather than the actual damage caused by their actions. As a tactic its impact is more psychological than physical. The 'propaganda of the deed' showing people jumping from skyscrapers or bodies pulled from the London Underground creates an atmosphere of panic, a mood that empowers the terrorists by creating the impression that, militarily speaking, they dispose of forces beyond their numbers or the size of any constituency for which they may speak.

The tactic is fully consonant with the 'vanguardism' one finds in many terroristically-inclined ideologies: the 'vanguard' or terrorist hit-squad sees itself as spearheading much larger political forces which in time will rally to their cause. Vanguards – from the self-styled revolutionaries of the Red Army Faction (the Baader-Meinhof group) to the 'knights' of al-Qaeda – see themselves as 'unmasking' the inherently unjust or repressive character (whether 'fascist' or 'infidel') of the existing political order. If the authorities over-react, the terrorists' analysis becomes self-fulfilling. In Northern Ireland, repression of the republican Catholic community (the 1970 Falls Road curfew; the thuggery of the B-Specials and the Royal Ulster Constabulary (RUC); internment in 1971; 'Bloody Sunday' in 1972; the use of sensory deprivation techniques; and the avoidable 1981 IRA hunger strike, for example) de-legitimised the British state in the eyes of the Catholic minority, making the climb-back to constitutional government lengthier and more painful than it might otherwise have been. President Bush's 'disastrously managed war on terror', whose operations exposed a litany of horrors including 'rendition' and 'waterboarding', as revealed by compelling images from Guantanamo Bay and Abu Ghraib, yields an even starker conclusion. When the state 'fights dirty', it undermines its own moral basis and legitimacy in the rule of law. As English explains, virtually 'all cases where terrorism is found involve profound problems of political legitimacy', whether caused by ethnic, religious or national dissatisfaction. In the struggle for legitimacy, a state that loses the higher moral ground may endanger its own existence.

His insights lead to the conclusion that the preponderance of terrorism in the Arab–Islamic world, as indicated statistically by bodies such as the US National Memorial Institute for the Prevention of Terrorism, has less to do with cultural, social and economic factors (hostility to Western values, high unemployment or social dislocation), however widespread these may be, than with the fundamental problem of constitutional legitimacy. The modern national state with its battle-forged frontiers, linguistic hegemony and rule by consent of the governed (however imperfectly realised) did not grow organically from Middle Eastern soil (where different arrangements had prevailed satisfactorily for many centuries) but was largely imposed by European powers for their own convenience. Here, terror is the flip-side of repression: the violence that shatters bodies in the street is the outward and visible manifestation of violence occurring in the secrecy of police torture chambers. English concludes his book with the unexceptional argument that we must learn to live with terrorism while attempting to address the root problems that give rise to it. Unfortunately, in much of the Islamic world at present it is the nature of the state itself that lies at the root of the problem.

Published in *Prospect* magazine, 18 November 2009.

The book reviewed was:

Richard English (2009) *Terrorism: How To Respond.* Oxford, UK: Oxford University Press.

7

Signposts on the Road

A week or two after the skybombings of New York and Washington, DC, on 11 September 2001, Terry Jones, the former member of the Monty Python comedy team, made one of the more memorable remarks about the 'war on terrorism' by asking in a radio interview 'Can you wage a war against an abstract noun?' The very use of the word 'war' in this context makes an important concession to the terrorists by elevating them to the status of combatants, rather than treating them as outlaws and criminals. In Northern Ireland, the British government resisted demands of Republican prisoners to be granted political status for precisely this reason. While the hunger strikes and 'dirty protests' eventually led to concessions being made in the prisons, the insistence of successive British and Irish governments on continuing to criminalise terrorism by use of police methods and court proceedings has yielded long-term benefits. Irish terrorism has been (almost) defeated without significant loss to the authority and legitimacy of either of the states involved. To adapt the Maoist metaphor, the only way to destroy pests is to drain the swamps in which they breed.

To state the problem in these terms, however, is to be made immediately aware of the immense difficulty posed by al-Qaeda. The organisation or network, as Peter Bergen discloses with painstaking, documented detail, is a global conglomerate, with limbs or tentacles stretching westwards from the Philippines to the United States. Its operatives are only loosely connected organisationally. In this respect it resembles a 'multinational holding company, headquartered in Afghanistan, under the chairmanship of bin Laden'. Given that the 'traditional structure of a holding company is a core management group controlling partial or complete interests in other companies', the degree of control Osama bin Laden exercises over subsidiary operations is, to say the least, problematic.

According to Bergen, bin Laden formulates general policies in consultation with his board, known by the Islamic term of the *Majlis al-Shura* (consultative council). This body makes executive decisions for the group. There are other, subordinate committees responsible for 'military' affairs (that is, terrorism), business interests, legal rulings (*fatwa*) and the media. Once decisions on overall policy have been made by bin Laden and his closest advisers, they are relayed to the relevant committee and then, at the appropriate moment, to lower-level members on a strictly 'need to know' basis. The ordinary foot soldiers are organised into cells which receive instructions and carry them out without questioning them or being able to see how they fit into an overall strategy. Reports from FBI investigations suggest that some of the 19 hijackers involved in the 9/11 attack were unaware of its suicidal nature: they thought this would be an 'ordinary' hijacking, which they had a reasonable chance of surviving. As an FBI agent testified at the trial in New York last March of the al-Qaeda members accused of complicity in the suicide bombings of the US embassies in Kenya and Tanzania in 1998, the lower-level operatives do not necessarily receive their instructions directly from bin Laden.

Bin Laden's overall complicity in the New York and Washington atrocities may be clear from the gloating videos he has released, as broadcast by the Al Jazeera channel in the Arabian Gulf, and from materials recently found in Kabul. Whether this would satisfy the exacting requirements of a legal system which produced an acquittal in the murder trial of O. J. Simpson is another matter altogether. What with the security implications of a bin Laden trial, not to mention the politically embarrassing disclosures he might make about Saudi and Pakistani complicity in his organisation, *it is not unreasonable to suppose that Washington would rather have him dead than alive.* In any event, as Bergen makes clear, the death of bin Laden hardly disposes of the problem posed by al-Qaeda.

Bin Laden's charismatic personality and organisational skills have held the organisation together, but on the 'holding company' analogy the different 'assets' acquired by al-Qaeda since the early 1990s existed before his organisation took them over. A good example is the Egyptian *Jihad* group headed by Ayman al-Zawahiri, who served three years in prison for being implicated in the murder of President Anwar al-Sadat of Egypt in 1981. Al-Zawahiri, an Egyptian surgeon from an upper-class background, joined bin Laden in Afghanistan after he was outvoted in the armed Islamist group he had previously headed in Egypt. During the 1990s, the group and its affiliates were responsible for killing some 1,200 people, notably Christians, government officials, police officers and foreigners, culminating in the massacre of 58 tourists and four Egyptians at Luxor in 1997. Realising they were losing public support, the groups announced a 'ceasefire' in their war against the government. Al-Zawahiri and other members, like the Real IRA, dissented and carried on their activities. Their departure for Afghanistan may have caused a sigh of relief in Egypt, but it brought important new blood into al-Qaeda. The softly spoken surgeon is said to be the most powerful mind behind the organisation, and would be well-placed to take over should bin Laden be removed.

By the same logic, the destruction of the al-Qaeda training camps in Afghanistan, achieved by US bombing, may secure a short-term respite from Islamist terrorism, but not much more. As Bergen points out, it is the training camps which 'turn raw recruits with a general and inchoate antipathy to the West into skilled bomb-makers'. However, like the poppy-fields and coca plantations, which produce most of the world's illegal narcotics, terrorist training camps are subject to the 'balloon effect'. Suppress them in one area, and they will pop up somewhere else. The 'war against terrorism' sounds disconcertingly similar to the 'war against drugs'.

What shocks and surprises most from reading Bergen's book is not that there should be terrorists who claim Islamic legitimacy for their actions – the history of Islamist terrorism in Egypt goes back 30 years – but that the US security services should have been so easily caught off-guard. The CIA's special Counter-Terrorist Center (CTC), founded in 1986, works closely with other agencies, including the FBI, the National Security Agency, the Secret Service, the Federal Aviation Agency, the Department of Defence, the State Department and the Bureau of Alcohol, Tobacco and Firearms (BATF). There is an anti-terrorism budget of more than $11 billion. The American people are very far from getting value for money.

One example of many cited by Bergen in this complex trail of ineptitude should suffice: the World Trade Center, the third-tallest building in the world and a primary symbol of American wealth and economic power, was attacked in 1993. Nine people were killed and many others injured in what Bergen regards as a dress rehearsal for the September 2001 attack. Ramzi Yousuf, who masterminded the 1993 bombing, was eventually arrested in 1995 in Islamabad after spending time in Manila, from where he fled after almost blowing himself up with a home-made device. Sheikh Umar Abd al-Rahman, spiritual leader of the Egyptian Jihadist group responsible for the assassination of Anwar al-Sadat, now serving a life sentence for his part in this crime, visited New York in 1987 and again in 1990, when he decided to stay. Despite being indicted in Egypt for his part in the plot to assassinate Sadat in 1981, he was given a visa in 1987 and a multi-entry visa in 1990. Later, government officials would claim that the visas were issued as a result of 'computer errors' because of the different way his name was transliterated from Arabic; but according to Bergen, at least one of these visas was issued by a CIA officer working undercover in the consular section of the American embassy in Sudan.

The militant Islamist sheikh's stay in New York from 1990 was arranged by Mustafa Shalabi, a chemist with an electrical contracting business in Brooklyn. Three years earlier, Shalabi had founded the Alkhifa Refugee Center, registered as a charitable organisation 'to provide for the needs and welfare of the Afghan people, particularly the refugees due to the Soviet invasion'. In fact it had very little to do with refugees, but acted as the recruitment hub for Muslims living in the United States who wanted to fight the Soviet invasion. More than 200 volunteers for the *jihad* in Afghanistan passed through the Center. Activities such as these, as is well known, received a fair wind from the CIA, even though, as Bergen explains, most of the support for the anti-Soviet campaign in Afghanistan was channelled through the SIS, the Pakistani secret service, since the CIA did not want to hand the Russians a propaganda weapon by having any of their agents caught on the ground. The SIS became the primary supporters of the Taliban, bin Laden's protectors. Judging from recent press reports, they have continued to support the Taliban against the Northern Alliance despite American bombing and the Musharraf government's support for the 'war against terrorism'.

Following the Soviet withdrawal in 1989, Shalabi and Abd al-Rahman had a falling out which was much publicised in New York Muslim circles. Shalabi, who had a reputation for honesty and piety, wanted to consult the donors about what to do with a considerable quantity of cash in hand. The Sheikh wanted to divert it to the *jihad* against America's ally, the 'infidel' Egyptian government. In his sermons he began accusing Shalabi of being a 'bad Muslim'. Posters appeared in mosques all over the New York area, accusing him of financial mismanagement. On 1 March 1991, Shalabi was found stabbed to death in his Coney Island apartment, two days before he was due to join his family in Pakistan. No one was charged with the murder. Thereafter, the Alkhifa Center was taken over by the Sheikh's loyalists. In a country where homicides are commonplace, Shalabi's murder evidently attracted little official attention, even though the finger of suspicion pointed towards acolytes of a man well known for his extreme views, and the known associate of the assassins of a friendly foreign head of state.

From his numerous interviews with the intelligence agencies, Bergen concludes that the 'strong religious orientation' of bin Laden's followers, combined with its diffuse organisational structure, makes al-Qaeda 'hard to penetrate', even on US soil. The Muslim ban on alcohol, according to these agents, posed an additional problem. As one of them explains: 'In the old days I could have a drink with a secular terrorist – there is no way with the bin Laden guys. Also these guys have a shared history and outsiders are viewed with suspicion.' What strikes one most about this remark is the parochialism it reveals about the US intelligence community (which may well apply to our own as well). Millions of Americans are teetotallers, among them 5–6 million Muslims, the vast majority of whom are loyal to their country of birth or adoption. Religious discussion groups are legion. Just as the FBI and BATF failed to heed the advice of trained theologians, with disastrous results after the siege of a ranch occupied by a Protestant religious sect, the Branch Davidians, at Waco, Texas, in April 1993, the intelligence community has signally failed to adjust to a contemporary political environment in which religious motivations *matter*. Sermons delivered in publicly accessible places can have security implications, whether preached by Egyptian mullahs or the 'Identity Christian' pastors linked to the Oklahoma City bomber, Timothy McVeigh. The culture engendered by the radical separation of church and state, in which religion is supposed to be harmlessly left to its own devices, has deeply infected the official mind.

None of this means, of course, that the security services could have prevented the New York and Washington attacks. The existence of Mohamed Atta, now believed to have been the overall commander of the operation, who flew the American Airlines Boeing into the North Tower of the World Trade Center, never came to the attention of the intelligence authorities, despite the lack of interest he showed in take-off and landing techniques at the flying school he attended in Florida. As a former inspector general of the CIA explained in a recent newspaper article, the CIA are woefully short of people with Arabic and Islamic expertise. Yet expertise in both the cultures and languages of modern Islam exists in abundance on American University campuses. The intellectual mentor of modern Islamist terrorism was Sayyid Qutb (1906–66), who lived in the United States from 1949 to 1951. Bergen notes that all the key members of al-Qaeda, like Qutb, have been Egyptians: 'One cannot overestimate the influence of Qutb on the jihadist groups in Egypt and by extension on Osama bin Laden.' Bin Laden was strongly influenced at university in Saudi Arabia by Abdullah Azzam, a Palestinian preacher in the Qutbist mould, and by Muhammad Qutb, Sayyid's brother, who shared many of the Egyptian martyr's extremist views.

Qutb, celebrated during his lifetime as one of Egypt's leading intellectuals, has been the subject of numerous essays and monographs by American academics, including Yvonne Haddad, Leonard Binder, John Calvert and Robert Lee (not to mention studies by Europeans such as Gilles Kepel and Johannes Jansen). Binder in particular has explained how Qutb courted martyrdom in order to resolve the tortured contradiction between a personal identity forged in the traditional faith of an Egyptian village and the reality of the 'godless' or 'pagan' (*jahili*) world he encountered in America and Cairo. In a book published in 1988 [*Islamic Liberalism*, University of Chicago Press], Binder suggests that Qutb's 'ontological' or Heideggerian version of Islam was linked to his concept of the 'ownmost being' of the believing Muslim, in a manner that urged him 'to act out, to realise, to practice that faith as an expression of his being' without regard for the consequences:

> *When we consider ... that the absolute foundation of Islam, and of the freedom of the individual Muslim to act, is the* hakimiya *(sovereignty) of God, then the characteristic Islamic act becomes the defiance of jahili activity.* Thus is the groundwork laid for acts of martyrdom which appear to be suicidal and/or hopeless acts of political terrorism.

Mohamed Atta, an outstanding student of architecture at the Hamburg Technical University, fitted the Qutbist mould in almost every respect. There is, however, a vital difference between them. Unlike Qutb, a pre-eminent man of letters whose adherence to the Qur'an was rooted in fascination with its language, Atta, along with almost all the Islamists who followed Qutb's path, shunned literary-critical approaches to the Islamic scripture. Indeed, Atta, in conversation with a German colleague, Ralf Bodenstein, expressed his approval for the condemnation for apostasy of Nasr Hamid Abu Zaid, an assistant professor at the Arabic Department at Cairo University, for applying modern linguistic methods when analysing the Qur'an.

Like Atta, nearly all the ideologues who make up the leadership of the Islamist movements in Egypt are graduates in technical or scientific subjects. One explanation for this is that, while students in the arts and humanities have to deal with texts, whether religious or secular, by making comparisons and exploring ambiguities, students in the 'hard' sciences treat texts mono-dimensionally, as sources of factual information. Qutb in his writings eschewed the apparatus of traditional scholarship in his interpretation of the Qur'an. The Prophet Muhammad's contemporaries, he wrote in his most influential tract, *Signposts on the Road*, composed in prison prior to his execution in 1966, did not approach the Qur'an for the purpose of acquiring culture and information, nor for taste or enjoyment. They approached it in order to act on what they heard immediately, 'as a soldier on the battlefield reads "Today's Bulletin" so that he knows what is to be done'. There are plenty of verses in the Qur'an which, taken singly and out of context, can be used as 'operational briefings' in the Islamist 'war against paganism'.

What was particularly disturbing about the New York attack – apart from the appalling casualties – was the technical proficiency with which it was executed. As a graduate of Cairo University's faculty of architecture, as well as from Hamburg, Atta knew exactly where to hit the buildings, using planes at the start of transcontinental domestic flights that were fully loaded with fuel. It was the fires, not the impact of the planes, that destroyed the structural supports, causing the buildings to collapse with devastating loss of life. In terms of sophistication and accuracy, the attack on New York had the 'surgical precision' claimed by the US in its bombing of Taliban positions in Afghanistan: the crucial difference being the use of living human brains instead of electronic guidance systems to actually hit the targets. Bergen draws our attention to the use of 'twenty-first-century communications and weapons technology in the service of the most extreme, retrograde reading of holy war' as well as to the 'grafting of entirely modern sensibilities and techniques' on to a 'pre-modern' religious message. But the issue is even more complicated than this.

The Islamist message, though it draws on 'pre-modern' readings of the Qur'an and other religious texts, is wholly modern in its revolutionary existentialism. The first Islamist group to emerge in Egypt after Sayyid Qutb's execution was inspired not only by Islamic writings, but also by the 'propaganda of the deed' advocated by ultra-leftist radicals such as the German Baader-Meinhof gang. This unholy alliance between pre-modern and modern pervades the entire Muslim world, where modernist or accommodationist readings of *jihad* ('struggle' or 'holy war') have been undermined by radical conservatives, many of them funded and supported by Saudi Arabia. As Bergen points out, the 'Afghan Arabs' originally recruited for the *jihad* against the Russians who now form the core of al-Qaeda, were initially funded by such respectable institutions as the Saudi-financed Muslim World League. The 'pattern of Saudi funding of militant Islamist organisations, known as *riyalpolitik*, which is supposed to shore up Saudi legitimacy … actually undermines it, because it funds the very groups most opposed to the Saudi regime'.

This contradiction, however, may suggest that bin Laden's aims are less far-reaching than is usually supposed. For while he fulminates against the 'Jews and Crusaders', drawing his supporters from the quintessentially modern, alienated, anomic disciples of Sayyid Qutb, who share the Egyptian martyr's disdain for the materialism and spiritual emptiness of the West and its 'pagan' imitators among the ruling elites of the Islamic world, bin Laden's targets are political rather than cultural. His rage is primarily against Saudi Arabia, particularly at the presence of infidel American troops in the peninsula, the 'Land of the Two Sanctuaries': 'For all his denunciations of the Jews, al-Qaeda has so far never attacked an Israeli or Jewish target.'

British and European governments have made it clear that they believe a Middle East settlement is a prerequisite to keeping the Arab states on side in the 'war against terrorism'. The Algerian, Egyptian, Syrian, Russian, Pakistani, Indian, Turkish and several other governments have joined the anti-terrorism bandwagon with varying degrees of enthusiasm, seeing in it an opportunity to enlist international support for the suppression of domestic opposition or local nationalist revolts. But if Bergen is correct, the 'war against terrorism' – with the very uncertain consequences it holds for the Middle East, and Central and South Asia, not to mention human rights across the world – is an over-reaction to what was admittedly an appalling act of mass murder. The origins of this atrocity, as the bin Laden story makes clear, lies in Saudi Arabia, both in the way the ruling family has tried to buy off religious opposition by sending it abroad, and in the industrialised world's reckless dependency on inexpensive Saudi oil. No solution which fails to address the Saudi–American nexus at the heart of this crisis can carry much hope for success.

Published in *The Times Literary Supplement*, 7 December 2001.

The book reviewed was:

Peter L. Bergen (2001) *Holy War Inc: Inside the Secret World of Osama bin Laden.* Weidenfeld & Nicolson.

8
Faces of Islam

In the immediate aftermath of the attacks of 11 September 2001, US President George W. Bush visited the Islamic Center in Washington, where he told his audience: 'These acts of violence against innocents violate the fundamental tenets of the Islamic faith ... The face of terror is not the true faith of Islam. That's not what Islam is all about. Islam is peace.' In Britain, his sentiments were echoed by Prime Minister Tony Blair, who told the Arabic newspaper, *al-Hayat*:

> *There is nothing in Islam which excuses such an all-encompassing massacre of innocent people, nor is there anything in the teachings of Islam that allows the killing of civilians, of women and children, of those who are not engaged in war or fighting.*

However reflective such views may be of the 'moderate' Muslim majority, they are not uncontested. As John Kelsay shows in his new book, *Arguing the Just War in Islam*, debates about the ethics of conflict have been going on since the time of the Prophet Muhammad. The scholars who interpreted the Prophet's teachings addressed issues such as the permissibility of using 'hurling machines', or mangonels, where non-combatants, including women and children, and Muslim captives or merchants, might be endangered. In the 'realm of war' outside the borders of Islam a certain military realism prevailed; for example, the eighth-century jurist, al-Shaybani (who died in 805) stated that, if such methods were not permitted, the Muslims would be unable to fight at all.

There may be a vast distance in time and technology separating al-Shaybani's authorisation of mangonels and the attacks on New York and Washington, but the boundaries of legal discussion remain remarkably consistent. In their 1998 *Declaration Concerning Armed Struggle Against Jews and Crusaders* following the deployment of US troops in the Arabian Peninsula, Osama bin Laden, Ayman al-Zawahiri and their co-signers belonging to the 'World Islamic Front' cited rulings by thirteenth-century scholars, including the celebrated jurist Ibn Taymiyya, in order to justify their ruling that 'to fight the Americans and their allies, civilians and military, is an individual obligation for every Muslim who can do it in any country in which it is possible'. In a recent video, bin Laden invites Americans to embrace Islam, a requirement the classical authorities insist upon before a non-Muslim enemy may legitimately be attacked. The critiques of bin Laden's statements coming from religious authorities focus on the means by which the ultimate objective of a 'restored' Islamic polity under *Shari'a* law may be achieved, rather than the objective itself.

For example, in a recent open letter to 'Brother Osama', the prominent Saudi cleric Sheikh Salman al-Oadah made a scathing attack on bin Laden for the excessive violence and damage to Islam inflicted by his campaign – including the 'destruction of entire nations' and the 'nightmare of civil war' in Afghanistan and Iraq, with their impact on surrounding countries. But the sheikh's quarrel with bin Laden is essentially about means rather than ends. The burden of his attack is that al-Qaeda's methods – and the political fallout they engender – are counter-productive. Even if the radicals take power somewhere in the world, the sheikh writes, they will not have the experience or competence to govern in accordance with Islamic law.

None of these arguments are really new. The debate has been raging since before 9/11. Will the militant actions taken in the service of justice yield more harm than good? Should a distinction be made between actions against 'near enemies' occupying Muslim lands in Palestine or Chechnya and the 'far enemy' in Washington? As Kelsay explains, 'statements by al-Qa'ida are best understood as attempts to legitimate or justify a course of action in the terms associated with Islamic jurisprudence'. He usefully terms this discourse 'Shari'a reasoning'.

The word *shari'a*, usually translated as 'law', refers to the 'path' or 'way' governing the modes of behaviour by which Muslims are enjoined to seek salvation. The way may be known to God, but for human beings it is not predetermined. A famous *hadith* (tradition) of Muhammad states that differences of opinion between the learned is a blessing. *Shari'a* reasoning is therefore 'an open practice'. In Islam's classical era, up to the tenth century, scholars exercised *ijtihad* – independent reasoning – to reach an understanding of the divine law. *Ijtihad* shares the same Arabic root as the more familiar *jihad*, meaning 'effort' or 'struggle', the word that is sometimes translated as 'holy war'. *Ijtihad* is in effect the intellectual struggle to discover what the law ought to be. As Kelsay remarks, the legal scholars trained in its sources and methodologies will seek to achieve a balance between the rulings of their predecessors

and independent judgements reflecting the idea that 'changing circumstances require fresh wisdom'. The *Shari'a* is not so much a body of law
but a field of discourse or platform for legal reasoning. Recently, it has
become an arena for intellectual combat.

It is therefore open to question whether the hijackers and the terrorists automatically put themselves beyond the bounds of Islam by killing
innocents, as statements by Bush, Blair and dozens of Muslim leaders
and scholars suggest. With no churches or formally constituted religious
authorities to police the boundaries of Islam, the only universally accepted
orthodoxy is the *Shari'a* itself. But the *Shari'a* is more of an ideal than a
formally constituted body of law. While interpreting the law was once the
province of the trained clerical class of *ulama*, any consensus governing its
correct interpretation has broken down under pressure of regional conflicts
and the influence of religious autodidacts, whose vision of Islam was formed
outside the received scholarly tradition.

None of the three most influential theorists behind Sunni militancy,
Abul Ala Maududi (1903–79), Hasan al-Banna (1906–49) and Sayyid
Qutb (1906–66), undertook traditional religious training. Yet both they
and the authors of the landmark texts examined by Kelsay in his admirably
lucid book (including the Charter of Hamas, which calls for the destruc-
tion of Israel, and bin Laden's 1998 *Declaration*) claim the mantle of the
Shari'a, as did the terrorists responsible for the atrocities in New York,
Madrid and London.

Like it or not, these terrorist campaigns were inspired by the example
of the Prophet's struggle – his 'just war' – against the Quraysh, the pagan
tribesmen of Mecca. In the context of the original conflict between the
early Muslims and the Meccans, the sources, including the Qur'an and the
narratives of Muhammad's life, suggest that 'fighting is an appropriate means
by which Muslims should seek to secure the right to order life according to
divine directives'. In militant readings of the *Shari'a*, the historical precedents are not so much interpreted as applied. For ultra-radicals such as
bin Laden's deputy, Ayman al-Zawahiri, there is, as Kelsay observes, 'little
room for a sustained process of discerning divine guidance' along the
lines enjoined by traditional scholars. An even more striking absence is
evident in the criticisms of militant readings advanced by official Islamic
authorities, including the widely respected Sheikh al-Azhar, head of the
mosque-university in Cairo and once the single most important voice in
Sunni Islam. While questioning the methods of the militants on grounds
of practical ethics – will the 'actions taken in the service of justice yield
more harm than good?' – their criticisms usually fall short of challenging
them on the grounds of political legitimacy. Conservative Muslim critics of

militancy 'do not in fact dissent from the militant judgment that current political arrangements [in most Muslim majority states] are illegitimate ... In its broad outlines, the militant vision articulated by al-Zawahiri is also the vision of his critics'.

The core of this consensus – shared by traditionally trained scholars and more populist leaders such as al-Banna, founder of the Muslim Brotherhood, and Maududi, his South Asian counterpart – is the belief that the abolition of the caliphate by Kemal Atatürk in Turkey in 1924 must not mean the end of Islamic government. In this vision, which is also shared by Shi'a jurists such as the late Ayatollah Khomeini, parliaments and elections are only acceptable within the frame of Islamic supremacy. They 'cannot compromise on Muslim leadership', Kelsay writes. Full-blown democracy, where the Muslim voice might simply be one among many, implying a degree of moral equivalence between Islam and other perspectives, would be 'dangerous, not only for the standing of the Muslim community, but for the moral life of humankind'.

In the majority, Sunni, tradition this sense of supremacy was sanctified as much by history as by theology. In the first instance, the truth of Islam was vindicated on the field of battle. As Hans Küng acknowledges in *Islam: Past, Present and Future* – his 767-page overview of the Islamic faith and history, seen from the perspective of a liberal Christian theologian – Islam is above all a 'religion of victory'. Muslims of many persuasions – not just the self-styled jihadists – defend the truth claims of their religion by resorting to what might be called the argument from manifest success.

According to this argument, the Prophet Muhammad overcame the enemies of truth through divinely assisted battles as well as through preaching. Building on his victories and faith in his divine mission, his successors, the early caliphs, conquered most of western Asia and North Africa as well as Spain. In this view, the truth of Islam was vindicated by actual events, through Islam's historical achievement in creating what would become a great world civilisation.

The argument from manifest success is consonant with the theological doctrine according to which Islam supersedes the previous revelations of Judaism and Christianity. Jews and Christians are in error because they deviated from the straight path revealed to Abraham, ancestral patriarch of all three faiths. Islam 'restores' the true religion of Abraham while superseding Judao-Christianity as the 'final' revelation. The past and the future belong to Islam even if the present makes for difficulties. Küng asks:

> In the history of religions, did any religion pursue a victorious
> course as rapid, far-reaching, tenacious and permanent as that

of Islam? Scarcely one. So is it any wonder that to the present
day Muslim pride is rooted in the experience of the early period?

This formative experience of victory is what interests Michael Bonner in his scholarly essay, *Jihad in Islamic History*. Viewing what has become an increasingly crowded field, he points out that the word *jihad* has acquired different resonances for a wide variety of actors, from the Islamist radicals for whom it forms the heart of a militant ideology, to mystical quietists who regard the 'greater *jihad*' as the struggle against the 'lower self' of baser human impulses. Some observers, notably the political theorist Benjamin Barber, in his widely read book of 1995, *Jihad vs. McWorld*, have stretched the definition to encompass local resistance to globalisation. Other definitions mirror that of the militants themselves: the *jihad* doctrine is cited as proof of Islam's innate tendency toward violence and its incompatibility with democratic norms. At the opposite end of the spectrum are those scholars, such as Abdulaziz Sachedina – a professor at the University of Virginia who studied in Iran, whose readings of the sources convinces them that *jihad* is purely defensive.

In clearing a path through this highly-charged intellectual undergrowth, Bonner adopts a thematic approach aimed at uncovering 'the inner logic' or 'structural' sense underlying the Qur'anic teachings, even when 'they sometimes appear to be in contradiction with one another'. He concludes that 'where the Qur'an treats of war, we usually find a rhetoric of requital and recompense'. God grants the Muslims permission to fight 'those against whom war has been made, because they have been wronged'. The law of reciprocity applies to goods as well as to warfare: whatever the faithful spend in the 'path of God' will be amply repaid. After the Arab conquests of the Middle East and North Africa shortly after Muhammad's death in 632, the law of recompense was institutionalised: the fighters received a fixed stipend from a treasury staffed by clerks who inscribed the recipients' names in a special register.

This expanding 'conquest society' was funded by rewarding the fighters with taxes extracted from the defeated, with a 'relatively small elite of Arab warriors' becoming recipients of taxes contributed by 'an enormous, taxpaying majority'. It was the purse, rather than the sword, that was an incentive to conversion, since Muslims, including converts, paid less tax than the non-Muslim majority. Eventually, from the ninth century onwards, the Arab fighters lost their privileged position, and the conquest society was replaced by systems under which Muslim rulers recruited specialised military units from non-Arab tribes, including Turks, Sub-Saharan Africans, Berbers and Slavs. For example, the Fatimids, who founded Cairo in 969, depended for their military power on Berber mercenaries and Sudanese slave-soldiers. But the notion of reciprocity remained embedded in *Shari'a* reasoning. The 'martyr' who dies on the field of battle is 'rewarded' in heaven for his courage. Proper religious motivation is paramount, but since 'only God has full knowledge of the fighter's intention', those slain in battle are given the benefit of the doubt and treated as martyrs.

Whatever the limitations imposed on the conduct of war by the jurists, *jihad* became deeply embedded in Islamic discourse. In Bonner's words, it is 'an indissoluble part of the transcendent, transforming Message' that 'provides motivation and pride'. Given the expanding frontiers of the formative period when the laws of *jihad* were developed, it would be wrong to regard the classical *jihad* as being purely defensive. As Bonner has it: 'The historical experience of pre-modern Islamic states, together with the pronouncements of many classical Islamic jurists, would all tend to undermine this modern view of *jihad* as being preeminently defensive in character.'

After an extensive survey of the best scholarly literature available in European languages, Hans Küng arrives at a similar conclusion:

> *The apologetic argument often advanced by Muslims that armed* jihad *refers only to wars of defence cannot be maintained. It is contradicted by the testimonies of the Islamic chroniclers, who show that the* jihad *was of the utmost political and military significance. It is hard to imagine a more effective motivation for a war than the 'struggle' ... which furthers God's cause against the unbelievers.*

As 'an ecumenical theologian committed to fairness to all religions', Küng sets himself the task of making a 'critical reconnaissance' of Islam with a view to assisting in its 'renewal'. His volume completes the ambitious threefold project that has already resulted in massive books on Christianity and Judaism. No religion, he says,

> *can be satisfied with the status quo in this time of upheaval. Everywhere there are amazingly parallel questions about a future renewal. In the face of antisemitism and increasing Islamophobia, what are called for are not uncritical philosemites or Islamophiles ... but rather authentic, truthful friends of Judaism and Islam.*

By 'authentic' one assumes that Küng means 'believing'. The believer's route to an understanding of religious traditions other than one's own is more risky and demanding than that of the sceptical outsider, because, in addition to the intellectual challenges, there are formidable emotional issues at stake. Since the God in which a vast amount of emotional energy has been invested appears to have said different things to the various individuals claiming to speak on His behalf, belief in the certainties held by one tradition necessarily excludes the others. This is especially so in the Abrahamic family of Western monotheisms, where confessions are deemed to be exclusive. In the mainstream, orthodox versions of these faiths, one cannot at the same time be a Muslim and a Christian, or a Christian and a Jew (though hybrid versions, such as 'Jews for Jesus', undoubtedly exist). In a globalised culture, where religions are in daily contact with their competitors, denial of pluralism is a recipe for conflict.

Yet acceptance of pluralism relativises truth. Once it is allowed that there are different paths to ultimate truth, an individual's religious allegiance becomes a matter of personal choice, and choice is the enemy of the certainties that religions – especially monotheistic ones – are supposed to uphold. Fundamentalism is one contemporary response to the crisis of faith brought about by awareness of differences. Another – diametrically opposite – response is the global ecumenicism promoted by Küng. In approaching the prospect of dialogue with other religions, Küng is surely right in proposing that participants must abandon the literalist interpretation of their sacred texts, since every tradition must acknowledge its local origins: 'A conversation with Jews and Muslims, or with Hindus and Buddhists, Chinese and Japanese, is doomed to failure if the linguistic tradition of a regional culture, whether that of the Greek East or the Latin West, makes absolute claims.'

Outside the ranks of a small intellectual elite, the theological obstacles to dialogue are indeed formidable. In the ninth century, the caliph al-Ma'mun and his immediate successors tried, and eventually failed, to impose as orthodoxy the belief that the Qur'an had been created in time (with the implication that its teachings might be contingent and time-specific). In reaction to this policy, the majority Sunni tradition espoused an anti-rationalist theology that holds the Qur'an to be 'uncreated' or co-eternal with God. In consequence, the extraordinary veneration of the Qur'an has dominated Muslim religious thought and popular culture for more than a millennium.

Whereas historical criticism of the Bible has been accepted by most Protestants (apart from fundamentalist diehards) as well as by Reform Judaism and, belatedly, by the Catholic Church (following the Second Vatican Council of 1962–5), 'higher criticism' of the Qur'an has yet to take root despite the impressive achievements of individual scholars such as (the late) Fazlur Rahman, Mohammed Arkoun and Farid Esack (all of whom work, or have worked, in Western universities). For Küng:

> *It can only help Islamic faith if Islamic scholars begin to tackle the historical problems. This can still be dangerous for a Muslim today, just as a heterodox view was for a Catholic at the height of the Inquisition or for a liberal Protestant in Calvin's Geneva.*

What is needed, he concludes, elaborating on the term made popular by Thomas Kuhn, is a 'paradigm shift' towards modernisation comparable to those that occurred in the Christian and Jewish traditions.

Küng's paradigm theory, which he illustrates with a complicated series of charts, makes structural comparisons between different stages in the evolution of the three monotheistic religions. The results, like some of the discursive threads in his monumental book, are at times confusing. Despite the apparent rigour, the detail is somewhat daunting, with the shape of the vast forest he sets out to map obscured by the density of the trees. His case could have been made more clearly in a shorter, leaner book.

But the direction of his argument is sound. Like other religious systems, Islam has no option but to enter the waters of post-Enlightenment modern society, a universal milieu where religion is no longer, as it was in the Middle Ages and the Reformation, an institution set over the social system to guarantee its unity, but merely a factor, a sphere, a one-part system among several.

There are precedents for this necessary paradigm shift – for example, in the expansion from the Arab empire with its limited cultural horizons to the world religion Islam eventually became, incorporating the non-Arab peoples who now make up the vast majority of Muslims. The intellectual groundwork for change has been laid in the works of modernist reformers who have been revisiting the sources of Islam for more than a century. They include Sir Sayyid Ahmed Khan (1817–98) and Syed Ameer Ali (1848–1928) in India, and Muhammad Abduh (1849–1905), the influential chief jurist of Egypt. The problems do not lie in the realm of theology, where Muslim intellectuals have charted retreats from the received certainties of the medieval paradigm that are just as ingenious and (for true believers) just as plausible as the efforts of Western theologians. The obstacle lies rather in the absence, in the majority traditions, of structures of leadership through which reformist ideas can be effected at the popular level.

The size of the mountain that must be scaled before many Muslim societies can undergo Küng's 'paradigm shift' may be gauged from Ayaan

Hirsi Ali's remarkable memoir, *Infidel*. Born in Somalia in 1969, Hirsi Ali became a celebrity in Europe when her collaborator, the film-maker, Theo van Gogh, was murdered in an Amsterdam street in broad daylight two months after the airing of a television film they had made depicting the plight of Muslim women. A note pinned to van Gogh's body warned Hirsi Ali that she would be next. The ten-minute film, *Submission, Part 1*, showed the opening verses of the Qur'an – a universal prayer for Muslims of all persuasions – displayed over a woman's body. Hirsi Ali states:

> My message was that the Qur'an is an act of man, not of God.
> We should be free to interpret it; we should be permitted to apply
> it to the modern era in a different way, instead of performing
> painful contortions to try to recreate the circumstances of a
> horrible distant past. My intention was to liberate Muslim minds
> so that Muslim women – and Muslim men, too – might be freer.
> Men, too, are forced to obey inhumane laws.

In the ensuing fracas, Hirsi Ali – who had recently been elected to the Dutch parliament – was forced into protective custody and, like the author, Salman Rushdie, has now emigrated to the safer and more congenial haven of America, where Muslim immigrants tend to be less isolated, better educated, more prosperous and less hostile to Western values than their co-religionists in Europe. Critics have labelled Hirsi Ali an 'enlightenment fundamentalist'. This interesting charge places her in the distinguished company of, among others, the late Ernest Gellner, the philosopher–anthropologist and one of the most sophisticated yet sympathetic observers of modern Islam.

It might be more appropriate, however, to describe Ali as a 'born-again' believer in Enlightenment values. *Infidel* has the hallmarks of a spiritual autobiography in which she progresses through various stages of illumination, from childhood trauma in Somalia (entailing genital mutilation inflicted by her own grandmother), through an adolescence in Saudi Arabia and Kenya, where a brief espousal of the ideas of the Muslim Brotherhood empowers her to question her family's tribal values within the frame of the movement's stultifying, still patriarchal, religiosity, towards eventual enlightenment and emancipation in the Netherlands, aided by encounters with Dutch fellow students and readings from Spinoza, Voltaire, Darwin, Durkheim and Freud. This remarkable spiritual journey is interlaced with a classic story of personal courage in the face of a parochial and misogynistic social system that systematically brutalises women in the name of God, and in which women routinely submit to neglect and violence. Told with a rare combination of passion and detachment, it is a *Seven Storey Mountain* in reverse: a pilgrimage from belief to scepticism.

Yet for all Hirsi Ali's questioning, there is a spiritual quality about her rebellion. The final break with her family occurs when senior members of her clan arrive in the Netherlands to persuade her to rejoin the husband chosen by her father, in order to save the family's honour. Her refusal seems divinely mandated: 'I paused for a moment, and then the words just came out of my mouth. "It is the will of the soul", I said. "The soul cannot be coerced".' The clan leaders, and her husband, accept the verdict. The soul cannot lie.

Hirsi Ali's political trajectory takes her from Labour to the Liberals, and then out of Dutch politics altogether, and beyond the soft boundaries of Islam. She now works for the conservative American Enterprise Institute in Washington. In Küng's terminology, she has negotiated a double paradigm shift, from the aristocratic clan-based identity into which she was born, through the new-style 'disembedded' religiosity promulgated by the Muslim Brotherhood, towards the individualism of the Occident, whose values she espouses in full. Her residual feelings for her religion evaporated after 9/11, when she saw television images of ordinary Dutch Muslim children celebrating in the streets:

> It was not a lunatic fringe who felt this way about America and the West. I knew that a vast mass of Muslims would see the attacks as justified retaliation against the infidel enemies of Islam … True Islam, as a rigid belief system and moral framework, leads to cruelty. The inhuman act of those nineteen hijackers was the logical outcome of this detailed system for regulating human behavior.

There are none of the ethical nuances here that one finds in the discourse of *Shari'a* reasoning. Indeed, she is infuriated by the claims of 'stupid analysts – especially people who called themselves Arabists' – that Islam is 'a religion of peace and tolerance'. Such statements she regards as being no more than 'fairy tales'. Her understanding of Islamic discourse is based exclusively on experience. Even though she acknowledges that female circumcision is not exclusive to Islam and is rarely practised outside of Africa, she shows little awareness of the diversity of Muslim practices outside her own Somali culture. Her angry musings about the Qur'an are muddled:

> I found myself thinking that the Qur'an is not a holy document. It is a historical record, written by humans. It is one version of

> events, as perceived by the men who wrote it 150 years after the Prophet Muhammad died. And it is a very tribal and Arab version of events. It spreads a culture that is brutal, bigoted, fixated on controlling women, and harsh in war.

Seemingly unaware of the basics of Islamic scholarship, she confuses the holy text with the Prophet's biography. But, disarmingly, she acknowledges her limitations:

> Most Muslims never delve into theology, and we rarely read the Qur'an; we are taught it in Arabic, which most Muslims can't speak. As a result, most people think that Islam is about peace. It is from these people, honest and kind, that the fallacy has arisen that Islam is peaceful and tolerant.

As a Dutch MP, Hirsi Ali mounted a successful campaign to expose the honour killings of young women in Muslim families for alleged sexual misdemeanours, and the scandal of circumcisions performed on little girls on Dutch kitchen tables. Finding the Labor Party less sympathetic to her agenda, she switched her allegiance to the Liberals before being forced, in effect, to emigrate to America. It is far from clear that she wants to influence the debate about gender and Islam now taking place throughout the Islamic world. Unlike Muslim feminists such as Fatima Mernissi or Leila Ahmed, who challenge the misogynistic and patriarchal interpretation of the holy texts, she confronts, and rejects, the canon in toto. This is not a position from which she is likely to have much impact on Muslims with a deeper knowledge of their own religious traditions.

In the Netherlands, as in Britain, multiculturalism or even 'cultural sensitivity' can provide a cover for the abuse of women and children, not to mention neo-fascist tendencies, such as Holocaust denial and the rampant anti-Semitism prevailing in some Muslim circles (a subject on which Hirsi Ali has been courageously eloquent).

In France, the situation is somewhat different. Debates about multiculturalism occur under the overarching canopy of *laïcité*, a term that loosely but inadequately translates into English as 'secularism'. Olivier Roy, in his short, discursive essay, *Secularism Confronts Islam*, exposes the historical roots of *laïcité* and its implications for France's Muslim communities. Though underpinned by the 1905 law of separation between church and state, *laïcité* extends far beyond the setting of institutional boundaries. It is a full-blown statist ideology whose pedigree stretches back to the Jacobin phase of the French Revolution. *Laïcité*, Roy insists, must not be confused with secularisation. With secularisation – a universal process integral to modernisation – 'a society emancipates itself from a sense of the sacred that it does not necessarily deny'. With *laïcité*, the state actively 'expels religious life beyond a border that the state itself has defined by law'. *Laïcité* actually fosters religion by making it a separate category. It reinforces religious identities rather than allowing them to dissolve into more diversified social practices.

Roy's essay was originally published in France at the height of the debate over multiculturalism that followed the government's decision to ban the veil and other conspicuous manifestations of religiosity in schools. He objects to the one-sided way in which politicians insisted on regarding the veil as a symbol of female oppression. One of the most astute observers of Islam writing today, Roy believes that strong enforcement of the policy of *laïcité* distorts the complex evolution towards secularisation that is occurring in the Islamic world, as it is in other faith systems. Disembedded from its various regional cultures, Islam is evolving into a distinctive faith system comparable to Christianity and other religions. The counterpart of the intensified religiosity that is found in fundamentalist movements of all traditions is a de facto acknowledgment of secularisation that can be observed, for example, in the behaviour of Muslim youth. Self-assertiveness among young Muslims should not just be attributed to 'Islam'. Roy writes:

> *Adolescents' intentions to assert themselves by wearing provocative clothing is a banality in secondary schools, but the affair of the veil has been experienced as the penetration of the school system by Islamism. A girl wearing the veil wants simultaneously to assert herself as an individual, escape from the social constraint of her milieu by adopting a sign that grants her both value and autonomy, make herself noticed, affirm a form of authenticity.*

The state should not interfere with this process. Rather than intervening theologically (for example, by trying to boost 'moderate' or liberal religious leaders against 'fundamentalists'), the state should leave religious communities to evolve under their own internal dynamic. According to Roy:

> *Many very conservative Muslims have adapted very well to secularisation and to laïcité by reformulating their faith in terms of values rather than norms, along the lines followed by Christian conservatives. They defend the family, sexual difference, and the criticism of morals; they oppose homosexual marriage and*

> *even abortion and divorce (two categories that hardly cause any*
> *difficulties in traditional* shari'a*); but they remain within the*
> *framework of legality.*

Roy's analysis chimes in well with Küng's own strictures on *laïcité* as an 'anticlerical secularism' that has outlived its purpose: 'Today the French Republic is no longer confronted with an over-powerful ultramontane political Catholicism (the religion which embraces the majority of the French) but with an often marginalised Muslim minority to whom the freedom of the individual brings little.'

As indicators for policy guidelines, Küng's and Roy's analyses make sense – but within crucial limits. There remains a strong body of evidence that the terrorist atrocity of July 2005 in London, and subsequent unsuccessful attempts, were inspired, at least in part, by radical preachers working out of British mosques. Saudi Arabia, the world's largest oil producer and exporter of the fundamentalist Sunni ideology known as Wahhabism, may be actively opposed to jihadism in its present forms. But as Roy explained previously in *Globalized Islam*, the oil-rich kingdom and neighbouring Gulf states have helped to extend Wahhabi or Salafist (fundamentalist) influence 'through an intensive outpouring of *fatwas* and short conferences or lectures, spread through the internet, television stations … or via cheap booklets'. These products, he argued, are

> *an important part of the curriculum of worldwide Muslim insti-*
> *tutions that are subsidised by Gulf money. Through informal*
> *networks of disciples and former students, [Wahhabi preachers]*
> *reach a lay audience far larger than the madrasas [seminaries] in*
> *which they teach.*

A recent survey of jihadists in Europe concluded that 'activists invest considerable time and energy in self-study of Wahhabi Islam and subsequently the jihadi strain of Salafism'.

There are countervailing tendencies, for example, in the appeal of Sufi ideas and religious disciplines (to which Wahhabis are adamantly opposed) in some literary and artistic circles, and in related mystical traditions imported from India/Pakistan. But so long as there remains a generation of European Muslims who feel alienated from their parents' traditions yet rejected by the wider society, the style of religiosity supported from Arabia will remain a powerful 'ultramontane' force.

Published in *The New York Review of Books*, 8 November 2007.

The books reviewed were:

Ayaan Hirsi Ali (2007) *Infidel.* New York: Free Press.

Michael Bonner (2006) *Jihad in Islamic History: Doctrines and Practice.* Princeton, NJ: Princeton University Press.

John Kelsay (2007) *Arguing the Just War in Islam*. Cambridge, MA: Harvard University Press.

Hans Küng (2007) *Islam: Past, Present and Future*, translated from the German by John Bowden. Oxford, UK: Oneworld.

Olivier Roy (2007) *Secularism Confronts Islam*, translated from the French by George Holoch, Jr. New York: Columbia University Press:

9
The Rise of Muslim Terrorists

In London, eight men – all British nationals – are currently [2008] on trial for an alleged 2006 plot to destroy seven transatlantic aircraft in mid-air, using liquid explosives disguised as soft drinks. According to the prosecution, they could have killed some 1,500 people, nearly half the number of those who died in the 9/11 attacks. The airport security staff were to have their attentions distracted by 'dirty' magazines in the would-be suicide bombers' hand luggage – a neat example of *jihad*-by-pornography, fighting the infidel West with its own salacious habits.

In a video testament intended for posthumous transmission, one of the would-be martyrs berates the British people for their apathy toward their government's policies in Iraq and Afghanistan:

> *This is revenge for the actions of the USA in the Muslim lands and their accomplices such as the British and the Jews ... Most of you [are] too busy ... watching Home and Away and EastEnders [two popular TV soaps], complaining about the World Cup, drinking your alcohol, to even care about anything ... I know because I've come from that.*

What are the forces that drive young men such as these to commit mass murder? The question is addressed from different perspectives in all the books under review.

A convincing analysis is offered by Marc Sageman, a forensic psychiatrist and consultant to the US government, in his *Leaderless Jihad: Terror Networks in the Twenty-First Century*. After examining some 500 individual cases using 'open source' data from court proceedings, media accounts, academic writings and selected internet materials, Sageman fixes his gaze on what he calls the 'middle range'. These are the social networks and intellectual milieus through which defendants in terrorist trials are recorded as operating. Contrary to widespread assumptions, he finds that they are not to be distinguished from their non-terrorist peers by extremes of hatred for the West:

> *It is actually difficult to convince people to sacrifice themselves just because they hate their target ... On the contrary, it appears that it is much more common to sacrifice oneself for a positive reason such as love, reputation, or glory.*

A common theme, however, was geographical displacement. A very high proportion of his sample – 84 per cent – belonged to the Muslim diasporas, with the majority joining global Islamist terrorist movements in a country where they did not grow up. The Hamburg cell that provided the leadership for 9/11 was typical of his wider sample: they were Middle Eastern students in Germany, who travelled to Afghanistan to join the fight against America.

Sageman pays close attention to family networks, with about a fifth of his sample having close family ties with other global Islamic activists. His point is strongly reinforced by Bilveer Singh in *The Talibanization of Southeast Asia*, his study of jihadist groups in Southeast Asia. Singh sees kinship as being a vital element in the makeup of al-Jamaat al-Islamiyah – the organisation responsible for the Bali nightclub bombings in October 2002. The people who form terror groups have to know and trust one another. In most Muslim societies it is kinship, rather than shared ideological values, that generates relations of trust.

Though drawn from the professional middle classes, the terrorists and 'wannabes' studied by Sageman are not pious intellectuals who may be persuaded – or dissuaded – by religious arguments. Most of them – especially those belonging to the younger generation or 'third wave' of Islamist terrorists – are less well-educated than earlier generations, especially in religious matters. Indeed, he suggests that this very ignorance contributes to their susceptibility to extremism. Sageman writes: 'The defendants in terrorism trials around the world would not have been swayed by an exegesis of the Qur'an. They would simply have been bored and would not have listened.'

In Sageman's view, the appeal of *jihad* is not so much narrowly religious as broadly romantic and consonant with the aspirations of youth everywhere. The young Moroccans with whom he spoke outside the mosque where the Madrid bombers used to worship equated Osama bin Laden with the soccer superstars they most admired. Their utopian aspirations are inspired as much by iconography as ideology. The images of Sheikh Osama, the rich civil engineer, and his deputy Ayman al-Zawahiri, once a promising physician from an elite Cairo family – both of whom are seen as having sacrificed everything for the sake of their beliefs – send powerful messages to aspirants far removed from the grimy realities of tribal Waziristan.

As Omar Saghi, a scholar of Islam at Sciences Po, Paris, points out in his introduction to *Al-Qaeda in Its Own Words*, the Harvard University Press selection of al-Qaeda statements and writings, bin Laden's first appearance after 9/11 dressed in Afghan garb sitting cross-legged at the mouth of a cave sent a powerful message to the Muslim umma – or world community – by means of a '"psycho-acoustic bubble" ... floating like gas through cyberspace':

> *The challenge he posed to America as an ascetic stripped of all worldly goods and hiding out in Afghanistan's miserable mountains was multiplied by the gaping breach that – as he delighted in emphasising – separated him from the United States' predatory opulence. The cave has powerful symbolic resonances: the Prophet Muhammad received his first revelation in a cave, and took refuge in one during his journey from Mecca to Medina.*

None of this means, of course, that the new *jihad* is devoid of theological content. The collections produced by Harvard University Press, and Routledge, who have published a *Sayyid Qutb Reader*, usefully link the new *jihad* with the ideas of its founders and the anchoring of these ideas in classical sources. Bin Laden's statements have already appeared in a more comprehensive volume in English. While the Harvard reader contains a much smaller selection of his utterances, it has the advantage of tying them to the works of his close associates, including his former mentor, Abdallah Azzam (assassinated in Peshawar, Pakistan, in 1989), and al-Zawahiri. Some 80 pages of explanatory notes usefully flesh out the political and contextual details, with citations in the Qur'an and *Hadith* (sayings or traditions of the Prophet Muhammad passed down the centuries).

The bin Laden section includes his famous 'World Islamic Front Statement', co-signed by two qualified Islamic scholars, declaring the *jihad* to be an 'individual duty' incumbent on all Muslims, because the Americans and their allies are supposedly occupying both of Islam's holy places – Jerusalem and Mecca. Al-Zawahiri's contribution includes excerpts from the much-quoted *Knights Under the Prophet's Banner*, published by the Saudi-financed daily newspaper, *Al-Sharq al-Awsat*, in London in December 2001. *Knights* contains this chilling threat: 'It is always possible to track an American or a Jew, to kill him with a bullet or a knife, a simple explosive device, or a blow with an iron rod.'

More pertinent for political analysis are the excerpts from al-Zawahiri's *Loyalty and Separation*, a polemical 2002 tract whose title is borrowed from a text by the nephew of Muhammad Ibn Abdul Wahhab, co-founder of the original eighteenth-century Saudi theocracy and a primary source of religious legitimacy for the kingdom's current rulers. All these writings are laced with Qur'anic references and citations from the *Hadiths*, carefully chosen to hark back to Islam's heroic age while containing tropes culled from Western sources, such as the Nazi fantasy that Jews are ruling the world. The language is deliberately archaic and patriarchal, weaving contemporary events into the fabric of salvation history.

It is now widely acknowledged that Sayyid Qutb, born in 1906 and hanged by Egyptian President Gamal Abdel Nasser in 1966 on trumped-up charges of subversion, is the intellectual godfather of modern Islamist activism and an enduring influence on Islamic radicalism. Qutb popularised the term jahiliyya in his writings, taking it to mean a condition of contemporary arrogance, ignorance and irreligion. Traditional mainstream scholarship viewed jahiliyya as the condition of barbarism that prevailed among the Arabian tribes before the coming of the Prophet Muhammad. Though he had been an admirer of Western literature, and especially the English Romantics, Qutb's sojourn in America in 1949 crystallised his disdain for Western culture. His is the paradigmatic case of the 'born-again' Muslim who, having adopted or absorbed many modern or foreign influences, makes a show of discarding them in his search for personal identity and cultural authenticity.

The term 'fundamentalism' that Albert Bergesen applies to Qutb's thought in his introduction to *The Sayyid Qutb Reader*, however, is open to question. Far from espousing received theological certainties in order to defend 'Muslim society' against foreign encroachments, Qutb's understanding of Islam is almost Kierkegaardian in its individualism. His 'authentic' Muslim is one who espouses a very modern kind of revolution against the deification of men, against injustice, and against political, economic, racial and religious prejudice. Bergesen says that, 'from a civilisational perspective, Qutb doesn't seemed to have hijacked Islam for political purposes as much as called for a return to Islam's original religio-political compact'. While this is true so far as it goes, he undervalues the way Qutb and other Muslim ideologues absorb values and influences derived from the Enlightenment while professing to deny them. One of Qutb's statements that Bergesen cites should be challenged explicitly: 'It is not possible to find a basis for Islamic thought in the modes and products of European thought, nor to construct Islamic thought by borrowing from Western modes of thought or its products.' This claim – which crassly denies a vast history of cultural borrowings – might have been balanced with a reference to Leonard Binder's important 1988 book, *Islamic Liberalism*, which teases out the Western lineages and resonances in Qutb's thought.

A more serious omission from Bergesen's *Reader* is Qutb's notorious 1950 diatribe, *Our Struggle with the Jews*, republished in 1970 and distributed throughout the world by the government of Saudi Arabia. In *Jihad and Jew-Hatred*, Matthias Küntzel, a political scientist and former adviser to Germany's Green Party, argues that this text, which has been available in English since 1987, blends traditional Islamic Judaophobia with imported Nazi ideas.

In Qutb's analysis, Jews appear to be inherently decadent and anti-religious. They are actually worse than the idolators fought by Muhammad, since they are cunningly able to undermine and destroy Islam, the only true religion, from within. During Muhammad's struggles in Medina, they joined the 'hypocrites' in resisting his divine authority, and made treacherous alliances with the polytheists. Qutb wrote that

> the Muslim community continues to suffer from the same Jewish machinations and double-dealing ... This is a war which has not been extinguished ... for close on fourteen centuries, and it continues to this moment, its blaze raging in all the corners of the earth.

Although there are no explicit references to Nazi sources, the Saudi editor of the 1970 edition helpfully appended references to *The Protocols of the Learned Elders of Zion* as 'proof' of the correctness of Qutb's ideas. Imported European anti-Semitism is now embedded in the charter of Hamas, whose 32nd article cites the *Protocols* explicitly as 'proof' of Israeli conduct. As Sari Nusseibeh, the Palestinian philosopher and former PLO representative in Jerusalem, has observed, Hamas' charter 'sounds as if it were copied out from the pages of *Der Stürmer*'.

In drawing attention to the anti-Semitic writings of Qutb and others, Küntzel has performed a necessary task. His analysis, however, draws the wrong conclusions. His statement that al-Qaeda and other Islamist groups are 'guided by an anti-Semitic ideology that was transferred to the Islamic world in the Nazi period' is overdrawn. It would be more correct to say that the Islamists exploit traditional theological Judaophobia, mixed with a sprinkling of imported Nazi ideas, in pursuit of their own, more ambitious, purposes. Bin Laden and his associates uniformly couple Jews with the Christians or Crusaders in their polemics.

Conventional wisdom generally holds that a resolution of the problems of Palestine and Jerusalem is the sine qua non for addressing wider geopolitical issues afflicting relations between the Islamic and Western worlds. By removing images of Palestinian persecution from Muslim television screens, a peace settlement would take the sting out of an issue that carries a formidable symbolic charge. But the Israeli occupation, though a constant source of pain and humiliation, is only one of many issues the global jihadists have in their sights.

Abu Mus'ab al-Suri, the Syrian ideologue who is the subject of a fascinating study by the Norwegian scholar, Brynjar Lia, is quite explicit about this. In his *Global Islamic Resistance Call* – a 1,600-page document widely available on jihadist websites and now translated by Lia – he states that 'Israel creates a motive for a global Islamic cause, and the American occupation [of Iraq] adds a revolutionary dimension, which is an excellent key to *jihad*'. The broader agenda, according to al-Suri, is to drive the Americans from the region, 'to fight the Jews, remove idolators from the Arabian Peninsula and to free its oil and other resources from the American hegemony' and to remove all the 'injustices and afflictions' caused by the occupation of the Islamic lands by America and its allies.

Al-Suri, who was captured in Pakistan in 2005 and is believed to have been repatriated to his native Syria, is the most articulate exponent of the modern *jihad* and its most sophisticated strategist. A mechanical engineer from Aleppo, his russet hair and fair complexion lend him a European look. He claims descent from the Prophet Muhammad through both his grandfathers – a claim that gives him high social status among the jihadis. He has Spanish citizenship and a Spanish wife and uses numerous aliases. His fellow jihadis teasingly call him 'James Bond'.

A veteran of the Muslim Brotherhood uprising in Syria in 1982, when the city of Hama was virtually destroyed by the Baathist regime of Hafez al-Assad, al-Suri has been a persistent critic of bin Laden's strategy and approach to *jihad*. Holding to the view that the 'road to Jerusalem lies through Cairo' (meaning that Palestine could only be liberated after the Mubarak regime had been toppled and replaced by an 'Islamic' one), he was quick to criticise al-Qaeda's 1998 attacks on the US embassies in East Africa. The centralised structure the jihadis had built in Afghanistan, with its emphasis on training camps, made them vulnerable to US missile attacks.

Al-Suri was dismayed by the disdain with which bin Laden and the 'Afghan-Arabs' – especially the Saudis among them – treated the Taliban rulers in Afghanistan, and by their habit of making unilateral decisions without regard to the feelings of their hosts. He was cautiously critical of the 9/11 operation, which put a 'catastrophic end' to the jihadist struggle that had begun in the 1960s. For al-Suri, the new condition imposed by the 'war on terror' calls for a new strategy. Al-Qaeda and the jihadis must abandon the 'Tora Bora mentality' of holding on to physical bases with a top-down command structure, and opt for a 'secret guerrilla war' using 'unconnected cells' of varying and different types.

Al-Suri's new strategy fits neatly into the conception of 'leaderless *jihad*' or third-wave terrorism described by Sageman, where jihadists recruit each other in chat rooms and can download bomb-making materials from the internet. Sageman makes the plausible argument that the dangers are greater in Europe than in America, a milieu less amenable to home-grown terrorism because of its traditions of community policing and the fact that the majority of Muslim immigrants in the United States belong to the professional middle classes and are more inclined than their European counterparts to identify with American values. When Sageman's book went to press, there had been 2,300 arrests for terrorist offences in Europe compared to 60 in the US. When the differences in population are taken into account, the rate of arrest is six times higher in Europe than in the United States.

Jihadis are not the only political activists seeking an Islamic state that will restore the *Shari'a* – the holy law of Islam – to the position it held in pre-colonial times. In a short but masterful exposition, *The Fall and Rise of the Islamic State*, Noah Feldman seeks to answer a question that puzzles most Western observers: Why do so many Muslims demand the 'restoration' of a legal system that most Occidentals associate with 'medieval' punishments such as amputation for theft and stoning for sexual transgressions? What do they mean by, and expect from, an Islamic state?

Feldman's analysis focuses on the crucial responsibility of the Ottoman state for the decline of the *Shari'a*. Pre-modern Islamic societies were for the most part governed according to an informal division of authority between the military rulers (often outsiders such as the Mamelukes, recruited from warrior societies, which were far removed from Islam's cultural centres) and the religiously trained class of legal scholars conversant with the law. The informal compact comparable to, but different from, the feudal arrangements in the West conferred legitimacy on the military men on condition that they upheld the authority of the scholars. The system of scholarly control over the law encouraged 'stability, executive restraint, and legitimacy'. Feldman writes:

> *Through their near monopoly on legal affairs in a state where God's law was accepted as paramount, the scholars … built themselves into a powerful and effective check on the ruler. To see the Islamic constitution as containing the balance of powers so necessary for a functioning, sustainable legal state is to emphasise not why it failed, as all forms of government eventually must, but why it succeeded so spectacularly for as long as it did.*

Under pressure from their European rivals to modernise their empire, the Ottoman sultans, beginning in the nineteenth century, began to enact a series of administrative reforms that brought legal administration under direct state control: 'The single most durable feature of the reforms turned out to be the removal of effective lawmaking authority from the scholars through the substitution of written legal codes for the common law of the shari'a.'

In effect, the sultans 'tamed' the *Shari'a* by encoding it in a book. The scholars were rendered impotent, with their freedom to interpret the law emasculated. Their incorporation into the Ottoman bureaucracy deprived them of the real authority they had previously enjoyed as upholders and interpreters of God's law. Initially, this concentration of legal power in the hands of the sultans was balanced by a European-style constitution, including an elected assembly, which the Ottoman modernisers saw as useful engines of reform. But within a year of its first sitting in 1876, Sultan Abdul Hamid dismissed the legislature and suspended the constitution, ruling as an absolute monarch for the next 30 years.

As Feldman sees it, the absolutist state became the dominant model in most of the Sunni world in the twentieth century. The 'distinctive distortions of many Muslim states in this era were products of unchecked executive authority'. However, the idea of *Shari'a* law – of rule 'in accordance with God's law' – retained its utility; hence contemporary demands for an Islamic state that includes its 'restoration'.

Unfortunately, Feldman does not flesh out his thesis with much historical detail. It would have helped his argument if he had provided specific examples of interventions by scholars in cases of disputed successions. An important example he does cite, however, is the establishment of the waqf, or Islamic trust, which, beginning in medieval times, was one of the most important institutions of the pre-colonial era. These foundations, which were immune from government interference, allowed the transmission of wealth down the generations while sustaining public welfare by providing hospitals, schools, mosques, inns, public drinking fountains and other services independently of the state.

Waqfs were the primary civil society institutions in the Islamic world. As such they represented a threat to the modernising schemes of governments facing the challenge of growing European power. The Ottoman sultans and other would-be reformers gradually took them over and incorporated them into the apparatus of state – a movement that facilitated the emergence of the autocratic regimes that prevail in much of the Islamic world to modern times because the increase in the power of the state was not balanced by advances in democratic accountability.

In his book, *Islam and the Secular State*, Abdullahi Ahmed An-Na'im – from Sudan, now a professor at Emory Law School, Atlanta, USA – covers some of the same ground as Feldman, and reaches similar conclusions. As a practising Muslim, however, he takes the discussion much further, making a powerful theological case for abandoning the very notion of an Islamic state. He argues that the claims of these so-called states to enforce the *Shari'a* repudiate the fundamental right of religious choice implicit in a Qur'anic verse that says there can be 'no compulsion in religion'. The *Shari'a* cannot be codified as state law without violating this provision. It is not a code but a process of legal reasoning. An-Na'im writes: 'Whenever the state has been used to enforce Shari'a, the outcome has been a highly selective set of principles in total isolation from their legitimate methodological sources.' Under modern conditions, he argues, recognition of this fact requires the separation of religious and secular institutions – in effect, a model similar to the system of church–state separation prevailing in the United States. A secular state provides the most welcoming environment in which people can practise their religion out of 'honest conviction'.

Such an institutional separation, however, need not entail a separation between Islam and politics. Under a formal system of separation, the connection between the two can be maintained, allowing for 'the implementation of Islamic principles in official policy and legislation', subject to certain safeguards. The Islamist ideology An-Na'im appears to have in mind – though this is not spelt out – would be comparable to the outlook of Christian democratic parties in Europe and Latin America: parties that subscribe to a political philosophy informed by religious values without being dogmatically religious.

In postulating his model, however, An-Na'im reveals the size of the theological mountain that must be climbed before such ideas can take root. To begin with, his approach demands a comprehensive reappraisal of Islamic origins. In returning to Islam's earliest sources, he follows the path cleared by the Sudanese humanist scholar Mahmoud Mohamed Taha, founder of the Sudanese Republican Brotherhood, who was hanged in 1985 after being convicted of apostasy. Taha had argued that a distinction must be made between the universal message of Islam proclaimed by Muhammad in Mecca, and the time-specific and hence changeable messages proclaimed in Medina, where he founded the first Islamic state. The changeable texts would include principles such as the 'guardianship' of women, punishment for apostasy and discrimination against religious minorities – issues that pit traditional interpretations of Islam against the constitutional provisions of most modern states, including most that have Muslim majorities.

An-Na'im argues that the dhimma system (entailing legal discrimination against 'protected minorities' such as Jews and Christians) is 'neither practiced nor advocated anywhere in the Muslim world today'. However, reality says otherwise. Of some 70 terrorist attacks in Southeast Asia that Bilveer Singh has attributed to the al-Jamaat al-Islamiyah group since 1994, 45 were against churches. When state institutions are weak, sectarian hatred, fuelled by Islamist rhetoric that demonises Christians and Jews, becomes the default position on the ground. It is difficult to see how such progressive views as An-Na'im's can entrench themselves in the face of 14 centuries of cultural programming.

A further reality check is provided by Roy Gutman's important study, *How We Missed the Story*. A searing critique of US policy in Afghanistan after the departure of Soviet troops in 1989, it traces the policy shifts in Washington and in particular the loss of focus that assisted the rise of the Taliban. Gutman's central claim, that the inability of the United States to prevent the 9/11 attacks was not so much an intelligence or military failure as a strategic foreign policy failure, will not make comfortable reading for Hillary Clinton's advisers.

Foremost among the errors he documents in detail was the failure of US President Bill Clinton and his Secretary of State, Madeleine Albright, to give adequate support to Ahmed Shah Massoud, the most able of Afghanistan's mujahidin commanders, in the face of pro-Taliban pressure from the Pakistan military. Massoud, the Tajik leader, headed a multi-ethnic coalition and practised a moderate version of Islamism that contrasted starkly with Taliban extremism. His troops were much more disposed to observe the rules of war than were their opponents.

Because of the Monica Lewinsky scandal and complications arising from Pakistan's nuclear policies, Clinton was distracted, with ultimately devastating consequences. Gutman is equally scathing about the role of the international press – or rather, its absence. The atrocities committed by the Taliban during their attempted conquest of central and northern Afghanistan received little coverage. They included 'every war crime on the United Nations' list of summary executions and massacres'. Few of these actions were spontaneous: in the case of the worst atrocity of the war, the massacre of at least 2,000 mainly Shi'a civilians in the town of Mazar-i-Sharif in 1998, 'there is overwhelming evidence of advance planning, central direction, and clarity of purpose, namely, revenge'.

Gutman provides many details of bin Laden's growing ascendancy over the Taliban and their leader Mullah Omar, and of various ways in which the 'Arab-Afghans' humiliated their Taliban hosts and subjected them to a Wahhabite religious agenda. The destruction of the Bamiyan Buddhas, giant sandstone statues that had stood for more than 1,500 years, was the most egregious of the iconoclastic acts carried out under pressure from the Arabs and Pakistani mullahs.

The Islamist movement is a mixture of forces comprising many strands of tradition, culture, allegiance and belief. Its most noxious ingredient is a style of religious imperialism fuelled by Arabian petrodollars. As Feldman points out, Saudi Arabia is unique in not having inherited the Ottoman state system. Its scholars influence state policies while also having the freedom to propagate versions of Islam that diverge from the interests of the ruling family. By helping to supply the religious arguments that support jihadist trends, the Wahhabi scholars have a political impact well above their intellectual and theological weight, even when specific outcomes, such as attacks on Western targets, run counter to the Saudi state's policies.

The dangers of jihadism, however, have been needlessly exacerbated by the 'war on terror' and the folly of the US invasion of Iraq, which, as Sageman suggests, galvanised a whole new generation of 'third-wave' jihadists. Yet the 'leaderless *jihad*' he discusses is inherently self-limiting. As a transnational social movement – rather than an ideology with a coherent political agenda – it generally lacks the organisational capacity to gain and hold power. The exceptions lie in the atypical situations of Iran, where the Shi'a clergy constitute an 'estate' comparable to their equivalents in early modern Europe, and of Gaza, occasioned by the continuing Israeli occupation of Palestine.

Contrary to the alarmist views of Henry Kissinger, who insists that 'radical Islam rejects claims to national sovereignty based on secular state models', Islamist attitudes towards the national state are ambivalent. There are no insuperable obstacles, historical or theological, to the de jure acceptance of the post-colonial state that most of the Islamist movements already acknowledge, de facto, as being the arena of politics. The challenge for policy-makers in Islamic and Western worlds must be to harness these movements' positive energies (including their democratic aspirations and social concerns), while criminalising terrorism and relentlessly exposing the bigotry that drives it.

Published in *The New York Review of Books*, 30 April 2008.

The books reviewed were:

Abdullahi Ahmed An-Na'im (2008) *Islam and the Secular State: Negotiating the Future of Shari'a.* Cambridge, MA: Harvard University Press.

Albert J. Bergesen (ed.) (2007) *The Sayyid Qutb Reader: Selected Writings on Politics, Religion, and Society*, London: Routledge.

Noah Feldman (2008) *The Fall and Rise of the Islamic State.* Princeton, NJ: Princeton University Press.

Roy Gutman (2008) *How We Missed the Story: Osama bin Laden, the Taliban, and the Hijacking of Afghanistan.* Washington, DC: United States Institute of Peace Press.

Matthias Küntzel (2007) *Jihad and Jew-Hatred: Islamism, Nazism and the Roots of 9/11*, translated from the German by Colin Meade. New York: Telos Press.

Brynjar Lia (2008) *Architect of Global Jihad: The Life of al-Qaida Strategist Abu Mus'ab al-Suri.* New York: Columbia University Press.

10

Deception over Lockerbie?

In his new book, *Terrorism: How to Respond*, Richard English, a historian who has written the definitive history of the IRA, argues that terrorism is best understood as a 'subspecies of war' that embodies – among other things – 'the exerting and implementing of power, and the attempted redressing of power relations'.

The furore over the Scottish government's decision to release Abdel Basset Ali al-Megrahi, the convicted Lockerbie bomber, and the speculations surrounding the whole affair prove his point. The festive welcome Megrahi received from President Muammar Qaddafi himself on arrival in Libya was met with predictable fury on both sides of the Atlantic. The explosion aboard Pan Am Flight 103 on 21 December 1988, which caused the Boeing 747 to disintegrate in flames over the Scottish town of Lockerbie, was the worst terrorist atrocity ever to have been perpetrated on British soil; 270 people died, including 11 Lockerbie residents. The majority of the victims, 189 of them, were US citizens returning for the Christmas holidays.

President Obama's spokesman, Robert Gibbs, described the jubilant crowds that greeted the frail figure of the returning Libyan intelligence agent as 'outrageous and disgusting'. Robert Mueller, Director of the FBI – who as assistant Attorney General had been involved in the investigation that led to Megrahi's indictment and conviction by a Scottish court sitting in the Netherlands – took the unusual step of releasing the text of a letter he had sent to the Scottish Justice Secretary, Kenny MacAskill, in which he complained that MacAskill's action, 'blithely defended on the grounds of "compassion"', would give 'comfort to terrorists around the world'.

The devolved Scottish government – under the Scottish National Party (SNP), which has announced its intention to hold a referendum on full independence – has robustly denied claims that business interests or pressures from the UK government had any part in its decision to release Megrahi. Its position was supported – after a lengthy and deafening silence

– by British Prime Minister Gordon Brown, whom the opposition has accused of 'double-dealing' over the Lockerbie affair:

> I made it clear that for us there was never a linkage between any other issue and the Scottish government's own decision about Megrahi's future ... On our part there was no conspiracy, no cover-up, no double-dealing, no deal on oil, no attempt to instruct Scottish ministers, no private assurances by me to Colonel Qaddafi. We were absolutely clear throughout with Libya and everyone else that this was a decision for the Scottish government.

In an effort to support their position, the UK and Scottish governments released a pile of documents, including previously leaked correspondence between MacAskill and Jack Straw, his counterpart in London. The British Justice Secretary explained that in his dealings with the Libyan authorities he had been unable to persuade them to exclude Megrahi from a prisoner transfer agreement between Britain and Libya under which prisoners would serve their sentences in their respective countries. The documents also reveal that when the Libyan minister for Europe told his British counterpart that Megrahi's death in a Scottish prison would have 'catastrophic effects' on UK–Libyan relations, he was told that 'neither the Prime Minister nor the Foreign Secretary would want Mr Megrahi to pass away in prison but the decision on transfer lies in the hands of Scottish ministers'.

In fact, the medical prognosis giving Megrahi less than three months to live provided both governments with a loophole in their dealings with Libya. Scottish prison service guidelines state that compassionate release 'may be considered where a prisoner is suffering from a terminal illness and death is likely to occur soon', with a life expectancy of around three months an 'appropriate time' to consider release. Doctors had earlier concluded that Megrahi might have a year or more to live, rendering him ineligible for release in time for the celebrations marking the 40th anniversary of the coup on 1 September 1969 that overthrew the Libyan monarchy and brought Qaddafi, a 27-year-old army captain, to power.

The three doctors – two British and one Libyan – who produced a revised prognosis in July were paid by the Libyan government. One of them, the British oncologist, Professor Karol Sikora, medical director of CancerPartners UK, a private health care organisation, admitted that the period of three months had been suggested by the Libyans. After examining Megrahi in prison and looking at the clinical details 'in much greater depth' than previous doctors, Sikora concluded that Megrahi's tumour 'was behaving in a very aggressive way, unlike [tumors afflicting] most people with prostate cancer' and that 'the three-month deadline seemed about right'. The Libyan doctor concurred. The third doctor would only say that Megrahi 'had a short time to live'. After it became clear that Megrahi could not be excluded from the prisoner transfer agreement, it seems the Scottish and British governments actively encouraged him and his legal team to seek a release on compassionate grounds.

At stake, for the British, were contracts for oil and gas exploration worth up to £15 billion ($24 billion) for British Petroleum (BP), announced in May 2007, as well as plans to open a London office of the Libyan Investment Authority, a sovereign fund with £83 billion ($136 billion) to invest. Libya refused to ratify the contracts until Straw abandoned his insistence on excluding Megrahi from the prisoner transfer agreement. Shortly after Brown's statement, Straw admitted – in apparent contradiction to his prime minister – that oil had been 'a very big part' of his negotiations. British leaders were also warned that trade deals worth billions could be cancelled. 'The wider negotiations with the Libyans are reaching a critical stage,' Straw wrote to MacAskill in December 2007, 'and in view of the overwhelming interests for the United Kingdom I have agreed that in this instance the PTA [prisoner transfer agreement] should be in the standard form and not mention any individual.' Within six weeks of the British government's concession, Libya had ratified the BP deal. The prisoner transfer agreement was finalised in May 2009, leading to Libya formally applying for Megrahi to be transferred to its custody.

For the SNP government in Edinburgh, the 'compassion loophole' made it possible to avoid authorising Megrahi's release under an agreement negotiated by London. The decision was widely condemned in Scotland, with the minority SNP administration losing a vote by 73–50 in the Scottish Parliament on a government motion that the release of Megrahi on compassionate grounds was 'consistent with the principles of Scottish justice'. But there was a further twist to this story. Before his release from Greenock Prison near Glasgow and his flight to Tripoli in a chartered Libyan jet, Megrahi agreed to drop his appeal against the life sentence he received from the specially convened Scottish court sitting at Camp Zeist in the Netherlands in 2001.

Megrahi has always insisted on his innocence, and doubts about his conviction have been expressed by several influential figures, most notably Dr Jim Swire, a spokesman for the UK families of Flight 103, whose daughter Flora died in the crash, and Professor Hans Köchler, official UN observer at Megrahi's trial at Camp Zeist. In his reports to the UN Secretary-General, Köchler deplored the political atmosphere of the trial and the failure of the court to consider evidence of foreign (that is, non-Libyan) government involvement that formed part of a special defence – inculpating others – that is available under Scottish law.

He was even more forthright in condemning the rejection of Megrahi's first appeal in March 2002 – calling it a 'spectacular miscarriage of justice' – which took place at the same time as discussions with Libya over compensation for the victims' families. The presence of a Libyan 'defence support team' hampered the efforts of the Scottish defence lawyers, who failed to raise vital questions about the withholding of evidence and the reliability of witnesses. Two notable omissions Köchler highlighted were the alleged coaching of a key prosecution witness by Scottish police, and the appeal court's failure to consider evidence of a break-in at the baggage storage area in London's Heathrow airport on the night before the bombing.

Conspiracy theories have plagued the bombing ever since the clearing-up operation, when unidentified Americans, thought to be CIA agents, were seen sorting through the debris alongside officially authorised Scottish police. The most plausible theories do not necessarily exonerate Megrahi, but do suggest that at most he was little more than a small cog in a much larger and more complex machine.

A widely held suspicion at the beginning of the investigation pointed towards the culpability of a Palestinian faction, the Popular Front for the Liberation of Palestine – General Command (PFLP-GC), working under the protection of Syria. The theory held that the PFLP-GC, who specialised in aircraft hijackings using Semtex bombs concealed in tape recorders, may have been 'sub-contracted' by Syria's Iranian allies to bring down Pan Am Flight 103 in revenge for the accidental shooting down of an Iranian civilian airliner by the USS *Vincennes* in July 1988, just months before the bombing of Flight 103.

At the time, Iran's Supreme Leader, Ayatollah Khomeini, vowed that the skies would 'rain blood' in revenge for the loss of 290 civilian lives, including 66 children. Two defectors from Iranian intelligence agencies – or alleged defectors – subsequently accused the Iranian government of being behind the attacks, for which the PFLP-GC was said to have been paid $10 million. Some analysts have argued that leads pointing towards the Palestinian–Syrian–Iranian connection were purposefully deflected after the 1990 Iraqi invasion of Kuwait, when Syria became – albeit temporarily – a US coalition ally. Libya, the only Arab state to support Saddam's invasion, remained a more tenable target for exacting exemplary justice.

After a decade of sanctions and interventions by UN Secretary-General Kofi Annan and South African President Nelson Mandela, the Libyans in 1999 gave up Megrahi and his alleged associate Lamin Khalifah Fhimah, who would later be acquitted. The case against Megrahi hinged on a fragment recovered at Lockerbie of a timing device traced to a Swiss manufacturer, Mebo. The firm had sold timers to Libya that differed in design from those allegedly used in cassette bombs of the type attributed to the PFLP-GC. The clothing in which the bomb was said to have been wrapped inside a suitcase was traced to a shop in Malta that Megrahi was alleged to have visited, travelling under an assumed name, on 20–21 December 1988.

Though the evidence was purely circumstantial (there was no direct evidence that either Megrahi or Fhimah had placed the device aboard the aircraft), the judges wrote in their decision that the preponderance of the evidence led them to believe that Megrahi was guilty as charged. He was sentenced to life imprisonment, with a recommended minimum of 27 years, to be served in a Scottish jail. A major reason for US anger at Megrahi's release has been the repeated assurances given by the British government that he would serve his full term.

In December 2003, as part of its campaign to end UN sanctions and abandon its pariah status, Libya accepted responsibility for the bombing, and agreed to pay compensation to the victims' families, though it continued to maintain Megrahi's innocence, as he had done throughout his trial. His position divided observers: some see his continuing denial as the standard response of a professional intelligence officer, as summarised by the unofficial motto of the CIA's Office of Technical Services – 'admit nothing, deny everything, make counter-accusations'.

Others, including a significant group of Scottish lawyers and lay people, take a different view. In June 2007, after an investigation lasting nearly four years, the Scottish Criminal Case Review Commission delivered an 800-page report – with 13 annexes – that identified several areas where 'a miscarriage of justice may have occurred' and referred Megrahi's case to the Court of Criminal Appeal in Edinburgh. The Commission considered evidence that cast doubt on the dates on which Megrahi was supposed to have been in Malta, as well as the testimony of the Maltese shopkeeper who claimed to have sold clothing to Megrahi. The shopkeeper changed his testimony several times, and had been shown Megrahi's photograph before picking him out of a line-up. It was expected that the fresh appeal would also consider new evidence about the timing device, as well as the reported break-in at Heathrow airport, which indicate that the bomb could have been planted in London rather than in a suitcase checked-in from Malta to New York, as the prosecution had claimed.

In July 2007, Ulrich Lumpert, a former engineer at Mebo and a key technical witness, admitted that he had committed perjury at the Camp Zeist trial. In a sworn affidavit he declared that he had stolen a handmade sample of an MST-13 Timer PC-board from Mebo in Zurich and handed it to an unnamed official investigating the Lockerbie case. He also affirmed that the fragment of the timer presented in court as part of the Lockerbie wreckage had in fact been part of this stolen sample. When he became aware that this piece was to be used as evidence for an 'intentionally politically motivated criminal undertaking', he said, he decided to keep silent out of fear for his life.

Though it would have been necessary for Megrahi to drop his appeal under the prisoner transfer scheme, this was not a precondition for release on compassionate grounds. Nevertheless it seems likely that he was pressured into abandoning the appeal. Oliver Miles, a former British ambassador to Libya, has suggested that the dropping of the appeal, rather than 'a deal involving business', was the real *quid pro quo* behind Megrahi's release. According to Miles, Scottish legal sources had been talking of a mood of 'growing anxiety in the Scottish justice department that a successful appeal … would severely damage the reputation of the Scottish justice system'.

Though many British and American victims' families are demanding a fuller inquiry, Megrahi's decision means the end of any formal legal investigation into the Lockerbie atrocity. However, this is unlikely to be the end of the controversy, whatever the unpublicised hopes of the Scottish, UK and US governments. Mark Zaid, the Washington lawyer who represents 30 American families and launched a lawsuit against the Libyan government, securing compensation of up to $2.7 billion, has announced that he is filing a suit under the Freedom of Information Act to try to ascertain what agreements and discussions have taken place between the United States and the UK, not just with respect to the release of Megrahi, but dating back to before the 1991 indictment. 'It is ironic,' he told the BBC, 'that in the latest release of documents from the British authorities the US viewpoint was redacted [that is, parts of it were omitted] at the specific request of my government.'

In retrospect, the connection between the downing of the Iranian Airbus in July 1988 and of Pan Am Flight 103 five months later has never been adequately established, and probably never will be. In settlements ending hostilities, justice is often the victim.

Published in *The New York Review of Books*, 9 September 2009.

Part **Three**

Muslim Societies

This section covers a variety of topics relating to Muslim beliefs and societies, starting with the first review I published in the London Review of Books in 1981. This was three years before the publication of Islam in the World, a book that received some flattering scholarly attention when it first appeared in 1984. I had, however, already been working on the book, which originated in a series of articles commissioned by Events, an English-language sister magazine of Al Hawadess, the Lebanese weekly owned and edited by Salim al-Lawzi. Lawzi, a warm-hearted man and a fearless editor, was cruelly murdered in 1980, it is thought by members of the Syrian intelligence services. In addition to Marshall Hodgson, Ernest Gellner was a the major influence on my work at this time. His collection of essays in Muslim Societies is reviewed below, along with V. S. Naipaul's Among the Believers. As might be expected, the two perspectives are utterly different. Naipaul, a Trinidadian of South Asian origin, is a writer of mesmerically brilliant prose, and one of the most compelling voices at large in the anglophone literary world. But his take on Islam lacks empathy and may be informed, unconsciously perhaps, by the disdainfulness of his Brahmin ancestors. He deals with his subjects with a certain magisterial arrogance, without appearing to have done the basic homework of engaging historically with their cultural systems. This makes for a seductive read, but one that can easily mislead. Gellner comes from the opposite end of the intellectual spectrum – a Central European heavyweight with an impressive command of both literature and fieldwork. As he stated memorably, 'orientalists are at home with texts. Anthropologists are at home in villages'. Though no orientalist, Gellner was both a philosopher and an anthropologist (he held university chairs in both disciplines) and his take on Islam was informed both by the anthropological field work he conducted in the Atlas Mountains of North Africa and his readings of the great Arab savant Ibn Khaldun (1332–1406).

The second essay in this section has direct contemporary relevance in the aftermath of the Arab uprisings in Tunisia and Egypt, where the Islamists of the Ennahada party (which won 40 per cent of the vote in Tunisia) and the Muslim Brotherhood in Egypt are poised on the brink of power. What could democratically-elected Islamist governments mean in terms of economic management and policy? What is 'Islamic economics'? Is it neo-liberal or neo-Keynsian? Charles Tripp, a scholar with a deep knowledge of the literature, shows that the slogan 'Islam is the solution', beloved of the Islamists, means little in terms of real economics: many so-called Islamic economic theories are simply mainstream economic theories to which green labels have been attached.

The essays on Central Asia and Syria, like my review of Gellner, reflects my debt to Ibn Khaldun and his concept of 'asabiyya – solidarity or 'group-feeling' based on the patrilineal kinship structures that have proved so durable in the Islamic world. In Central Asia these structures proved remarkably resilient, despite more than six decades of Soviet-directed communist rule. In Tajikistan, the resurfacing of these structures in the aftermath of the Soviet collapse led to a bitter civil war costing thousands of lives. The same brutal logic applies in Syria, where the Alawite-dominated regime of Bashar al-Assad was still clinging to power, in the teeth of external and internal opposition, when this book went to press. The outcome of this increasingly bitter conflict does not necessarily bode well for Syria's other minorities.

11
Onward Muslim Soldiers

Fourteen centuries ago, the Prophet Muhammad united the tribes of Arabia under the banner of Islam and reconquered for the One True God the Holy City of Mecca, which had long been a centre of pilgrimage. Within a generation, his successors – the caliphs – were in control of territory stretching from the Atlantic to the Indus valley. This was not just an astonishing feat of world conquest, comparable to the achievements of Alexander the Great and the Caesars: it had religious and social implications as far-reaching as the death of Christ and the Bolshevik Revolution. While Christianity merely revitalised the ancient Roman Empire, providing it with a new legitimacy that enabled it to overcome the crises posed by nationalism and barbarian invasion, Islam created a brand new polity – in effect, the world's first ideological state.

The Muslim world today is heir to what was at once a religious and a political aspiration. The state created by Muhammad barely survived its founder. Within four decades, it had become a monarchy ruled by the very Meccan aristocrats who had been the bitterest opponents of Muhammad's reforms. Further dynastic changes and something approaching a social revolution only delayed the inevitable collapse. No government at that time and in that region could have held together such a vast expanse of territory. Power passed into the hands of regional governors, royal body-guards or usurping dynasties. But the failure of Islam at the political level was compensated by its success in creating a normative social system. The lawyers and divines of the eighth and ninth centuries developed, out of the Qur'an and the Prophet's Sunna (his alleged sayings and actions as originally recorded in oral tradition), a coherent system of laws governing community, family and religious life. The theocratic utopia remained an aspiration. The reality has been accurately described as a 'divine nomocracy'. Freed from its political shackles, Islam extended itself more or less autonomously. It was brought to the remoter regions of Africa and the Far East not, on the whole, by soldiers, but by wandering scholars, merchants and holy men.

Despite its failures in the political field, Islam has never renounced its political aspirations. To do so would mean abandoning one of the pillars of the Islamic way of life: the Prophet's Sunna. *Imitatio Christi* means renouncing worldly ambition and seeking salvation by deeds of private virtue. *Imitatio Muhammadi* must sooner or later mean taking up arms against those forces which seem to threaten the survival of *Dar al-Islam*, from within or from without. The Qur'an is full of allusions to Muhammad's battles, to the heroism of those who took part, and the cowardice of those who held back. The Mujahidin are those who struggle in God's cause. The munafiqin are those who try to opt out, or worse, to collaborate secretly with the enemies of Islam. Both words have become part of the modern political vocabulary. The Iranian Mujahidin (leftist supporters of Bani Sadr currently waging war on the Ayatollahs) are described as munafiqin in the official government media.

It is a part of this fragmented and turbulent world of political Islam that V. S. Naipaul sets out to investigate in his latest book. His travels take him to Iran, Pakistan, Malaysia and Indonesia – countries with distinctive Islamic traditions, all of them influenced by, but not contained within, the Arab culture in which Islam made its first appearance. This is the major weakness of this otherwise brilliant book.

Islam sits more lightly on the shoulders of the Arab peoples than on non-Arabs. The Qur'an, with its seductive rhythms and elliptical shifting images, its pervasive life-affirming message, its promise of reward to the just and punishment to the wicked, is universally accessible only to Arabs. The Cairo taxi-driver who plays the Qur'an on cassettes in his cab and plasters the interior with coloured stickers containing the name of God may be pious – but not strenuously so. Islam is part of his lifestyle, but not the key to his identity. Islam and Arabism merge imperceptibly into one another. Though the two may conflict at the intellectual and political levels (for example, within the ranks of the Palestinian national movement at the time of writing), the cultural homogeneity of Arab–Muslim society renders the conflict less intractable than it would at first sight appear. Among non-Arabs, Islam is more inclined to crystallise into regimented forms and fixed images. In the popular religion of Shi'ite Iran, the cult of the martyred Hussein replaces that of the Book, access to which is effectively limited to members of the religious establishment. In Pakistan, the emphasis is both legalistic and utopian: hence the obsession with barbarous punishments and the constant search for the vague and amorphous ideal of a modern Islamic state. Muslim activists in the Far East become even more desperate in the search for a distinctive Muslim identity, since in these parts Islam has been superimposed on the more ancient Hindu–Buddhist culture, and feels itself constantly threatened by it. As Naipaul observes, passion for the faith increases with distance from Arabia.

Without a part of the Arab heartland to counterbalance the Islam of the periphery, Naipaul's book inevitably creates a somewhat distorted impression. Moreover, despite his striking aperçus, his quiet sympathy for individuals and his intelligent grasp of political and social realities, he is not entirely at ease with the Muslim world and its culture. He does not appear to be widely read in its literature, even in translation. At times he maintains a fastidious detachment, a suspiciousness tinged with arrogance. He seems to lack the sense of concern, the desire to come to terms with a complex reality, that made *India, A Wounded Civilisation* so impressive.

As a person 'without religious faith' and with a Hindu family background, it is perhaps not surprising that Naipaul should have some difficulty in approaching Islam. His interest was inspired by the events in Iran, as viewed on a TV screen in Connecticut, USA. His only previous knowledge was of the small diaspora community in his native Trinidad, viewed, necessarily with some suspicion, across the communal divide. In Iran he is understandably nervous about his origins. He tells Ayatollah Shirazi that he is a Christian – only to regret the lie, knowing it must cloud that man's response to his questions. Though he decides never again to complicate matters like this, the sense of unease remains with him for much of the journey. The gentle and cultivated humanist is always in danger of exposure as a Hindu polytheist.

For all that, there is no doubting his courage. He is scared of the Tehran traffic, but ventures into the lion's den at Qom – that 'medieval Oxford' where men and women walk on different sides of the street. He is even entertained by the Revolutionary Prosecutor Ayatollah Khalkali – a murderous buffoon ('I am very clever, very intelligent') who boasts that the Islamic Republic will last 10,000 years. (Had he heard of Hitler's more modest 'Thousand-Year Reich'?) Unfortunately, he does not get to see Khomeini, a man with a mind still caught in the coils of medieval jurisprudence, who, for reasons peculiar to the Shi'ite faith, the Iranians have made their leader: 'the deputy of the hidden Twelfth Imam, the regent of God'. Naipaul's most illuminating encounter is with his guide Behzad, whose communist faith is as rigid, dogmatic and out of touch with political and social realities as the faith of Khomeini himself.

In the unfamiliar territory of Iran, Naipaul never quite succeeds in penetrating beneath the surface, though with his sharp eye for detail he draws a convincing picture of a Shi'ite society obsessed with martyrdom, determined 'to keep alive ancient animosities, to hold on to the idea of personal revenge even after a thousand years, to have a special list of heroes, martyrs and villains'. Even the picture-sellers in the Tehran streets purvey the same lugubrious opiate as the Ayatollahs. Along with dream-landscapes, blown-up photographs of Swiss lakes and German forests, there are portraits of beautiful women and children, all weeping: 'Big gelatinous tears, lovingly rendered, ran half-way down their cheeks.'

In Pakistan, Naipaul is closer to the Indian world he knows already. The Shi'ite ethos is still strong. The legend of the unfortunate Mr Bhutto's martyrdom at the hand of General Zia replicates that of the Imam Hussein at Karbala. In the Iranian stories and annual passion plays commemorating the death of the Prophet's grandson, much is made of the wickedness of the Umayyad soldiers in refusing to allow the dying Imam to quench his thirst. An almost identical story – suitably modernised – is told of Bhutto: 'In the jail at Lahore – I had been told – they had put him in a cell where the cruel summer sun fell for much of the day. He asked for his drinking water to be boiled; they brought him a flask of boiling water; it was evening before the water was cool enough for him to drink.'

But Pakistan is not just another Muslim state ruled by a military auto-crat. Islam is its *raison d'être*. More than a haven for Muslims, it was to be the first truly Islamic state since the days of the Prophet and his close compan-ions, 'a fusion of history and theology, the indestructible alloy of faith'. Like other Utopian fantasies, however, it contained the seeds of disaster.

This Islamic state could not simply be decreed; it had to be invented, and in that invention faith was of little help. Faith, at the moment, could supply only the simple negatives that answered emotional needs: no alcohol, no feminine immodesty, no interest in the banks. But soon, in Pakistan, these negatives were to be expanded: no political parties, no parliament, no dissent, no law courts. So existing institutions were deemed to be un-Islamic, and undermined or undone; the faith was asserted because only the faith seemed to be whole; and in the vacuum only the army could rule.

In his account of Pakistan and of the Muslim militants he met in Malaysia and Indonesia, Naipaul develops his principal theme. The emotional rejection of the West involves a kind of hypocrisy. The Islamic ideal (which, in modern times, in any case, has never been realised) is contrasted with the corrupt reality for which the West is blamed.

The West, or the universal civilisation it leads, is emotionally rejected. It undermines; it threatens. But at the same time it is needed, for its machines, goods, medicines, warplanes, the remittances from emigrants, the hospitals that might have a cure for calcium deficiency, the universities that will provide master's degrees in mass media. All the rejection of the West is contained within the assumption that there will always exist out there a living, creative civilisation, oddly neutral, open to all to appeal to. Rejection, therefore, is not absolute rejection. It is also, for the community as a whole, a way of ceasing to strive intellectually. It is to be parasitic; parasitism is one of the unacknowledged fruits of fundamentalism.

There is a further hypocrisy involved in this rejection: it employs the tools which the West has itself developed. Publications in Qom borrow the words of Schumacher and Toynbee about technology and ecology, to lash the West. In Malaysia, the teacher Mohammed gives Naipaul a tract he has written:

> It was in the style of Islamic missionary writing. One section was headed 'The Bankruptcy of the West' ('vice and lust, alcohol and women, wild parties and tempting surroundings'); another was headed 'The Perfectness of Islam'. There was a logic in this. The West, which had provided Mohammed with academic learning, was open to the criticism it had trained him in. Islam, which had not provided this learning, which provided only the restoring faith, was exempt from criticism.

There is force in Naipaul's argument, however one-sidedly expressed. It is consistent with the theme he developed earlier in *India, A Wounded Civilisation*. Where the emotional rejection of modernity is worked out in a practical way, it is either hypocritical, as already described, or it simply enthrones the status quo. In the India described by Naipaul, rural poverty dehumanises more than any machine, and industrialisation, where human beings take command of machines, can be a liberating force. The processes of Westernisation and urbanisation, denounced by Muslim militants who seek a return to the pristine Islam of a 'tribal or city state that, except in theological fantasy, never was', provide, as well as the 'bars brothels, casinos and opium' denounced by Khomeini in his jeremiads, a range of cultural choices and social opportunities impossible in 'traditional' small towns or village communities. The militant intellectuals who attack Western 'materialism' with language borrowed from Schumacher would die of boredom if they really had to live in the kind of societies whose merits they seek to celebrate.

The flaw in his case is that, in common with many Western critics of so-called 'fundamentalism', he ignores the divergences between the various Islamic movements. An enormous gulf separates the 'fundamentalism' of people such as Khomeini from that of enlightened reformers, in the tradition of Muhammad Abduh, who realised that the survival of all Muslim societies would depend on the success with which they accommodated and integrated the fruits of Western science within Islam's spiritual and social framework. In Iran, that gulf seems likely to be bridged only at the cost of civil war. The failure of the reformers to unseat the traditional religious authorities led to the process of secularisation to which we are now witnessing the reaction. But that reaction contains a variety of different and opposing strands, not all rejectionist or parasitical. While Naipaul is quite justified in drawing attention to the implicit contradictions in the attitudes of thinkers such as Abdul Ala Maududi, the guru of the Pakistani 'fundamentalists' who died in 1979, he creates the misleading impression that Maududism is in some way typical of the movement as a whole. Since the cultural epicentre of Islam must always be in the Arab world, he would have obtained a broader perspective of his subject had he visited at least one important Arab country.

The Islamic vision of society is closely bound up with its social origins in a part of the world where settled peoples were normally at the mercy of Bedouin invaders: a situation that lasted well into the twentieth century in Arabia and parts of North Africa. For this reason, anthropological studies in these regions can make an important contribution to our understanding, not just of the people who live in remote areas under primitive conditions, but also of the central religious tradition that informs their lives. In substituting loyalty to Islam for tribal leadership, and universalism for parochialism, Muhammad established a pattern that was to be repeated by religious-reformers-cum-political-radicals down to the present time. These patterns can be observed in the microcosm of the small village or tribal unit, as they can in the macrocosm of world history. On the social level, Islam supplies the common vocabulary through which the perennial conflict between the city and the countryside, the townspeople and the pastoralists, is articulated. This dialectic originated in the agricultural conditions of the arid zone, but it contains far broader implications, which make it possible for its terms to be translated to suit the conditions of modern societies. The Muhammadan model of the tribesmen abandoning their polytheistic attachments and uniting under the banner of true religion has been imitated consciously by major reform movements within Islam from the Abbasids (CE 750) down to Abdul Aziz al Saud, the founder of modern Saudi Arabia. Moreover, under modern metropolitan conditions, the group loyalties characteristic of tribal formations can attach themselves to non-kinship groups, such as revolutionary brotherhoods. Islam, as Professor Gellner points out in this collection of his writings, is unique among world religions in 'maintaining its pre-industrial faith in the modern world': a feature which, when it combines with political aspirations, makes a potent agent for political mobilisation (surpassing, at present, even Marxism).

The classic theoretician of Muslim society is Ibn Khaldun (1332–1406), who, along with David Hume, Robert Montagne and E. E. Evans-Pritchard, Gellner acknowledges as his major influence. Ibn Khaldun's most celebrated theory, based on a profound understanding of Islamic history and a practical knowledge of North African politics, concerns the circulation of elites: 'Leadership exists through superiority, and superiority only through *asabiyya*' – social cohesion or group feeling. In desert conditions, the social solidarity of the tribe is vital to its survival. If and when the tribes decide to unite, their superior cohesion puts the city-folk at their mercy. Inspired by religion, they conquer the towns, which are incapable of defending themselves, and become the rulers until such time as, corrupted by luxury and the loss of their group cohesion, they are in turn replaced by a new nomadic dynasty (a process which usually takes three or four generations).

Gellner's central thesis is a sophisticated and modernised variation on Ibn Khaldun's original theme. Muslim city life lacks the cohesion of tribal existence. The division of labour and the absence of corporate institutions militate against the emergence of an urban polity capable of disarming the countryside. Government is thus the 'gift of the tribe to the city' and is informed by a central paradox: 'only those who refuse to be governed are themselves fit to rule: political education is to be had in the wilderness alone. If you wish to command you must not first learn to obey'. Thus an urban civilisation depends for its rulers on those whom it cannot itself rule.

The contrast with European polities is striking. For Plato, as for Marx, government is the consequence of social stratification, arising from the division of labour. Rulers are members of a dominant class, recruited from a professional caste of warriors who control the countryside (feudalists), or from the upper stratum within the city that exploits the labour of its fellow citizens (bourgeoisie). The European nation state emerged out of the transition from feudal to bourgeois government – both of which, in the first instance, depended on the suppression of pastoralism. In the arid zone, neither the feudal antecedents nor the bourgeois legatees were able to dominate the barbarians on the fringes. The national state is only now beginning to emerge, in the wake of colonial conquest of the 'land of insolence', of modern armaments, including air-power, and the internal combustion engine. The result is often an intermediate, neo-Ibn-Khaldunian type of government, in which democratic jargon ('government by the people for the people') cloaks kin-patronage politics. Though Professor Gellner doesn't say so, this is an accurate description of the political systems in Syria and Iraq. The Saudis, beneficiaries of an Ibn-Khaldunian game of musical chairs of a purer type, have no need to hide kin-patronage politics under populist verbiage.

The role of religion in this picture is very different from what it is in the Christian West. Muslim civilisation 'seems a kind of mirror image of traditional Christendom', Gellner explains:

> In Islam it is the central tradition which is egalitarian, scriptur-alist, devoid of hierarchy or formal leadership or organisation, puritanical and moralistic; whereas it is the marginal, question-ably orthodox movements which are fragmented, ritualistic, hierarchical, ecstatic and deeply implicated in, if not compro-mised by, local political structures.

Joseph de Maistre observed of Christianity that superstition constitutes the outer bulwarks of religion, meaning that the abandonment of such popular strong points must endanger the citadel itself. The same percep-tion, turned about, underlies the attacks of rationalists and Marxists. As Gellner remarks:

> religions in which the outer bulwarks and the central bastion form one integral whole face a terrible dilemma in modern times: if they defend those exposed outer positions, the entire system may fall when the outposts become indefensible, as nowadays they often do. If, on the other hand, they are abandoned and disa-vowed, the remaining inner redoubt is so narrow and constrained and minimal, and its retention seems so opportunist, that it barely looks worth defending, and inspires little enthusiasm.

In Islam, however, all is different: the tension between the outer bulwarks of rural superstition and the inner citadel of urban scripturalist unitarianism has been there from the beginning. The Qur'anic message is always avail-able to lead the attack on shirk (the 'association' of lesser beings with God):

> The perforation is ever ready, marked 'tear off here when modern world arrives' … So when modern conditions did make it socially and intellectually attractive to separate a true, pristine, pure faith from the superstitious accretions, it could be done with real conviction.

The Divine Law, as revealed in the Qur'an and elaborated through the 'science' of fiqh (jurisprudence), is the province of the urban scholar-lawyers (ulama): but they are not as a rule in a position to enforce it beyond the realm of private social conduct. Though the rulers will appoint them as judges, there is a marked reluctance on the part of the *ulama* to compromise the purity of the Divine Law by serving the Establishment. The failure of Islam as a polity is compensated for by its success as a normative system of social conduct. The absence of caliphal legitimacy, which accounts for almost continuous political turbulence, is counterbalanced by a stabilising social morality which enables society to weather the storms of the surface. The 'divine nomocracy' presided over by the *ulama* may be utopian, because contemporary conditions will never allow a restoration of the purity of Muhammad's reign: but it provides the burghers, who are weak, with a moral and ideological sanction against their rulers. In the right conditions, they will ally themselves with the wild men of the 'lands of insolence', providing, under the banner of a reformed Islam, the crucial alliance between the urban populace and a new military outgroup which can bring about a change of government.

Professor Gellner finds that Ibn Khaldun's theory dovetails neatly with the theory of cyclic oscillations between monism and pluralism outlined by Hume in his *Natural History of Religion*. In Hume's hands, the theory is unduly psychologistic. Taken in conjunction with Ibn Khaldun, it accommodates successfully the range of religious possibilities encompassed by the urban nomad complex. Gellner's fieldwork was conducted in North Africa and he is an expert on the role of Sufi orders and maraboutic lineages. Sainthood in Islam does not require celibacy. Muslim saints (like the Prophet himself, who enjoyed several wives over and above the four permitted to ordinary believers) often combine spiritual with sexual energy and form lineages through which their charisma is transmitted to posterity. In a segmentary society they perform a variety of functions, such as supervising the elections of chiefs, guaranteeing the movement of caravans and managing tribal boundaries. The faith of the illiterate tribesman, unlike that of the literate townsman, requires the mediation of special and distinct holy personnel. Thus (while Gellner does not mention it) the functions of sainthood in many ways correspond to the pagan rituals of the jahiliya – the period of 'ignorance' before Muhammad's reforms.

The undercurrent of conflict between a fetishistic, pluralistic tribalism and a puritanical monistic urbanism helps to explain some of the paradoxes in the relationship between Islam and the modern world. In Turkey we find reformism with a decidedly secularist bent, while in Algeria it has a scripturalist and puritanical character. Shi'ite Iran, at the time of writing the scene of a full-blooded 'Islamic Revolution', represents a further complication.

As Gellner points out, the Ottoman state contradicted Ibn Khaldun's model on a number of important points: 'It was stable, strong and long-lived by any standards, not only those of Muslim society.' It represented the development of a pattern of which mamlukism was the intermediate stage. The *mamluks* (slave warriors purchased as boys from Central Asia and trained as a special military caste) gave Egypt a relatively stable government for more than five centuries and successfully defended it against the Mongol invaders. Under the mamluk system, which the Ottomans took over and developed,

> *political cohesion at the top was attained by the artificial creation of a new élite, technically slaves, ideally free of kin links to distract them from their duty, not by the shared hardships of tribal life, but by systematic training and education for wars and administration.*

The Ottomans ruled with *mamluks de robe* as well as *mamluks d'épée*: there were slave-bureaucrats as well as slave-soldiers, holding the front line of Islam against the West. Official Islam became closely shackled to the state, and proved to be incapable of finding any original solution to the problems eventually raised by Western cultural and political dominance. The result was a secularist attack on Islam, which drove its reformist and traditional wings into uneasy opposition.

In Algeria, on the other hand, the French authorities had allied themselves with or tolerated the unregenerated, traditional forms of Islam associated with tribalism. Nationalist struggle began in the guise of Islamic reform, which the French found difficult to oppose. After the departure of the French, who, like other colonial governments, had brought Ibn Khaldun's recruiting ground, the 'lands of insolence', under central control, 'reformist Islam, scripturalist and puritanical, was virtually the only usable ideology, deeply implanted and intelligible inside the country'.

Shi'ite Iran, of course, is a special case. Like Christianity, Shi'ism began its career as an underground movement opposed to the state – in this case, the official Muslim state of the Umayyads. Here again, the Islamic inversion of Christian patterns is apparent. The cult of martyrdom and the sacred person is an offshoot of the scripturalist mainstream – 'Protestantism', as it were, being the norm, and 'Catholicism' the deviant version. The occultation (disappearance) of the Twelfth Imam places religious authority in the hands of the mullahs, who, in his absence, are in a position to de-legitimise the ruler. We are witnessing the consequences:

> *The Pahlavis, unlike the Romanoffs, were overthrown without prior defeat in war, with their military power intact and whilst endowed with enormous financial resources – an astonishing feat*

and an impressive testimony to the capacity of Shiism for revolutionary mobilisation.

However, as Gellner points out, it is one thing to overthrow a dynasty, and quite another to govern a modern state. The fall of the Shah has brought to the fore internal divisions within the class of Shi'ite *ulama*, in which scripturalist reverence for the law, common to all Islamic reform movements, comes up against the cult of the sacred person. The time will no doubt come, he predicts (the book was written in 1979), when 'the two kinds of scholars, the Shi'a with PhDs and the populist mullahs, come to fight it out for the inheritance of the Iranian revolution'. With the continuing slaughter of the leaders of the Islamic Republican Party by the Shi'ite PhDs, the battle lines in this life-and-death struggle have already been joined. In the devious, contradictory and paradoxical world of Muslim society, Gellner's essay should prove a useful, if somewhat difficult, guide. However, the reader should not be misled by the title of the book into supposing that it gives a general account of Muslim society. As Gellner himself says, 'orientalists are at home with texts. Anthropologists are at home in villages'. Despite his claim that 'the time has come to assert the thesis of homogeneity' in Muslim society, if only as a problem or point of departure, his remains a partial view of the subject, as seen mainly from the village.

Published in *London Review of Books*, 1 October 1981.

The books reviewed were:

Ernest Gellner (1981) *Muslim Society*. Cambridge, UK: Cambridge University Press.

V. S. Naipaul (1981) *Among the Believers: An Islamic Journey*. London: André Deutsch.

12
Pasting Green Labels

During the Cold War era, the developing world seemed to be presented with a clear-cut choice between the socialist path of 'top-down' industrialisation and social modernisation through the agency of an all-powerful state, and liberal models that relied on the operations of supposedly benign market forces. In the Islamic world the ideological divide was influenced profoundly by the experience of peoples such as the Egyptians, Indo-Muslims, Algerians and Indonesians, who had just broken free from the tutelage, and humiliations, of the Western European colonial powers. A leftward slant seemed inevitable in the circumstances; Western governments were seen to have exploited their power or political leverage to impose unfavourable terms of trade or to make compliant regimes sign agreements that mortgaged their export commodities, such as oil. Despite the repression of Islam in the Caucasus, Central Asia and China, the Soviet and Chinese models of development seemed more benign. Islamic scholars and ideologues, co-opted by governments, argued that Muhammad was the original socialist, and that the early caliphs were all socialists at heart. As the Egyptian writer, Mahmud Shalabi, put it in 1962: 'We have an independent socialism springing from our history, our beliefs and our nature.' However, the appropriation of Islam and its symbols by authoritarian states with single-party, Eastern-European-style governments led rapidly to disillusionment among Muslim intellectuals – especially after the catastrophic defeat of Egypt, Jordan and Syria by Israel in the June 1967 war. Voices that had always expressed scepticism about official, left-leaning Islam became more voluble and gained a wider hearing.

Honed by persecution in Egypt and Syria, and fuelled by injections of patronage from conservative oil-bearing states, the Islamist movement in its various guises tried to forge a more authentic idea of an 'Islamic' political economy. The slogan 'Neither East nor West, Islam is Best' encapsulated the idea that 'Islam' was not 'just a religion' but a full-blown 'ideology' rooted in the Qur'an, the exemplary life of Muhammad and the comprehensive system of jurisprudence that flowed from them. This ideology was supposed to supply distinctive 'Islamic' solutions to issues of development, economic management, finance, gender relations and political power. The movement reached its climactic moment in 1978–9 with the overthrow of the Shah of Iran and the proclamation of Khomeini's revolutionary Islamic Republic.

Any lingering suspicion that Islamism might lean more towards socialism than liberalism was destroyed by the USSR's invasion in 1979, under the Soviet leader Brezhnev, of Afghanistan. Forget that pro-Soviet governments in Kabul had brought electricity, female education, decent if basic hospitals, and some solid infrastructural necessities such as clean water and paved roads, to regions of a country where poverty and illiteracy had ruled for centuries. The great *jihad* supported by the Saudis (and covertly by the Americans) not only destroyed the left-leaning government in Kabul. It also set in motion the momentous train of events in Eastern Europe and Central Asia that brought an end to the Soviet Union itself. For Panglossian Western voices such as Francis Fukuyama, the 'end of history' signalled by the triumph of capitalism was complete. For Muslim ideologues such as Abdullah Azzam, one of Osama bin Laden's intellectual mentors, however, the message of Soviet collapse was quite different. Just as the early caliphs had destroyed the armies of Persia before gaining control of Roman Byzantium's wealthiest provinces, so the Islamist movement – the Third or Middle Way between the empires of East and West – would triumph against the crusading armies of the United States and its Muslim lackeys. Territories once held by Islam (including Spain) would be restored to Islamic rule. In a globalised world, moreover, ambitions were no longer confined to restoring territories lost many centuries before. For Sayyid Abul Ala Maududi, the influential Indo-Muslim ideologist, who died in 1979, the ultimate objective of *jihad* must be the establishment of a 'universal Islamic order which would use the spirit of *jihad* and the instrument of revolution to capture power through the existing state system and thereby guarantee the rule of Islam' in perpetuity.

Where Islamism has come to power, as in Iran and Sudan, the political forms seem no less authoritarian than the systems they intend to replace. Nor is it at all clear what the actual content of Islamist government may be in terms of the universal categories that define modernity: namely, liberal market capitalism and its (perhaps only temporarily eclipsed) former rivals and counterparts – state socialism and communism. This is the demanding task that Charles Tripp has set himself by examining the writings of the leading Muslim intellectuals who have grappled with this question. On a brilliant and comprehensive reading of the sources, both Muslim and occidental, he arrives at a conclusion that will dismay Muslim radicals without giving much comfort to the (now discredited) proponents of the 'war on terror'. Islamism rests on fragile intellectual foundations. Far from being rooted in the 'authentic' discourse of Islam, most of its ideas are borrowed from the West it claims to abhor.

Muslim responses to the transformation of local economies under the pressure of market forces ranged from the Luddite-style attacks on spinning machines and factories by the so-called 'Wahhabis' in Northern India, in defence of Muslim weavers, early in the nineteenth century, to the whole-sale adoption of capitalist institutions by reforming governments operating under Western colonial auspices. Despite the obvious contrast in methods, there were common ethical concerns. Islamic jurisprudence, derived from the Qur'an and Muhammad's precepts, places a strong emphasis on fair exchange and social harmony. An often quoted *hadith*, or saying, attributed to the Prophet states that 'wealth is the test of my community' – implying that its possession would test their moral fortitude. Many twentieth-century Muslim writings – echoing the criticisms of Christian socialists as well as Marxists – argue that capitalism removes all restrictions on the acquisition and spending of money, promoting excessive concentrations of wealth and the commodification of basic necessities such as food and sex, making money the measure of all things, to the detriment of moral values. At the start of the twentieth century, Talaat Harb, an Egyptian financier, was inspired to found Egypt's first national bank because of his concern that the foreign capital flooding into the country was eroding the social solidarity of the peasants, and with similar consequences for urban society. Yet he was far from being anti-capitalist, seeing in the modern banking system an effective machine for engineering growth and economic development. He hoped it could be 'tamed' by embedding it in the matrix of Islamic social values. Muhammad Abduh, the Islamic reformer who abandoned his former nationalism to collaborate with Lord Cromer, the British pro-consul in Egypt in the interest of modernisation, argued that capitalism diminished moral constraints, and particularly the quintessentially Islamic virtues of compassion, mercy, soli-darity and co-operation. His Turkish contemporary, Said Halim Pasha, went even further: 'Modern culture, based as it is on national egoism is … only another form of barbarism. It is the result of an over-developed industrialism through which men satisfy their primitive instincts and inclinations.' The consensus of progressive thinkers held that, while capitalism was dangerous – especially when its levers were held in irresponsible foreign hands – its effects could be mitigated by bringing it within the frame of Islamic moral precepts.

This hope, however, would prove to be elusive. The tradition of *fiqh* – Islamic jurisprudence – addressed the ethical responsibilities of the pious believer; it had little to say about society as such. Indeed 'society', as under-stood by Western social theorists, lies outside the conceptual universe of traditional Islamic thought. The need to accommodate society's needs, and to defend the Islamic social order against the depredations of capitalism, required the adoption of novel categories – though these were cleverly smuggled into a renovated Muslim discourse by the use of familiar termi-nology. Thus Abduh, an admirer of Herbert Spencer, elevated *maslahah*, the public interest as acknowledged by traditional *fiqh*, into a defining principle of his reformist agenda. Under the rubric of maslahah, the public good and social benefit became the yardsticks by which social transactions would be judged. As Tripp points out, a signal change in intellectual outlook occurred with a shift of emphasis towards the state as the guardian and implementer of maslahah. Traditional Islamic discourse, rooted in the history of nomadic incursions and the mamluk or 'slave' dynasties that flowed from them, took a highly sceptical view of state power. Though the sultans and amirs who took over after the collapse of the Arab caliphate were theoretically subject to the divine law of Islam, there were no mechanisms other than moral suasion for calling the rulers to account. Islamic civil society existed more-or-less independently of the state. Not only did the 'privileging of state power' represent a radical break with the 'decidedly cautious treatment of the state by generations of Islamic jurists'; it soon became apparent to ideologues such as Sayyid Qutb, executed by Nasser in 1966 but whose prison writings continue to inspire today's jihadists, that the state had a secular agenda wholly at variance with the aim of creating a 'good' Islamic society based on the example of the Prophet and his immediate succes-sors, the 'rightly-guided' caliphs. Disillusionment with state systems that were authoritarian, repressive and corrupt divided the Islamist movement between a pragmatic majority (represented by the main body of the Muslim Brotherhood) prepared to lobby for its values within the existing order, and the revolutionary utopians belonging to an array of different groups who followed Qutb's call for a vanguard preparing for power in order to subject society to true Islamic governance. As a result mainly of the military disas-ters in Iraq, Afghanistan and the continuing crisis in Israel–Palestine, the Qutbists are gaining ground after a period of eclipse when (following massa-cres of tourists in Egypt and the carnage inflicted by al-Qaeda in East Africa and New York) the radical hinterlands had been alienated by attacks on civilians and damage to tourism livelihoods.

The rebirth of Islamist extremism, however, tells us little about the alternatives to market liberalism and socialism proclaimed by the slogans. In the economic realm, ambiguity continues to reign, without a clear definition of what is meant by 'Islamic' economics. In many cases, as Tripp points out, Islamist writings echo the critiques of market forces advanced by Fabians and Christian socialists, while the influence of Keynes is pervasive. In essence, the moral critiques of capitalism, and of socialism, advanced by Muslim intellectuals are not substantially different from those offered by Fabians or neo-liberals, leaving the impression that in this arena (as in others, including arguments about political activism) 'Islamic' is simply a label attached to imported intellectual goods. Digging deep into texts of influential Islamist writers such as the Iraqi Ayatollah Muhammad Baqir al-Sadr (executed by Saddam Hussein), Tripp discerns the foundations of 'Islamic economics' as lying uneasily between the classical occidental model of the self-interested individual as the agent of economic motivation, and the construction of an ideal-typical 'Islamic personality' who is supposed to act in accordance with Islamic teachings because he remains mindful of his responsibilities before God. However, it is far from clear how a 'calculus of utility which incorporates the hereafter' can influence action in the world by contributing to greater social justice, or how it could transform economies configured around the existing right–left spectrum by creating innovative new methods or institutions. When institutionalised by governments, zakat – the charity to which Muslims are obliged to contribute – is liable to meet with resistance, since governments are considered unreliable; while, as socialists have often argued, charitable giving to the 'poor' may simply serve to uphold economic inequalities. Similarly, the prohibition of riba, or usury, widely interpreted by latter-day Islamists (though not by earlier reformers such as Abduh) as meaning fixed interest payments on deposits and loans, has generated an array of financial institutions in which lenders and borrowers are supposed to share the burden of risk in equal measure. The results are not impressive. In the Islamic Republic of Iran, the prohibition of riba has contributed to a flourishing black economy. And elsewhere, despite earlier promises that the new financial system would offer a 'third way' between socialism and capitalism, the whole system has become fragmented and subject to arbitrary rules, with well-paid Islamic scholars scouring the corpus of the legal tradition to find ways of legitimising transactions developed in the larger context of the global financial markets. 'In reality,' comments Tripp, 'the Islamic banks have challenged neither the idea nor the institution of the capital market which is at the heart of global capitalism. On the contrary, they have merely created a niche in that market for themselves.'

A comparable ambiguity in the relations between Islam and modernity in the era of global capital pervades the most egregious of the symbolic markers erected by the Islamists to distinguish themselves both from outsiders and from their ordinary co-religionists: the various forms of female covering loosely termed the 'veil' in English. In a chapter rich in irony, Tripp shows how women clad in these shapeless garments have turned on its head what was originally an exclusively male discourse in which women were 'passive participants on whom could be inscribed all the moral preoccupations of their male counterparts'. In fighting capitalist domination and colonial occupation, the Muslim family was seen as a final refuge, a 'strategic point of departure for a more general Islamic order', or even a 'revolutionary cell which, in concert with others, would organise effective resistance to the structures of political and economic power'. Disconcerting as it was for such male intellectuals, women 'were now determined to inscribe themselves into the narrative, not as ideally constructed clusters of virtues, but as active interpreters of their own fate'.

Far from heralding resistance to the pervasive capitalist order, the veil represents a type of accommodation, with 'license now given to women to join the labour force on a par with men'. This development, would have horrified Qutb – who argued that by going out to work women were contravening the divinely instituted natural order and threatening the very foundations of social life. The veil, however, is not just an empty token: while defining Islamic identity and symbolising rejection of the supposed 'commodification' of female sexuality, the veil has enabled a growing body of assertive women to 'emerge as actors in spheres the contours of which are not necessarily dictated by men' and to open up 'key questions about social roles, equal rights, social utility and the gendering of knowledge'.

This is a far more constructive response to capitalist hegemony than resorting to violence, the subject of Tripp's final chapter. Here, his insights are no less penetrating than his deconstruction of Islamic economics. The protean nature of capitalism renders violence both politically futile and symbolically meaningful. On the practical level, its use merely enmeshes its perpetrators in the coils of state power. Symbolically, however, the 'propaganda of the deed' such as 9/11 may succeed in its aim of removing the 'false consciousness' from Muslim minds, making them aware of the parlous nature of their situation: here, as elsewhere in the book, Tripp reveals how ideas adopted from European anarchists such as Bakunin and Malatesta are rebranded with Islamic labels. Appropriately for the world's most scripturally-driven creed, Islam provides the 'alphabet' by which ideas in the world's intellectual superstores are appropriated. But the 'grammar' is far from being 'Islamic'. It is already 'out there', external to the tradition, shaped by the hegemonic power of global capitalism.

Published in *The Times Literary Supplement*, 26 January 2007.

The book reviewed was:

Charles Tripp (2006) *Islam and the Moral Economy: The Challenge of Capitalism*. Cambridge, UK: Cambridge University Press.

13
Phantoms of Ideology

Will Islam replace communism as the governing political ideology of Central Asia? Neither of these books gives an unambiguous answer. Dilip Hiro's workmanlike survey, *Between Marx and Muhamad: The Changing Face of Central Asia*, chronicles Soviet involvement in Central Asia since the Russian Revolution, with impressive attention to the twists and turns of policy, but less insight into the complex religious and ideological currents flowing through the region. His is an outsider's view, based on materials generally available in the West. Vitaly Naumkin's selection of essays by Soviet specialists, *State, Religion and Society in Central Asia*, published during the *glasnost* era, makes a useful supplement to Hiro, by explaining in more detail how, despite official persecution and harassment, Central Asian Islam continued to sustain itself in secret during more than seven decades of communist rule.

In the period after the Revolution, as Hiro explains, anti-religious policies were implemented in the Muslim-majority areas with considerable caution, partly because the communists considered Muslim society to be 'feudal', lacking a revolutionary proletariat, and partly because of the way that Islam 'impinged on every facet of life, individual and social'. Nevertheless, institutional Islam was attacked during the 1930s, when mosques were placed in the hands of the Union of Atheists, to be turned into museums or places of entertainment, while two of the five 'pillars' of the faith, the pilgrimage to Mecca and the collection of zakat (the religious dues used to maintain mosques and provide funds for the needy), were forbidden. The religious establishment was further crippled by the state takeover of the *awqaf* (religious trusts), depriving mullahs of their income and starving mosques and theological schools of funds. The Shari'a and *Adat* (customary) courts were abolished. The ban on Arabic script imposed in 1929 ensured that future Soviet generations in Central Asia would have less access to their own history and to the Islamic canons, making them dependent on the Soviet authorities for material printed in Roman or Cyrillic scripts. The solidarity of the Central Asian Umma (Muslim community) was attacked by a deliberate policy of divide and rule.

Today's Central Asian states owe their territorial existence to Stalin, who responded to the threat of pan-Turkish and pan-Islamic nationalism by parcelling out the territories of Russian Turkestan into the five republics of Uzbekistan, Turkmenistan, Kazakhstan, Kyrgyzstan and Tajikistan. (Hiro also includes the Transcaucasian state of Azerbaijan in his survey, though strictly speaking it does not belong to Central Asia.) The prosperous Fergana valley, which lies at the core of the region and had always been a single economic unit, was divided between Uzbeks, Tajiks and Kyrgyz. Stalin's policies demanded that differences in language, history and culture between these mainly Turkic peoples be emphasised in order to satisfy the Leninist criteria on nationality, which required a common language, a unified territory, a shared economic life and a common culture. To the new territorial configurations were added the straitjackets of collectivisation and monoculture. Under Khrushchev's Virgin Lands scheme, vast tracts of Kazakhstan were given over to cereal production, and when the mainly pastoral Kazakhs resisted, Slavs and other nationalities were imported to do the work. In Uzbekistan, more than 60 per cent of domestic production was turned over to cotton. This served the interests of the ruling party elites, some of whose members became involved in frauds based on the systematic falsification of production figures, but left a devastating environmental legacy by starving non-cotton crops of irrigation and drying up rivers and lakes, including the Aral Sea.

Though there were undoubted benefits resulting from industrialisation and the introduction of almost universal literacy, the retreat of Soviet power following the war in Afghanistan has seen, not surprisingly, an upsurge of non-communist ideologies, including local nationalisms, pan-Turkism and militant forms of Islam. Suppressed for nearly three generations, Islam has made a remarkable comeback among ordinary people. Mosques and religious schools are flourishing. Yet, despite the retreat of Russia, the general disillusionment with Soviet rule and the collapse of the local economies, the old communist *nomenklatura* have, except in Azerbaijan, managed to cling to power under their new 'democratic' labels. Even in Tajikistan, where the opposition is sustained by the Afghan Mujahidin, the neo-communists have managed to claw their way back to power.

Though they were written in 1990, before the disintegration of the Soviet Union and the civil war in Tajikistan, several of the papers in Naumkin's collection of essays by Soviet specialists contain clues to, if not complete explanations of, this phenomenon. In the clotted jargon that reveals its Marxist–Leninist provenance, Yuri Alexandrov explains that 'contradictions artificially introduced into the indigenous economic and social structure by a foreign agent of change' can engender 'multiple ways of adapting traditional society to the economic relations imposed on it'. Whereas in European Russia the state succeeded in restructuring local communities in accordance with its requirements, in Central Asia the communities adapted state institutions to their own rules. Sergei Polyakov suggests that the Eurocentricity of the Soviet planners, and their very ignorance of local conditions, made it easier for Central Asians to impose their own patterns of authority on communist institutions. The privatisation of property in land, which was beginning when Central Asia was incorporated into the tsarist empire, was abruptly halted after the Revolution. Far from benefiting the peasants, the Bolshevik takeover had the effect of boosting 'an authoritarian–patriarchal type of management' in the collective-farm system, based on '"patron–client" relations between superiors and subordinates'. This, argues Polyakov, suited the traditional Islamic order, 'leaving the customary way of life unaffected'. In terms of their legal status and the official protection they enjoyed, the new Soviet institutions did not differ greatly from the Islamic *awqaf* in place before the Revolution.

In his essay on Tajikistan, Valentin Bushkov makes a similar point. For the Tajiks, the collectivisation of land introduced in the 1930s coincided with previous notions of clan property, and the first collective farms were actually organised on a clan basis, with the heads of families becoming farm chairmen and the collectivised property consisting of *aviod* or clan lands. In Central Asia, sovietisation reinforced, rather than undermined, traditional social structures. In Bushkov's view, however, this was not – as Polyakov and others have suggested – the result of faulty sociology, but rather of deliberate policy: 'It was central government policy to preserve village traditions and the underdeveloped economy because this encouraged Central Asian agriculture to accelerate and expand cotton production.' However, the details of how the clan system operated at the macro level, sustaining Soviet power, are not clear from Naumkin's selection of papers. To obtain a more precise picture, one would need to know how party and clan memberships overlapped, and how far Soviet institutions buttressed tribal authority.

The resilience of the clan system had an important bearing on the survival of the local power structures after the collapse of the Soviet Union. It may also account for the survival of Islamic praxis during seven decades of communist rule. Meshed into the social system, Central Asian Islam did not depend on official institutions for its survival. In his essay on 'Religious and Political Change in the Soviet Muslim Regions', Alexei Malashenko suggests that the local elites, attached to Islamic customs and recognising a degree of affinity between Islamic and socialist values, cheated on their anti-religious activities as assiduously as they faked their figures of cotton production. Gatherings of old men reading the Qur'an would be described to zealots of the Society for Scientific Atheism as meetings of Great Patriotic War veterans. The custom of taqiya, concealing one's beliefs to avoid persecution, was practised not only by the Shi'a, but also by Sufi orders, such as Naqshabandiya, which have deep historical roots in Central Asia. The public resurgence of Islam after 1989 was not so much a religious revival as the resurfacing of something that had always been there.

All of this should have provided fertile ground for the Islamic radical groups which mushroomed, especially in Uzbekistan and Tajikistan, during the period of *glasnost*; while the defeat of Soviet power in Afghanistan at the hands of the Mujahidin confirmed the failure of Marxism–Leninism, and added an immeasurable boost to the idea that Islam could fill the ideological void. Hiro attributes the unexpected survival of the *nomenklatura* mainly to Iranian self-interest and self-restraint.

Tehran, despite being demonised in the West, particularly the United States, was 'more interested in integrating the economies of [the] six Muslim majority states into its own than in aiding Islamic movements or groups in these countries'. This appears true in retrospect, when the Iranians are putting a good face on their reversal in Tajikistan, but as the Pakistani journalist Ahmed Rashid claimed in his recent book, *The Resurgence of Central Asia*, the Iranians were heavily involved in Tajikistan, and were far from restricting aid and support to their fellow Shi'ites. A more plausible explanation, hinted at by Malashenko, lies in the ambivalent nature of Central Asian Islam, which is suffused with the tolerant and apolitical spirit of Sufism: the fundamentalism with which the authorities felt themselves threatened, not only in Tajikistan, but rather with what Malashenko calls a 'phantom of ideologised consciousness'. Having scared themselves, and the Russians, with this spectre haunting Central Asia, they were able to win enough support for the ruthless methods necessary to sustain themselves in power. The danger, revealed by the continuing conflict in Tajikistan, is that such an over-reaction can be self-fulfilling, hardening the opposition and creating a militancy that was not previously present.

Published in *The Times Literary Supplement*, 26 August 1994.

The books reviewed were:

Dilip Hiro (1994) *Between Marx and Muhammad*.
Vitaly Naumkin (ed.) (1994) *State, Religion and Society in Central Asia*.

14

Storm over Syria

'Damascus has seen all that has ever occurred on earth, and still she lives,' wrote Mark Twain after visiting Syria's capital in the 1860s. 'She has looked upon the dry bones of a thousand empires, and will see the tombs of a thousand more before she dies.'

The turmoil in Syria, where hundreds of unarmed protesters have been mown down by the forces of President Bashar al-Assad, who comes from the country's Alawi minority, is much more menacing than the generally peaceful revolutions in Tunisia and Egypt, from which the Syrian protesters drew their initial inspiration. The regime of Zine al-Abidine Ben Ali in Tunisia capitulated in the face of spontaneous demonstrations sparked by the self-immolation of a 26-year-old man who had been reduced to scratching a living as a humble street vendor. Ben Ali, along with his hated wife and family, chose to go into exile before a single shot had been fired.

In Egypt, if press reports are to be believed, the generals unseated President Hosni Mubarak after tank commanders refused his orders to fire on civilians. The Egyptian revolution, which has seen some resistance from the military and police, has now taken a constitutional turn, with the country approving a series of amendments that could lead to the emergence of a parliamentary democracy. Much will depend on the willingness of the military to allow an open political process to take place.

The Syrian government's response to the Arab world's turbulent spring, by contrast, has been both violent and vacillating. Its initial response was to characterise the protests across the country as the result of a global conspiracy fomented by a clutch of unlikely allies, including the USA, Israel and Arab enemies in Lebanon, Saudi Arabia and Qatar, working with former regime officials and homegrown Salafists, or fundamentalists. President Assad tried to defuse the opposition by receiving protest delegations and announcing the lifting of long-standing emergency laws, apparently acknowledging the existence of legitimate grievances. But this proved to be no more than a gesture. In effect, the government's response has been contradictory to the point of incoherence: as the Brussels-based International Crisis Group pointed out in a report released on 3 May:

> The regime has lifted the emergency law but has since allowed the security services to conduct business as usual, thereby illustrating just how meaningless the concept of legality was in the first place. It authorises demonstrations even as it claims they no longer are justified and then labels them as treasonous. It speaks of reforming the media and, in the same breath, dismisses those who stray from the official line. It insists on ignoring the most outrageous symbols of corruption. Finally, and although it has engaged in numerous bilateral talks with local representatives, it resists convening a national dialogue, which might represent the last, slim chance for a peaceful way forward.

Over 700 people have been killed so far, more than 100 of them in the south-western city of Deraa, near the Jordanian border, where the Omari mosque – a centre of resistance – has been closed to worshippers after being shelled by tanks and taken over by snipers. Some 10,000 people are now said to have been detained by elite security forces backed by the army. According to Amnesty International, detainees have been beaten with sticks and cables, and sometimes deprived of food. Unlike the situation in Libya, there are no NATO forces to protect Syria's cities or parts of the country from the murderous attacks inflicted by a regime that is now losing the last threads of international legitimacy. Assad has a more effective army than Qaddafi, and powerful friends in Iran, Lebanon and Iraq.

In contrast to Libya, military action in defence of Syria's beleaguered population would hardly attract a shred of international support. While the Arab League voted unanimously for the no-fly zone to protect the people of Benghazi, in the case of Syria it has not even mentioned the country by name, merely declaring that pro-democracy protesters 'deserve support, not bullets'.

As *The New York Times* pointed out in an editorial, the UN Security Council 'hasn't even been able to muster a press statement. Russia and China, as ever, are determined to protect autocrats'. Israel has been watching and waiting with alarm as the outcome of the unrest in Syria becomes increasingly uncertain. Despite his alliance with Iran and refusal to recognise the Jewish state, Assad is the devil it knows best. Prolonged instability or a Salafist regime could only make matters worse.

On the ground, it is far from clear what is happening, since foreign reporters have been banned from entering the country, the internet service has been shut down, and mobile phone coverage limited to satellites or systems outside government control. Nevertheless, the protests, spurred by the funerals of victims and gatherings at Friday prayers – the only occasions on which large numbers of people are permitted to assemble, have spread from Deraa to at least a dozen other cities, including Baniyas and Latakia on the Mediterranean coast, as well as to the northern city of Homs and some suburbs of Damascus. With the Alawi-dominated regime under threat, the struggle is showing ominous sectarian overtones. At Baniyas, where the army moved scores of tanks and armoured vehicles into the city's southern outskirts, paramilitary groups were said to have massed in Alawi-populated northern suburbs. The city centres of Damascus and Aleppo, however, remained relatively quiet, as the government appeared to be organising rallies of its own supporters, with activists claiming that efforts were being made to bus in pro-government demonstrators from Alawi-dominated regions. Grainy mobile phone images sent clandestinely from Homs to the Al Jazeera TV network showed a speech by a senior defector from the ruling Baath party being greeted with shouts of 'Allahu Akbar' (God Is Greater), often regarded as the jihadist war cry.

At first sight, the defection of more than 300 members of the ruling Baath party in protest at the crackdown would suggest that Syria's one-party state, in place since 1963, is beginning to unravel. What some people are calling the Facebook Revolution, an unprecedented wave of visible public protest, is led by a generation of media-savvy young people, more aware of the outside world than their parents were, who are demanding an end to the system of repression, corruption and privilege that has been the hallmark of the authoritarian Arab regimes lying between the Atlas Mountains and the Persian Gulf.

Yet, unlike the Muslim Brotherhood's rebellion in Hama, which shook the government of Bashar al-Assad's father, Hafez, in 1982, the Facebook rebellion seems curiously faceless. There are some signs of opposition violence, with 'plausible reports of security forces being ambushed by unidentified armed groups, as well as of protesters firing back when attacked', according to the International Crisis Group. But these appear to be small and random incidents. The vast majority of casualties are the consequence of the regime's brutality. The protests are largely spontaneous. There seem to be no controlling organisations or identifiable leaders, and the opposition's ideological focus is unclear, beyond slogans calling for an end to corruption and repression.

Optimists see this as an implicit acceptance of democratic values and assumptions. Despite the increasingly desperate efforts of the region's authoritarian governments to keep their people in the dark about the realities of the outside world by restricting information, the younger generation identifies with its peers in the liberal West and it knows what it is missing regarding access to materials and educational benefits, as well as civil and democratic rights. The problem is that while the Facebook generation knows what it doesn't like, it is far from clear that there are structures in place, or being planned, that could provide the basis for an alternative political system if the regime collapses. Pessimists envisage a scenario encapsulated in the phrase 'one man, one vote, one time', leading to a Salafist takeover and a settling of scores against minorities (including Christians) who were protected by the regime or benefited from its pluralist approach. More than 70 per cent of the Syrian population are Sunni.

How did Syria come to this? While some observers see in recent events a parallel with 1989, and the break-up of the Eastern European-style system introduced by the Baathists in the 1960s, this is no velvet revolution, nor is Syria like Jaruzelski's Poland. The regime's violence is not ideological. It is far from being the result of an emotional or philosophical commitment to a party that long ago abandoned its agenda of promoting secular Arab republican values and aspirations. The regime's ruthless attachment to power lies in a complex web of tribal loyalties and networks of patronage underpinned by a uniquely powerful religious bond.

The Alawis of Syria, who make up only 12 per cent of its population, split from the main branch of Shi'ism more than 1,000 years ago. Before the twentieth century they were usually referred to as Nusayris, after their eponymous founder, Ibn Nusayr, who lived in Iraq during the ninth century CE. Taking refuge in the mountains above the port of Latakia, on the coastal strip between modern Lebanon and Turkey, they evolved a highly secretive, syncretistic theology containing an amalgam of Neoplatonic, Gnostic, Christian, Muslim and Zoroastrian elements. Their leading theologian, Abdullah al-Khasibi, who died in 957, proclaimed the divinity of Ali, the Prophet Muhammad's cousin and son-in-law, whom other Shi'ites revere but do not worship. Like many Shi'ites influenced by ancient Gnostic teachings that pre-date Islam, they believe that the way to salvation and knowledge lies through a succession of divine emanations. Acknowledging a line of prophets or avatars beginning with Adam and culminating in Christ and Muhammad, they include several figures from classical antiquity in their list, such as Socrates, Plato, Galen and some of the pre-Islamic Persian masters.

Nusayrism could be described as a folk religion that absorbed many of the spiritual and intellectual currents of late antiquity and early Islam, packaged into a body of teachings that placed its followers beyond the boundaries of orthodoxy. Mainstream Muslims, both Sunni and Shi'a, regarded them as ghulta, 'exaggerators'. Like other sectarian groups, they protected their tradition by a strategy known as taqiyya – the right to hide one's true beliefs from outsiders in order to avoid persecution. Taqiyya makes a perfect qualification for membership in the mukhabarat – the ubiquitous intelligence/security apparatus that has dominated Syria's government for more than four decades.

Secrecy was also observed by means of a complex system of initiation, in which insiders recognised each other by using special phrases or passwords, and neophytes underwent a form of spiritual marriage with the naqibs, or spiritual guides. At this ceremony, three superior dignitaries represent a kind of holy trinity of the figures who feature in other Nusayri rituals – namely Ali, Muhammad and Salman al-Farisi (the Persian companion of Muhammad who in several Islamic traditions forms a link between the Arabs and the wisdom of ancient Persia). Nusayri rituals, performed in private homes or out-of-the-way places, include a ceremony known as Qurban – almost identical to the Mass – where wine is consecrated and imbibed in the Christian manner. As Matti Moosa, a leading scholar of the Nusayris, states in his seminal study *Extremist Shiites: The Ghulat Sects* (1988):

> The Christian elements in the Nusayri religion are unmistakable. They include the concept of trinity; the celebration of Christmas, the consecration of the Qurban, that is, the sacrament of the flesh and blood which Christ offered to His disciples, and, most important, the celebration of the Quddas [a lengthy prayer proclaiming the divine attributes of Ali and the personification of all the biblical patriarchs from Adam to Simon Peter, founder of the Church, who is seen, paradoxically, as the embodiment of true Islam].

Moosa suggests that, like other schismatic groups residing in Syria, such as the Druzes and Ismailis, the Nusayris do not take their beliefs literally, but understand them as allegorical ways of reaching out to the Divine. While this may be true of the educated naqibs, or spiritual elders, such belief systems may have different ramifications for semi-literate peasants, reinforcing a contempt or disdain for outsiders who do not share these beliefs. Like the Druzes and some Ismailis, Nusayris believe in metempsychosis or transmigration. The souls of the wicked pass into unclean animals such as dogs and pigs, while the souls of the righteous enter human bodies more perfect than their present ones. The howls of jackals that can be heard at night are the souls of Sunni Muslims calling their misguided co-religionists to prayer.

It does not take much imagination to see how such beliefs, programmed into the community's values for more than a millennium, and reinforced by customs such as endogamous marriage – according to which the children of unions between Nusayris and non-Nusayris cannot be initiated into the sect – create very strong notions of apartness and disdain for the 'Other'.

The great Arab philosopher of history, Ibn Khaldun, who died in 1406, elaborated the concept of 'asabiyya – variously translated as clannism or group solidarity – that provides a more adequate explanation of the political systems operating in many Arab countries than notions based on imported ideologies such as communism, nationalism and socialism. Ibn Khaldun's analysis was based on his native North Africa, but it can be adapted to the conditions of the Mashreq, or Levant, where similar historical conditions prevailed. As Albert Hourani explained in his magisterial *History of the Arab Peoples* (1991), 'asabiyya is a force that informs the patriarchal family order that still underpins the structure of power in many Arab societies.

In the past, as Hourani pointed out, a ruler with 'asabiyya was well placed to found a dynasty, since the merchant classes of the cities, untrained in the military arts and without powerful corporate structures, tended to lack this quality. Moreover, when dynastic rule achieved in this way was stable and prosperous, city life flourished. But in Ibn Khaldun's time, every dynasty carried within itself the seeds of decline, as rulers degenerated into tyrants or became corrupted by luxurious living. In due course, power would pass to a new group of hardy rulers from the margins after a period of turbulence often described as fitna, or disorder (a term with overtones of sexual disharmony because, in the family context, fitna is seen as the outcome of sexual misconduct).

The rise and possible fall of the Assad dynasty would provide a perfect illustration of the Khaldunian paradigm under recent post-colonial conditions. Under Ottoman rule the Nusayris were impoverished outsiders struggling on the social margins. In addition to feuding among themselves, they were fierce rivals of the Ismailis, whom they expelled from their highland refuges and castles, forcing them to settle in the more arid lands east of Homs. The Ottoman governors regarded them as non-believers and tools of the Shi'ite Persians: they were not even accorded the dignity of a millet, or recognised religious community.

When the French took over Greater Syria after the First World War (including modern Lebanon and parts of modern Turkey), they flirted briefly with the idea of creating a highland Alawi state of 300,000 people separate from the cities of the plains – Homs, Hama, Damascus and Aleppo – with their dominant Sunni majorities. The French rightly believed that the Sunni majority would be the most resistant to their rule. Like other minorities, the Alawis, as they preferred to be called, saw the French as protectors. In 1936, six Alawi notables sent a memorandum to Leon Blum, head of France's Popular Front government, expressing their loyalty to France and their concern at negotiations leading to independence in a parliamentary system dominated by the Sunni majority. The memorandum includes the following points:

- *The Alawi people, who have preserved their independence year after year with great zeal and sacrifices, are different from the Sunni Muslims. They were never subject to the authority of the cities of the interior.*
- *The Alawis refuse to be annexed to Muslim Syria, because in Syria the official religion of the state is Islam, and according to Islam the Alawis are considered infidels.*
- *The granting of independence to Syria ... constitutes a good example of the socialist principles in Syria ... [But] as to the presence of a parliament and a constitutional government, that does not represent individual freedom. This parliamentary rule is no more than false appearances without any value. In truth, it covers up a regime dominated by religious fanaticism against the minorities. Do French leaders want the Muslims to have control over the Alawi people in order to throw them into misery?*
- *We can sense today how the Muslim citizens of Damascus force the Jews who live among them to sign a document pledging that they will not send provisions to their ill-fated brethren in Palestine. The condition of the Jews in Palestine is the strongest and most explicit evidence of the militancy of the Islamic issue vis-à-vis those who do not belong to Islam. These good Jews contributed to the Arabs with civilisation and peace, scattered gold, and established prosperity in Palestine without harming anyone or taking anything by force, yet the Muslims declare holy war against them and never hesitated in slaughtering their women and children, despite the presence of England in Palestine and France in Syria. Therefore, a dark fate awaits the Jews and other minorities in case the Mandate is abolished and Muslim Syria is united with Muslim Palestine ... the ultimate goal of the Muslim Arabs.*

One of the signatories to this document was Sulayman al-Assad, a minor chief of the Kalbiya clan and father of Hafez al-Assad.

The 'asabiyya of the Alawis was carefully exploited by the French, who polished the Khaldunian model by giving them military training as members of the Troupes Spéciales du Levant. In the turbulent years that followed full independence in 1946, their military know-how proved valuable. Bright members of the sect, such as Hafez al-Assad, whose families could not afford to send them to university, joined the armed forces and were drawn to secular parties, such as the Baath (renaissance) party jointly founded by two intellectuals, Michel Aflaq and Salah al-Din Bitar, with an agenda aimed explicitly at overcoming sectarian divisions.

It would be wrong to suppose that the Alawis deliberately sought to subvert or take over the Baath or the armed forces. Their primary impulse was their own security. After independence, the Syrian parliament abolished the separate representation for minorities instituted by the French, along with certain judicial rights. Nusayri sheikhs and notables encouraged young men to join the Baath because they believed its secular outlook would protect them from Sunni hegemony and persecution. Other minorities, including Christians, Druzes and Ismailis, tended to join the Baath (or in some cases the Communist Party and Syrian Socialist National Party) for similar reasons. The eventual dominance achieved by the Alawis may be attributed to their highland military background and the default logic by which 'asabiyya tends to assert itself in the absence of other, more durable structures.

The first three military coups that followed Syrian independence were engineered by Sunni officers. This was followed by the disastrous union with Nasser's Egypt in 1958, when Baath party leaders, following their pan-Arabist nationalist logic, merged their country's identity into that of their more powerful Sunni neighbour. After Syria united formally with Egypt, Nusayri officers who had joined the Baath party became increasingly alarmed that Arab nationalism, for all its secular rhetoric, was really a veil concealing Arab Sunni supremacy. They formed a clandestine military committee led by Salah Jadid, an Alawi, which took power in a military coup in 1963. Hafez al-Assad, trained as a fighter pilot, became the commander of the air force. Some 700 officers were purged, and most of their positions filled by Nusayris. A further coup against the Baathist old guard brought Assad into the cabinet as defence minister in 1966, a position he cleverly exploited after Syria's defeat by Israel in the Six-Day War of 1967, after which it was alleged that the regime had had secret dealings with the Jewish state. A 'palace coup' inside the leadership brought Assad to power as president in 1970.

Thereafter, the power of the state was concentrated firmly in Alawi hands. Of the officers commanding the 47th Syrian Tank Brigade, which was responsible for suppressing the Muslim Brotherhood's rebellion in the city of Hama in 1982 at a cost of some 20,000 lives, 70 per cent are reported to have been Alawis. When Hafez al-Assad died in June 2000, the constitutional niceties were rapidly dispensed with to ensure the succession of his son Bashar, who had studied ophthalmology in England. Fearful that

Hafez's exiled younger brother Rifaat al-Assad, who had commanded the Hama operation, would try to take over, a hastily convened session of the People's Assembly voted to lower the minimum age for a president from 40 to 34, the exact age of Bashar al-Assad.

In the welter of violence now accompanying the regime's determined efforts to suppress the demonstrations, its achievements should not be forgotten or ignored. While its massacre in Hama was horrific, and it has an abysmal record on human rights, engaging in torture and severe political repression, it had a good, even excellent one when it came to protecting the pluralism of the religious culture that is one of Syria's most enduring and attractive qualities. Some of these virtues are captured in Brooke Allen's engaging account of her travels in Syria, *The Other Side of the Mirror*, where she meets ordinary people from different backgrounds and rejoices in the natural friendliness of Syria's people and the extraordinary richness of its past. Instead of the Soviet-style greyness she expected to find from reading accounts in the US media, she discovered a sophisticated cosmopolitan society where life is being lived in many different styles and varieties, '*totally unselfconsciously*, just as it has been for thousands of years'.

In Aleppo, a jewel among cities, with its commanding citadel and labyrinthine, covered souk, she sees fully veiled ladies, exotic Bedouin women displaying bright splashes of colour, and wealthy Gulf Arabs wearing white robes, rubbing shoulders with men riding donkeys and mixing with 'trophy girlfriends' in miniskirts teetering perilously on the ultra-high-heeled shoes that Aleppans evidently consider to be the epitome of fashion.

Having been in Aleppo recently, I can vouch for the accuracy of her descriptions. Visiting several mosques, churches and shrines, she provides an impressive testimony to the country's religious diversity and the regime's commitment to religious freedom. It would be tragic if the pursuit of democracy led to the shredding of this bright human canopy, where religious and cultural differences seem to have flourished under the iron grip of a minority sectarian regime.

Published in *The New York Review of Books*, 9 June 2011.

The book reviewed was:

Brooke Allen (2011) *The Other Side of the Mirror: An American Travels Through Syria*. Philadelphia, PA: Paul Dry Books.

15
The Family

To date, the history of Saudi Arabia has largely been the story of its ruling family. No other modern state calls itself by its rulers' surname and labels its citizens with it. Though there is now a governmental system of growing complexity, and inefficiency, with ministries, departments of state, royal commissions and so on, power is still wielded in an arbitrary and personal manner. Every leading prince has his majlis, where ordinary citizens can meet him, take coffee and discuss their problems. But there are no corporate institutions or centres of power independent of the royal family. Even the formal *Majlis al-Shura* (consultative council), promised after the disturbances in Mecca and Qatif in 1979, has yet to come into being. Without us, the Al (family of) Saud seem to be telling the world, the state would not exist. Like it or not, they are probably right.

In theory, the Saudi state is an absolute monarchy. Under a royal decree of 1958, a council of ministers is responsible for the budget and internal affairs, but only the king can legislate, publish laws, treaties and concessions. A decree of 1961 forbids the formation of political parties, and prohibits the profession of any ideology other than 'Islam'. Anyone engaging in 'violent action against the state or the royal family' is liable to execution. In practice, the kingdom is governed by a consensus of 31 senior princes, all of them (including the present king) sons of the late Abdul Aziz ibn Abdul Rahman al Saud (c. 1880–1953), the Bedouin warrior who created the modern Saudi state.

None of this would seem extraordinary without the oil and the enormous weight of Saudi investment in the Western economic system. Saudi Arabia is the last great Muslim state to have been created in the classic manner, from an alliance between Bedouin warriors and the men of religion. The first Saudi state enjoyed a comparatively brief existence in the eighteenth century, when the religious reformer, Muhammad ibn Abdul Wahhab, made a pact with Muhammad ibn Saud, sheikh of Diriya, in central Nejd. Together, they pledged to restore the 'purity' of Islam as practised in the time of the Prophet, by purging it of all innovations and superstitious accretions, by executing adulterers, and so on. Their fanatical iconoclasm brought them into conflict with the Ottoman and Persian empires, and within a few decades the Saudi–Wahhabi state had collapsed, a victim of internal family quarrels and foreign intervention.

The modern revival of Saudi fortunes is largely a result of the genius of Abdul Aziz (also known as 'Ibn Saud' – a title comparable to 'The O'Neill' or 'The MacTavish'). Starting out from Kuwait in 1902 with a band of about 40 followers, he regained the stronghold of Riyadh from his family's Turkish-backed rivals, the Rashids, and proceeded, through war and diplomacy, to recover all the former Saudi dominions and much else besides. By 1913, he controlled the Gulf coast from Kuwait to Qatar, having eliminated the Turks from El Hasa – now the Eastern Province, where, in the 1930s, the world's largest oil deposits were discovered. In 1924, his most able son, Feisal, added Asir, on the Yemeni border, to the Saudi dominions. By 1926, he had realised his final ambition – the conquest of the Hejaz, Islam's holy land. The way had unwittingly been smoothed for him by the British, who had helped the local ruler, Sharif Hussein, to remove the Turks. The sharif was a vain and foolish old man with ambitions far beyond his ability. After some hesitation, the Saudi conquest of the Hejaz was greeted with general relief.

As always, the alliance between religion and politics was unstable. The storm-troopers on whom Abdul Aziz relied for his victories, known as the Ikhwan ('Brothers'), were Bedouin from the Mutair, Utaiba and other tribes who were settled in cantonments modelled on the Prophet's original military–religious Islamic state. Literalistic and imitative in their religious behaviour, the Ikhwan disposed of some 55,000 armed men in more than 100 settlements dotted around central Arabia. As an Arab wrote who saw them in action:

> I have seen them hurl themselves on their enemies, utterly fearless of death, not caring how many fall, advancing rank upon rank with only one desire – the defeat and annihilation of the enemy. They normally give no quarter, sparing neither boys nor old men, veritable messengers of death from whose grasp no one escapes.

Though acknowledging Abdul Aziz as their leader, the Ikhwan refused to recognise any territorial limits to their power. The Saudi leader's northern and eastern frontiers were controlled by the British, whose officials were invariably impressed by his charm and courtesy. Eventually his international undertakings (as well as his personal inclination) obliged him to deal with his over-zealous supporters – not least because, after conquering the Hejaz, he was anxious to reassure a nervous Muslim world that the holy cities and their pilgrims would be properly cared for. The Ikhwan were beaten back by the British in Iraq and Transjordan; and after a revolt by two of their leaders, Abdul Aziz finished them off himself. Their armed units were disbanded and absorbed mainly into what became the Saudi National Guard. By 1932, the genie was back in the bottle, religion rele-gated to its proper place: a prop to the social order, not a force to threaten it. Abdul Aziz, who was already describing himself as King of Nejd and its Dependencies and King of the Hejaz, gave himself a new title – King of Saudi Arabia. In the eyes of the religiously militant it was a classic instance of an ideological sell-out: instead of re-creating the Islamic state of their dreams, the Ikhwan (like so many of their predecessors, from the time of the early caliphs) had been used to further the ambitions of a dynast.

Religion, of course, is still employed to legitimise Saudi rule. As guard-ians of Islam's holy places and major financial contributors to Islamic institutions all over the world, Al Saud now enjoy a quasi-caliphal role, regarding themselves as non-titular heads of an increasingly politically conscious, pan-Islamic community. This gives them a moral influence within the most important bloc of Third World states, which complements their economic weight in the West. But it also makes them especially vulnerable to attacks from religious quarters, as was shown in the armed occupation of Mecca's Grand Mosque in 1979 by an eclectic group of extremists led by Juhaiman al-Utaibi. A child of the Ikhwan who grew up in the shadow of its defeat, Juhaiman and his 200 followers (who included Yemenis, Sudanese, Kuwaitis, Iraqis and Egyptians as well as Saudis) consciously imitated the style and behaviour of the Ikhwan, and called themselves by the same name. In a pamphlet published in Kuwait which circulated in Saudi Arabia before the attack on the Grand Mosque, Juhaiman denounced the corruption of the royal family ('They worship money and spend it on palaces, not mosques. If you accept what they say they will make you rich; otherwise they will persecute and even torture you') and pointed out that the people are not obliged to obey impious rulers, even if they rule in the name of Islam. During the occupation he broadcast his attacks over the mosque's loudspeakers, which enabled his voice to be heard all over central Mecca. He denounced the scandalous personal habits of the Saudi princes (drinking, gaming and visiting the fleshpots of Europe), mentioning by name the Governor of Mecca, Prince Fawwaz ibn Abdul Aziz.

After two weeks of hard fighting, the Saudi forces finally gained control of the mosque, and most of the surviving rebels were executed, with the full approval of the rest of the Muslim world. The faithful were generally agreed that, by bringing in arms, the rebels had gone much too far in violating the sanctuary. Nevertheless, religious attacks on the

Saudi establishment continue. In Iran, the Shi'ite mullahs (who have never forgiven the Wahhabis for destroying the shrine of Karbala in 1802) condemn the princes for their pro-Western policies and luxurious lifestyle. Within the country, the regime's critics are unlikely to have been impressed by the measures so far adopted publicly in the wake of the Mecca episode: further restrictions on the behaviour of foreigners, removal of the bibulous governor of Mecca, and more restrictions on Saudis travelling abroad. As the behaviour of the Saudi princes departs further from Wahhabi norms, the government finds it expedient to penalise ordinary citizens, or even more vulnerable creatures such as women and foreigners. The patriarch, Abdul Aziz, who epitomised both personal piety and desert hospitality, used to provide whisky and cigars for his European guests (as well as slave-girls for those, such as St John Philby, sensible enough to embrace Islam). He only banned alcohol for foreigners in 1952, after a British consul had been murdered by an inebriated Saudi prince. Nowadays the fleshpots of Europe provide a safety valve for those rich enough to afford them. If they were obliged to stay at home, social mores would probably have to be liberalised.

The story of modern Saudi Arabia, an impoverished state created by the political and military skills of a single desert chieftain, would have been epic stuff even without the oil. Given that the price of oil has risen 1,600 per cent since 2001, that the Saudis control Mecca, not just for the annual 2 million Muslim pilgrims, but for almost the same number of foreign businessmen, technicians and workers desperate to grab some of the material benefits on offer, you have the contemporary saga to beat them all: Dallas and the Klondyke, Moses and the Godfather merged into a single script. Not surprisingly, two highly successful journalists, David Holden and Robert Lacey, decided to turn their talents to an exposition of this fascinating modern legend.

Unfortunately, Holden, a distinguished reporter with many years' experience of the Middle East labyrinth, never lived to complete his book. He had written the first ten chapters (about 75,000 words) covering the career of Abdul Aziz, when, in December 1977, he was shot dead in Cairo while on a routine assignment for his paper, *The Sunday Times*. The cause, and exact circumstances, of his murder have never been established, despite extensive investigations by the staff of *The Sunday Times*. Richard Johns, Middle East editor of the *Financial Times*, who wrote most of the rest of the book, says in his introduction that he believes Holden 'aroused, unjustifiably, the suspicion of some persons in the paranoid world of intelligence and subterfuge of which, I trust and hope, he was no part'. Trust and hope are not quite the same as certainty.

Robert Lacey, also late of *The Sunday Times*, is widely known as the author of *Majesty*, a biography of Queen Elizabeth II written to coincide with her Jubilee year. His sympathetic treatment of Al Windsor evidently recommended him to Al Saud, judging from the interviewees listed in his voluminous bibliography, who include King Khalid, Interior Minister Prince Naif, Prince Salman (Governor of Riyadh) and Prince Abdullah, Commander of the National Guard, all of them sons of Abdul Aziz. Others whom he interviewed, or with whom he corresponded, include Henry Kissinger, Richard Nixon, Sheikh Yamani, the oil minister, and Adnan Khashoggi, the arms dealer now thought to be one of the wealthiest individuals in the world. Despite this co-operation, Lacey's book will not be allowed, officially, to enter the kingdom. Having sent a draft to the Ministry of Information, Lacey felt unable to make some 80 changes to the text requested by them. Most of these seem to have been concerned with family quarrels during the notorious reign of King Saud (1953–64). Al Saud are extremely suspicious about public discussion of 'family matters', and Lacey must have been very naïve to have thought that they would find an even remotely accurate account of these years acceptable. The late King Saud ibn Abdul Aziz is almost as much of a 'non-person' in official Saudi historiography as Trotsky is in the Soviet Union.

Despite their inordinate lengths, neither of these books really does justice to its subject. Holden, who had considerable talents as a descriptive writer, promised a lively and readable narrative, spiced with telling vignettes based on his own observations. The text written by his successor, Richard Johns, though strong on economic and political detail, is a stodgy chronology drawn largely from Western published sources, occasionally interspersed with gossipy anecdotes of the kind exchanged by journalists in hotel bars. The tedium is relieved, to some extent, by a lively and well-informed account of the Mecca Siege written by James Buchan, of the *Financial Times*. Johns is an unabashed Western chauvinist: he seems to dislike Saudi Arabia, and has little sympathy for its people and their ways. He would like to see them behaving, as nearly as possible, like readers of the *Financial Times*. His text is least dull when describing the indignities suffered by Western businessmen, forced to sleep in hotel corridors or even in taxis at $50 per night, during the mad rush for contracts in the late 1970s. Of the inconveniences, and dislocations, suffered by ordinary Saudis, not to mention thousands of foreign workers, we hear little.

Lacey's book would have been very much better had he not felt constrained to be over-polite about his influential Saudi hosts. He must have hoped that his book would be ordered in large quantities by the Ministry of Information, and handed out to worthy visitors. Thus the continuing discords and scandals that have upset family relationships since the death of Abdul Aziz are minimised. Political and industrial troubles, such as the strikes among oil-workers in El Hasa during the 1950s and 1960s (in which a number of workers were beaten to death), rate scarcely a mention. At times, the tone is sycophantic: the adjective 'royal', hardly suitable to the traditions of Arabian society unless Saudi pretensions are taken at face value, is sprinkled around the text like caster sugar. Even the title, *The Kingdom*, is misleading in this respect: *The Family*, with its over-tones of Chicago and New York, where kin-patronage politics also flourish in an urban milieu, would have been more appropriate.

Despite his self-censorship, however, Lacey does succeed in conveying more of Saudi Arabia's complex reality than does Richard Johns. He under-stands that, in a mainly oral culture, 'facts' are secondary to anecdotes. His text is skilfully interlarded with stories about the Family, as they might be told in the souks of Jeddah or the goat-hair tents of the Bedouin. Were he a more fastidious writer (or had he been served by a capable editor), his book would be a delight to read. As it is, it represents a partial attempt to see Saudi Arabia from the 'inside', in terms of its traditional attitudes and values. More's the pity, then, that so much of this effort was squandered in trying to appease the unappeasable.

Neither book reveals a really sound grasp of the country's social and political problems. Lacey, while capably summing up the reasons for the country's 'doveish' oil policies, appears to suppose that the present structure of princely hegemony can survive into the twenty-first century. Johns' prog-nosis is less sanguine: he reckons that 'within five years the Saudi sovereigns could have had their last page in history', but he fails to provide a cogent analysis of the forces most likely to undermine them.

On the face of it, given the state's monopoly of oil, and Al Saud's control over the state, the patronage at the disposal of the royal family is almost limitless. Unlike the Shah, they do not as a rule find it neces-sary to torture and murder their opponents: there are exceptions, of course, but their record in this respect is superior to that of most Middle Eastern states, including Israel. Most of the air force pilots who took part in an abortive coup in 1969 are, according to Lacey, living in freedom. Other former opponents of the regime, including the rebel Prince Talal ibn Abdul Aziz, who joined in Nasser's denunciations in the 1960s, are now living the lives of prosperous businessmen. Though there are pockets of social depri-vation among deracinated pastoralists who have drifted to the cities, and who now fall outside the tribal structure through which the government's subsidies are channelled, these are unlikely in themselves to constitute a political threat. Nor is the Shi'ite minority, which makes up about half of the Saudi Arabian Oil Company's (Aramco's) workforce of 20,000 in the Eastern Province, likely to pose a serious challenge. Despite the appeal of Khomeini's propaganda, they are too few, and can easily be bought off by improved wages and facilities. (The troubles in the early 1950s and 1960s, while they had political overtones, were really prompted by anger at the living conditions enjoyed by Aramco's American employees. Since Aramco was nationalised, with a growing proportion of its senior staff being Saudi-born, these differences have virtually disappeared.)

A much more serious problem is posed by the country's total dependence on foreigners in the construction and service industries. The official line is that these workers are necessary for the creation of the Saudi 'infrastructure', and that once this has been completed, they will all be sent home, to be replaced by a well-trained army of Saudis. To this end, prodigious sums are being spent on education, yet about 80 per cent of Saudis are still illiterate, and ill-equipped, according to Johns, to do anything other than to drive trucks and taxis, and to act as door-keepers and tea-makers to the country's princely and technocratic elite. Unofficially, the number of foreigners is estimated at 1.7 million out of a total population of only 4.3 million. (Saudis put the latter figure at over 6 million, but this has never been confirmed by a census regarded as accurate by outside observers.) Apart from a European and American elite and about 40,000 South Koreans, the vast majority of these workers are Muslims from Egypt, Sudan, Palestine, Libya, India, Pakistan and Malaysia. Many arrive there for the pilgrimage, and stay on illegally afterwards. It is difficult for the Saudis to justify their deportation from an Islamic point of view: traditionally, the Hejaz has been universally accessible to Muslims, and for centuries people from all parts of the world settled there.

It is not difficult to see how the Islamic ideology could be used by these foreign Muslims, allied to the small, but increasingly confident, Saudi merchant class, to de-legitimise the Saudi hegemony. The behaviour of the Saudi princes, both at home and abroad, is in continuous and flagrant violation of the puritanical and egalitarian norms of Islam, especially of the Wahhabi and Hanbali forms as practised in Saudi Arabia. In Islam generally, dynastic rule is only justifiable in defence of the faith. Rulers who are seen to violate its tenets are not merely worthy of condemnation: it becomes the positive duty of the faithful to overthrow them. For the present, the conservative *ulama* (religious scholars) are content to uphold the regime's legitimacy in return for social and economic privileges. Many, particularly the descendants of Muhammad ibn Abdul Wahhab, are personally related to the royal family and hold senior positions in the government. However, as the late President Sadat discovered, co-opting the religious leadership is no guarantee against attacks from religious quarters: like Protestantism, Sunni Islam confers no religious or sacerdotal authority on its clerics. By advancing the most ignorant and obscurantist religious leaders, such as Sheikh Abdul Aziz ibn Baz, a blind scholar who believes in a geocentric universe, to positions of authority, Al Saud are providing their government with the weakest available ideological defence.

There is a widely-held belief, both inside and outside Saudi Arabia, that Juhaiman al-Utaibi erred mainly by choosing the wrong target: if he had attacked one of the royal palaces (so King Khalid himself is quoted as saying), things might well have worked out differently. The coming decade will almost certainly witness more Islamic attacks on the government, despite cosmetic measures aimed at appeasing the most reactionary elements in the religious leadership. The size of princely commissions alone is a continuing subject of scandal: Richard Johns mentions the case of Prince Muhammad, the 25-year-old son of Crown Prince Fahd, who apparently stood to gain an astonishing $1.3 billion from a series of exclusive telecommunications deals with the Dutch-owned Philips company. After protests from rival US competitors (represented by Prince Muhammad ibn Abdul Aziz, eldest surviving son of the founder, and grandfather of the executed Princess Mishaal), the contract was modified, and the younger Prince Muhammad was obliged to settle for a mere $500 million. Characteristically, Robert Lacey puts a different gloss on this story, presenting it as a piece of intelligent enterprise on the part of the go-ahead young prince.

According to the traditional mercantile values of Saudi society, there is nothing wrong in taking commissions on deals: everyone down the line, so the argument goes, gets his rake-off – and what Westerners like to call 'corruption' is really an effective form of wealth distribution. While such arguments were no doubt relevant in the past, they scarcely hold water when the sums involved are such as to concentrate a country's economic and social power almost exclusively in the hands of a single ruling family consisting of some 4,000 members.

This is not to say that 'corruption' will bring down the House of Saud dramatically, in the Pahlavi manner. The merchant classes are still politically weak and numerically unimportant. There is no equivalent to the 'mosque bazaar' axis that helped to bring down the Shah's regime. Following the staggering increase in real-estate values after the 1974 oil hike (at one time, property prices in Riyadh were doubling *weekly*), many middle-class families have acquired a vested interest in the status quo. Its most able members, including Sheikh Ahmed Zaki Yamani, have been co-opted into serving the government. Nor, at the moment, would the elite units of the armed forces, a traditional source of danger for Arab governments, seem to pose a serious danger. There are princes (no one knows how many, but probably running into hundreds) holding commands in all branches of the security services. All the ministerial posts affecting national security are held by sons of Abdul Aziz.

The greatest source of danger to Al Saud hegemony must come from tensions within the family, in which personal rivalries are compounded by the religious and social conflicts in the country at large. After the disastrous reign of King Saud, his pious, cautious and conservative brother, Feisal, restored the family's credibility – and its finances – by instituting the minimal reforms necessary to counter the appeal of Nasser's Arab socialism. For the most part, the brothers trained or promoted by him (Khalid, the present king and titular prime minister; Fahd, Crown Prince and effective head of the government; Sultan, minister of defence; Naif, interior minister; Abdullah, commander of the national guard; and Feisal's son Saud, the foreign minister) are still the ruling group within the royal family. However, the fissures in this coalition are becoming increasingly apparent. The affair of the Philips contract revealed the limitless ambition of Fahd's own family group (which, in addition to his son, includes his full brothers Sultan, Naif and Salman, governor of Riyadh, all of them members of an inner caucus of princes sometimes known as the 'Sudairi Seven' after their mother Hassa bint Ahmed al Sudairi). A natural source of opposition to 'Al Fahd', whose politics and pleasures are generally 'pro-Western', could come from the capable and pious sons of the late King Feisal with the support of the more progressive Islamic elements. For the present, however, they are counterbalanced mainly by Prince Abdullah, commander of the national guard and a son of Abdul Aziz by a woman of the Rashid clan.

Political and tribal conflicts are therefore likely to be exacerbated by commercial rivalries. All of them threaten to undermine the cohesion of the Saudi 'fratrocracy'. According to Robert Lacey, King Abdul Aziz always forbade members of his family from participating in business activity: 'There are two things which do not mix,' he used to say, 'running a government and making money.' If the kingdom inherited by his sons does fall apart, it will be largely because of their failure to heed the patriarch's warning.

Published in *London Review of Books*, 17 December 1981.

The books reviewed were:

David Holden and Richard Johns (1981) *The House of Saud*. London: Sidgwick & Jackson.
Robert Lacey (1981) *The Kingdom*. London: Hutchinson.

Part **Four**

Iran in Focus

The 1979 Iranian Revolution came as a shock, not only to political strategists who had looked on the Shah's regime as Western bulwark against the Soviet Union, but to social scientists who had trouble coming to terms with what appeared to be a 'religious' revolution. Classic secularization theory, echoing the great sociologist Max Weber's idea that the 'disenchantment of the world' was integral to the processes of modernisation, was obviously in trouble. Stories appeared in the newspapers recounting that office windows in late-night Washington were ablaze with light as bureaucrats were 'speed-reading the Qur'an' to catch up with developments. The first article in this section, 'Fall of the Shah', looks at 'what went wrong' for Western policy through the brilliantly eclectic writing of Ryszard Kapuściński – a worthy compatriot of Joseph Conrad – as well as through the lenses of leading diplomats, including Britain's man in Tehran, Sir Anthony Parsons (an engaging personality and familiar presence on radio and television during the 1980s). The centrepiece of this part of the book, 'Was Weber Wrong?', addresses the intellectual crisis engendered by the Iranian Revolution through the work of two outstanding scholars, Gilles Kepel and Martin Riesebrodt. I was fortunate to meet both of them at a gathering of the Fundamentalist Project, hosted by the distinguished theologian, Professor Martin Marty, under the auspices of the American Academy of Sciences. The proceedings of this and subsequent conferences eventually produced several thousand pages, in five thick volumes, published by the University of Chicago Press. My own efforts in this area have been much more modest and succinct: Fundamentalism: A Very Short Introduction (around 70 pages), published by Oxford University Press.

The remaining essays in this section encapsulate – I hope – some of the best recent writing on Iran and its wayward, disorganised, confused and confusing revolution. In his Rose Garden of the Martyrs, Christopher de Bellaigue, to my knowledge the most talented journalist (apart from Kapuściński) to have covered Iran, brings the grim realities to life by engaging directly with individuals and

their experiences. Janet Afary, an American-Iranian and expert on the work of
Michel Foucault, explores some of the mysteries behind the ubiquitous chador,
and exposes the homosexual culture that served to preserve segregation – and
feminine 'honour' – in pre-modern times; while Ray Takeyh, a former US State
Department official, in contrast to the hysterical outpourings of the pro-Israeli
press, addresses Iran's nuclear aspirations in the light of cold, rational, strategic
common sense. The final essay celebrates Hamid Dabashi's brilliant, if flawed,
account of Shi'ism not just as a religion of protest, but as a psychic phenomenon
demonstrated in striking examples of cultural expression through the works of
Abbas Kiaorstrami and Shirin Neshat. I am particularly pleased to have had the
opportunity to struggle with this book (it is by no means an easy read) because it
made me aware of Dabashi's mentor, Philip Rieff, a great Freudian critic whose
work has been unjustly neglected.

16
The Fall of the Shah

The Iranian Revolution of 1978–9 is the most massive popular upheaval to have occurred in a developing country since the Second World War. Within a period of a few months the Middle East's most powerful military autocrat and the West's most trusted ally in the region had been overthrown by an unarmed but disciplined crowd of citizens acting under the instructions of their religious leaders. As with other major revolutions, including the French and Russian, to which this political earthquake can justly be compared, the new group that inherited power was virtually unknown outside the country. Who, before 1978, had heard of the Ayatollah Khomeini – or even knew what an ayatollah was? But more remarkable than the personalities of the leaders was the fact that this revolution – the first since the seventeenth century – was religious in inspiration and used the language of religion to articulate its aspirations. The goals of liberation and brotherhood, which are common to all revolutions, were subsumed under the rubric – strange and anachronistic to Western ears – of the Government of God.

How did this seeming reversal of history come about? As an Eastern European, a foreign correspondent attached to the official Polish news agency who has covered Third-World revolts in Bolivia, Mozambique, Sudan and Benin, and the employee of a state formally committed to the doctrine that revolutions are the inevitable concomitants of 'Progress', Ryszard Kapuściński is unusually qualified to provide us with an answer. He understands – as few Western writers can – how a regime can be based largely if not exclusively on terror; and that since the instruments of terror are primarily psychological, resistance begins when people cease to be afraid. As Kapuściński sees it, the government of the Shah was a despotism built on the twin pillars of terror and petroleum. His description of SAVAK, the Shah's security police, has a distinctly Eastern European colouring. As the eyes and ears of the regime, SAVAK is as ubiquitous as its communist counterparts, forcing ordinary citizens to restrict their vocabulary:

Experience had taught them to avoid uttering such terms as oppressiveness, darkness, burden, abyss, collapse, quagmire, putrefaction, cage, bars, chain, gag, truncheon, boot, claptrap, screw, pocket, paw, madness, *and expressions like* lie down, lie flat, spreadeagle, fall on your face, wither away, gotten flabby, go blind, go deaf, wallow in it, something's out of kilter, something's wrong, all screwed up, something's got to give — *because all of them, these nouns, verbs, adjectives and pronouns, could hide allusions to the Shah's regime, and thus formed a connotative minefield where you could get blown to bits with one slip of the tongue.*

If terror was the negative force sustaining the regime, oil and its by-products, bribery, corruption and extremes of wealth and poverty were its positive charge. Oil is 'a filthy, foul-smelling liquid that squirts obligingly up into the air and falls back to earth as a rustling shower of money', which the Shah's lackeys, starting with his own family, fell over each other to grab. Since the oil belonged to the state, and the Shah was the sole source of official preferment, most of this money ended up in his hands or those of his family, because anyone seeking a contract or wishing to start a business had to resort to bribery. The Shah's vast wealth enabled him to 'breathe life into a new class, previously unknown to historians and sociologists: the petro-bourgeoisie'. The lower members of this class think nothing of chartering a jet to take them to Munich for lunch; the upper echelons, who would find the journey tedious, hire an Air France jet to bring them lunch, complete with cooks and waiters from Maxim's. The petro-bourgeoisie builds itself lavish villas, costing a million pounds or more, in the suburbs. A few streets away, in the shanty towns, whole families of rural immigrants huddle in crowded hovels without water or electricity. This highly volatile mixture produced the explosion that destroys the petro-bourgeoisie, along with its creator and protector.

Why a religious revolution? Here the unstated parallel with Poland is clearly in the author's mind:

A nation trampled by despotism, degraded, forced into the role of an object, seeks shelter, seeks a place where it can dig itself in, wall itself off, be itself. This is indispensable if it is to preserve its individuality, its identity, even its ordinariness. But a whole nation cannot emigrate, so it undertakes a migration in time rather than in space. In the face of encircling afflictions and threats of reality, it goes back to a past that seems a lost paradise.

> *It regains its security in customs so old and therefore so sacred*
> *that authority fears to combat them … The old acquires a new*
> *sense, a new and provocative meaning.*

Shi'ism has been Iran's official religion since the early sixteenth century; and, as Kapuściński notes, its history of martyrdom and the sense of tragedy inflicted on the dispossessed imams of the Prophet's house and their followers provides it with an oppositional outlook that legitimises protest. Here, however, the parallel with Polish Catholicism ends, for a mosque is not, like a church, a 'closed space, a place of prayer, meditation and silence'. Its largest component is 'an open courtyard where people can pray, walk, discuss, even hold meetings'. The Shi'ite mosque is, for historical reasons, under relatively independent clerical control. Moreover, it lies at the centre of the 'colourful, crowded, noisy, mystical–commercial–gustatory nexus' known as the bazaar. It is here that the opposition that was to overwhelm and destroy the regime took root.

Was this destruction inevitable? Not according to this former employee of the Polish state media. Once the revolution got under way, the only aim uniting its various components was to remove the Shah. The monarch himself vacillated between repression and appeasement:

> *He tried shooting and he tried democratising, he locked people*
> *up and he released them, he fired some and promoted others, he*
> *threatened and then he commended. All in vain. People simply*
> *did not want a Shah any more; they did not want that kind of*
> *authority.*

Universal dislike, however, is not in itself enough to bring down an unpopular leader. The Shah's problem was that he took himself too seriously, too literally. Shocked by the sight of the people demonstrating against him, he felt he must react immediately: 'he lacked a certain dose of cynicism. He could have said: "They're demonstrating? So let them demonstrate. Half a year? A year? I can wait it out. In any case, I won't budge from the palace".' And the people, disenchanted and embittered, willy-nilly, would have gone home in the end because it's unreasonable to expect people to spend their whole lives marching in demonstrations. But the Shah didn't want to wait.

Shah of Shahs is politically more explicit than *The Emperor*, Kapuściński's justly-praised account of the last years of Haile Selassie's reign. There isn't, as there was in *The Emperor*, the feeling of being enclosed in a gothic nightmare, as a medieval edifice crumbled from within, but the book is every bit as impressive. Its sparkling images and sudden changes of focus give a cinematic immediacy to the events it recalls by the simple but effective device of a reporter, alone in his hotel room, trying to make sense of photographs and scraps of notes. The underlying suggestion of Eastern Europe is stronger than in *The Emperor* – not least, perhaps, because Iran is close to Russia, and the Shah's despotism had a strongly Russian flavour to it – but the writing has the same fable-like quality. Kapuściński's Iran, like his Ethiopia, is a region of the mind, as well as a real place where people suffer from the cruelties and follies of real men. And so it becomes part of our universe in a way that the accounts of scholars or journalists, secure in their Western liberties, usually fail to convey.

As Britain's ambassador to Iran from 1974 to 1979, Sir Anthony Parsons was a privileged witness to the momentous events surrounding the fall of the Shah. Like most other diplomats and a good many experts, Parsons was taken by surprise, and his book is in part an attempt to explain why. With unusual candour, he blames himself. Having previously served in Turkey and several Arab countries where the armed forces are the principal underpinning of government – a legacy of the Ottoman centuries – he underestimated the extent to which the Iranian monarchy depended on the support of other elements, including feudalistic barons and religious leaders. There had been abundant evidence, from previous occasions in Iranian history, the most notable being the Constitutional Revolution of 1906 which foreshadowed the fall of the Qajars, that the Shi'ite clergy were powerful enough to rock the government and that the armed forces, faced with such a challenge, would be liable to waver in their loyalty.

In the confrontation with the army, the religious dimension was decisive. As Dilip Hiro explains in his balanced and carefully-researched account of the revolution and its first five years, the first major problem that faced the disparate groups which made up the opposition – the industrial workers, the Bazaaris, the students, the clergy and the army of the mustazafin, the *misérables* of the shanty towns – was how to overcome a force of nearly half a million men which had hitherto been utterly loyal to the Shah. Khomeini's answer (delivered by cassette-tape, or word of mouth, from his place of exile near Paris) was simple and radical, inspired by Shi'ite traditions of martyrdom: 'Let the army kill as many as it wanted, until the soldiers were shaken to their hearts with the massacres they had committed, he said. Then the army would collapse, he predicted. And it did.'

More remarkable than the collapse of the Shah has been the survival of the clerical government presided over by the ageing, and increasingly frail, Khomeini. It has overcome secessionist threats from Arabs, Kurds and other minorities; a murderous onslaught by the leftist Mujahidin; and the massive external attack launched by Iraq in 1980. Though it has sacrificed tens of thousands of young men – many of them virtually children – in its attempts to avenge itself on Iraq by bringing about the overthrow of the Baathist regime, there are only a few signs that it is losing its popular base among the poor and socially deprived. The mixture of religious fervour and a nationalism bordering on xenophobia seems to have prevented things from falling apart; the continuing potency of this mixture is in no small part related to the Shah's own attitudes and policies. Parsons, in his elegant and very readable account of his ambassadorship, details a number of situations where the incumbent of the Peacock Throne seems to have gone out of his way to offend religious or national sensibilities. One of the fringe events at the Shiraz Festival of 1977 involved a rape scene performed on the pavement. When Parsons explained to the Shah that such a play would have caused outrage even in England, he merely 'laughed indulgently'. A more fundamental source of cultural alienation was the degree to which the Pahlavi regime relied, and was seen to rely, on the Americans. The Shah had been reinstated in the famous 'countercoup' organised by Kermit Roosevelt against the Mossadeq Government in 1953. As early as 1964 he incurred public odium by extending diplomatic immunity to US citizens engaged on military projects – a gesture reminiscent of the Capitulations granted to Europeans by his Qajar predecessors, and one that explains why the attack on the US Embassy and the holding of hostages after the revolution was generally popular.

In 1972, US President Nixon and Henry Kissinger, US National Security Adviser, under the Nixon doctrine of devolving strategic responsibility to America's 'trusted allies', presented the Shah with a virtual blank cheque for military development, thereby accepting the Shah's own inflated view of himself as the region's policeman, bulwark against Soviet expansionism and defender of enlightened Western values. One result of this was the dismantling of the USA's own intelligence operations in the country. Embassy officials were quietly discouraged from having contacts with the opposition. The British, who ought to have known better, slavishly followed the American lead. Parsons, who is disarmingly self-critical in his attempts to find out 'How we got it wrong', says he deliberately refrained from offering the Shah advice on internal affairs, in case it interfered with the lucrative business of obtaining contracts, especially in the military field: 'If we gave him advice to be more democratic, to ease up on the students, curb SAVAK etc., we would only receive a whole colony of fleas in our ear and reduce our access to and influence with him.' He is understandably reticent about the seamier side of this tacit connivance with despotism – the scandalous backhanders paid to members of the Shah's family and entourage in the hunt for contracts.

An unfortunate side-effect of Parsons' self-denying ordinance was that it left the Embassy almost as isolated as the Shah himself when it came to domestic intelligence. The Embassy went wrong, Parsons admits, in its assumption that the Shah

> must be better informed about the domestic situation in his own country than we were. We had experienced his shrewdness and mastery of foreign and strategic matters and not unnaturally concluded that, with all the information-gathering facilities at his disposal, he was also master of internal affairs ... It never occurred to me ... that he actually believed the unconvincing theories which he advanced to me, a conspicuous example being that the widespread student discontent was only a minority manifestation stimulated by a handful of foreign-inspired agitators.

This admission is remarkable for its disingenuousness. Most foreign observers knew what the Shah's 'information-gathering activities' involved: the systematic and wholesale torture of anyone suspected of opposition – in other words, government by terror. Such intimidation is customarily inflicted, as it has been in Northern Ireland, under the guise of intelligence-gathering, though those who have studied the matter usually conclude that torture is not a satisfactory way of obtaining information. Parsons was certainly not ignorant of SAVAK's methods, since he alludes to them on several occasions. He evidently assumes that the Shah 'went along', as a kind of *politesse*, with the conspiracy theories dished up by the SAVAK chiefs – to avoid alluding to something disagreeable. Nor was his over-sophisticated disbelief in the Shah's ignorance counterbalanced by reliable information reaching the Embassy from elsewhere. He admits he deliberately gave priority to the Embassy's commercial work – advising businessmen against making long-term investments, just in case things went wrong. This was a gamble which Parsons is probably right in claiming paid off well. As Hiro points out, by 1978, Iran had become Britain's second trading partner in the Middle East, with two-way trade running at $1.5 billion for the sake of a mere $170 million invested. In short, the Embassy did not bother to inquire too closely into the regime's stability, or its methods, because it was too busy helping British businessmen to make money.

Such a policy, of course, can be justified on narrow, chauvinist grounds – British jobs before Persian limbs, or even lives. It is the duty of diplomats to represent their countries' interests, not to try to administer the *Universal Declaration of Human Rights*. However, this is not quite the line that Parsons chooses to take. While admitting that his primary concern was to persuade

British businessmen to make as much money as they could for the least possible investment, he also defends his embassy's record in the matter of political intelligence-gathering:

> we did identify the principal elements of opposition to the Shah, namely the religious classes, the bazaar and the younger generation of the intelligentsia … Where we went wrong was that we did not anticipate that the various rivulets of opposition, each of which had a different reason for resenting the Shah's rule, would combine into a mighty stream of protest which would eventually sweep the Shah away.

The failure, according to Parsons, occurred in the analysis of the intelligence, and for this he blames himself 'unreservedly'. Even now, he seriously underestimates the ideological factors that contributed to the merging of opposition forces. The name of Ali Shariati, the Islamic intellectual who forged a bridge between secular and Islamic radical outlooks, does not appear in his book – an omission comparable to writing an account of the Russian Revolution without mentioning Karl Marx, or of the French Revolution without Rousseau. Shariati died in London in 1977 (reputedly at the hand of SAVAK agents, though the British coroner recorded a verdict of natural causes), but pamphlets and cassettes of his famous lectures delivered at the Husseiniya Ershad seminary in Tehran were circulating throughout the revolutionary period. It is astonishing that the embassy appears to have had no Farsi expert sufficiently aware of the intellectual currents to provide Parsons with accurate briefings.

William Sullivan, US Ambassador to Iran during the crucial two years of the revolution, seems to have been better-informed in this respect, even if his understanding was superficial. 'Shariati,' he says, 'attempted to reconcile socialism with Islam, and thereby introduced the basic tenets of Marxist thought into a vernacular that would be acceptable to the urban poor.' This is about as accurate as referring to George Orwell as a Marxist. It is true, however, that Shariati sought out the common ground between Marxist activism and Islamic radicalism, and this certainly helped to forge the links between leftists and Khomeinists, without which the revolution could not have succeeded. Sullivan, who had previously served as ambassador in Laos and the Philippines, resigned from the foreign service after a row with Zbigniew Brzezinski, President Carter's National Security Adviser, who wanted to launch a 1953-style counter-coup to save the Shah. Sullivan had urged the USA to make overtures to Khomeini at an earlier stage, having rightly decided that the Shah was unsavable. For a man who was closely involved in some of the United States' outstanding policy failures – in Southeast Asia, Iran and probably the Philippines – his tone is remarkably complacent: a mixture of bland self-righteousness and anecdotal bonhomie. Though he was right to resist Brzezinski's attempt to rescue the Shah, based as it was on a misreading of the dangers posed by the Soviet Union in the 'Arc of Crisis', the alternative he proposed, a moderate government supported by Khomeini that would still be friendly to the USA, never had a chance because of the extent to which the opposition to the Shah was united by anti-American feeling.

Has the 'loss' of Iran really proved to be such a setback for the USA? Though the Americans lost prestige and a good deal of sophisticated weaponry, as well as their listening-post on the Soviet border, there has been no Soviet thrust to the Gulf. The Iran–Iraq war has not led to the super-power confrontation that some predicted; and the West's 'jugular', the Strait of Hormuz, remains obstinately open. Though the war is taking its toll of Western shipping, there still seem to be plenty of tanker-owners and captains prepared to face the hazards of sailing in these waters. The Marxists in South Yemen have come to terms with Oman; and though the Russians remain in Afghanistan, their presence has been made more, not less, difficult by a regime in Iran that gives unconditional support to the Mujahidin. In general, the spectre of Soviet expansionism in the Middle East has been a fantasy encouraged by local regimes (including, at various times, Iran, Iraq, Israel, Jordan, Saudi Arabia, Egypt, Ethiopia, Turkey and Libya), which have solicited US military aid to consolidate their grip over their own territories or those of their neighbours.

Why do local powers find the USA such a soft touch? After a career spent largely in the cause of anti-communism, Sullivan almost gives the game away:

> From Truman through Nixon, our international actions were justified by statements that catered to the traditional jingoism of the American imperium. In order to command the support of Congress and the votes of the great American public Presidents had to stress American national security and American hegemony more than the facts would warrant. Even while their actions were deliberately reducing our international imperium, some leaders felt compelled, for reasons of domestic policy, to rationalise them in Cold War terms.

The trouble with using this Cold War rhetoric, as Sullivan found to his cost, is that it often places genuine 'cold warriors' and their advisers in the White House.

George McGhee, an Oxford-educated Texan oil man who became Dean Acheson's Assistant Secretary of State for Near-East, South-Asian and African Affairs, and later President Kennedy's Ambassador at Large, is almost as candid when he remarks that America's 'excessive preoccupation' with the communist threat in the early 1950s provided a useful way of 'enlisting American interest in Africa'. Yet, in summing up the thrust of US diplomacy in his region from 1945 to 1951, he makes the typically simplistic assumption that the neutralism to which most of the states emerging from colonial rule aspired would lead them to communism:

> *We wanted to convince the new states of the dangers of Soviet Communism and help them develop internal security forces adequate to protect themselves from Communist subversion. We tried to persuade them that neutralism would weaken their defences against Communism, and to encourage them to accept a generally pro-Western and democratic point of view.*

The internal security apparatuses, trained in 'interrogation' and counter-revolution, complemented the more conventional forces that the USA supplied to its anti-communist allies. As in Latin America, though perhaps to a lesser degree, 'counter-subversion' became the means by which undemocratic regimes maintained themselves in power. It was perhaps inevitable that, when one of these regimes was overtaken by nationalist revolution, the new elite would find in these same techniques convenient ways of suppressing dissent. But it cannot be entirely accidental that, of all the countries where McGhee tried to promote his anti-communist crusade, the one that most determinedly resisted American blandishments, and insisted on retaining a good relationship with the Soviet Union to protect its neutrality, was India – the only effectively functioning democracy in McGhee's 'Middle World'.

The Americans, of course, are not the first to have used the Russian bogey to obtain support for an imperialist foreign policy. In the nineteenth century, the Tsarist threat to India played a similar role, lending respectability to British ambitions in Persia. The Persians themselves had good reason to fear the Tsars, who had absorbed part of Azerbaijan and most of Caucasia by 1830, and by 1870 had swallowed up much of Turkistan. The Qajar shahs looked increasingly to the British to protect them.

A growing number of Persians – princes, students, diplomats, ministers and eventually two of the shahs themselves – made visits to Britain and wrote accounts of their journeys, some of which found English translators.

One of the first to make the journey was Mirza Abu Taleb, son of an Azerbaijani exile in India, who spent 30 months in England between 1800 and 1803. After a visit to the House of Commons, which reminded him of 'two flocks of Indian paroquets, sitting on opposite mango trees, scolding at each other', he returned convinced that 'many of the customs, inventions, sciences and ordinances of Europe, the good effects of which are apparent in these countries, might with great advantage be imitated by Mohammedans'. The Persian elite took this advice so much to heart that by the time of Reza Shah's coronation in 1926 a totally English performance was insisted on down to the last detail. Vita Sackville-West found that 'there was no point, however humble, on which [the Persians] would not consult their English friends' (Harold Nicolson was at that time Counsellor at the British Legation):

> *They would arrive with little patterns of brocade and velvet; they would ask us to come down and approve the colour of the Throne Room ... They must have red cloth for the palace servants like the red liveries worn by the servants of the English legation. They must have a copy of the proceedings at Westminster Abbey for the Coronation of His Majesty King George V; one of the Ministers who prided himself on his English came to ask me privately what a Rouge-dragon Poursuivant was, evidently under the impression it was some kind of animal.*

The somewhat one-sided love-affair between the Persian elite and the British is the main theme of Denis Wright's entertaining and informative book. The more sophisticated Persians, as so often happens, adopted the forms rather than the substance of their models, which usually meant that the ordinary people got the worst of both worlds. The first Pahlavi was a despot who ordered his subjects to wear Homburg hats and exhibit their wives, unveiled, in public. For all their apparent conservatism, the mullahs were much more discerning when, in 1906 and in 1977, they demanded Anglo-Saxon constitutions without the Anglo-Saxon monarchical trimmings.

Published in *London Review of Books*, 4 July 1985.

The books reviewed were:

Dilip Hiro (1985) *Iran under the Ayatollahs*. London: Routledge & Kegan Paul.

Ryszard Kapuściński (1985) *Shah of Shahs*, translated by William Brand. London: Quartet Books.

George McGhee (1983) *Envoy to the Middle World: Adventures in Diplomacy*. New York: Harper & Row.

Anthony Parsons (1984) *The Pride & the Fall: Iran 1974–1979*. London: Jonathan Cape.

William Sullivan (1984) *Obbligato: Notes on a Foreign Service Career*. New York: W. W. Norton.

Denis Wright (1985) *The Persians Amongst the English: Episodes in Anglo-Persian History*. London: I.B.Tauris.

17
Was Weber Wrong?

In the 1960s it was widely assumed that politics were becoming divided from religion and that, as societies became more industrialised, religious belief and practice would be restricted to private thoughts and actions. The processes of modern industrialism, which Max Weber had seen as being characterised by de-personalised relationships and increasing bureaucratisation, were leading, if not to the final 'death of God', at least to the 'disenchantment of the world'. The numinous forces that had underpinned the medieval cosmos would be psychologised, subjectivised and demythologised.

On the face of it, the 1979 revolution in Iran dented this conventional wisdom seriously. Here was a revolt deploying a repertoire of religious symbols that brought down a modernising government and placed political power in the hands of a religious establishment steeped in medieval theology and jurisprudence. Moreover, this was clearly an urban, not a rural, phenomenon – a response, perhaps, to 'over-rapid' or 'uneven' development, but not in any sense a peasant *jacquerie*. Some commentators (myself included) argued that the mix of politics and religion was peculiarly Islamic, or even uniquely Shi'ite. Unlike Christianity, Islam, it was said, had a built-in political agenda: the Prophet Muhammad had combined the role of state-builder with that of revelator, and all who sought to follow his path must sooner or later be drawn into the political game. Shi'ism was a variant on this theme: originally a protest movement against the usurping of Islam's righteous empire by the worldly Umayyads, it developed into a tradition of radical dissent, one that oscillated over the centuries between quietism and activism, withdrawal and revolt. The Khomeini Revolution – like the rise of the Hezbollah in Lebanon – represented the swing of the Shi'ite pendulum towards activism, after decades of sullen acquiescence under 'unrighteous government'.

By the early 1980s, it was becoming clear that religious activism was very far from being confined to the Islamic world, and that newly politicised movements were appearing in virtually every major religious tradition. In

America, the New Christian Right challenged and temporarily checked the steady secularisation of politics. Commenting on the growth of evangelical and fundamentalist churches, Peter Berger, doyen of Weberian theorists, was forced to admit that 'serious intellectual difficulties' had been created 'for those (like myself) who thought that modernisation and secularisation were inexorably linked phenomena'. Brushing aside the Muslim world, Berger offered a theory of American exceptionalism. Like India, the USA was in some way irredeemably religious. Secularism of the sanitised, Scandinavian type was confined to university campuses and other privileged cultural enclaves. When it came to religion, America was 'an India, with a little Sweden superimposed'.

A theory of modernisation that excludes America, India and the Muslim world from its purview faces some major problems. One need hardly add that the collapse of communism in Eastern Europe has brought about a marked resurgence in public religiosity, while Latin America and parts of Africa appear to be undergoing far-reaching religious transformations, with Pentecostalism poised to replace Catholicism as the dominant tradition. With Japan and South Korea ranking high in the list of countries nurturing new religious movements, only secular Western Europe and Australia – areas that Martin Marty, the American historian of religion, calls 'the spiritual ice-belt' – appear to be conforming to Weberian predictions. And even in Western Europe, as Gilles Kepel's study of neo-Catholic movements indicates, there are symptoms of a spiritual thaw.

Is the whole world undergoing a religious revival? Can such varied phenomena as the siege of the Branch Davidians in Texas and the Hindu attack on the mosque at Ayodhya, which brought Indian democracy to the brink of collapse, be subsumed under a common label of 'fundamentalism'? In his survey of revivalist currents in the Abrahamic tradition, Kepel, a political scientist, avoids the term, preferring the more cumbersome 'movements of re-Judaising', 're-Christianisation' and 're-Islamisation'. Coming as it does from the lexicon of modern American Protestantism, 'fundamentalism' fits uneasily into other traditions. It is widely applied by Western writers to Islamic movements, but there is no exact equivalent in the languages of Islam. Two widely-used Arabic terms, salafi and 'usuli (pertaining respectively to ancestors and roots) were adopted by previous reformers in the Sunni and Shi'a traditions and have lost their radical bite. A similar difficulty faces attempts to attach a common fundamentalist label to neo-orthodox and ultra-nationalist Jewish groups, including both the anti-Zionist Neturei Karta, who regard the State of Israel as a monstrous impiety and refuse to participate in elections, and the Gush Emunim, who believe Israel's right to the Occupied Territories to be divinely ordained.

Each can be described as 'fundamentalist' in its own, diametrically opposite, way. But can a single term that embraces such different positions be analytically useful?

Students of comparative fundamentalism, notably Martin Marty, who has just completed a five-year investigation of the phenomenon for the American Academy of Arts and Sciences, have tended to exclude Catholic movements of renewal from consideration, while including syncretic movements in Asia that combine elements of Buddhism, Taoism, Shintoism and Christianity. Yet, as Kepel's analysis reveals, the revolutionary Islam of Ayatollah Khomeini and Sayyid Qutb, lodestar of the Sunni militants, has more in common with the Catholic liberation theology of Gustavo Guiterrez than with the Protestant fundamentalism of, say, Pat Robertson or Jerry Falwell. Similarly, much common ground can be found between the pietistic Jamaat-i-Tablighi, one of Europe and South Asia's most rapidly growing Islamic movements, and Father Luigi Guissani's Communione e Liberazione, a Catholic movement dedicated to countering the allegedly secularising agenda flowing from Vatican II.

Kepel makes an important distinction between movements seeking to achieve power or impose their authority 'from above', and those whose primary concern is to create communities 'from below'. In the Abrahamic tradition, the seizure of power 'from above' is frequently linked to a messianic eschatology that postulates some form of divine intervention. Many of those who supported Khomeini's successful bid for power in February 1979 identified him with the Hidden Imam of the Shi'a, who is expected to return as Mahdi, or Messiah, at the end of time. The murderers of Anwar Sadat in 1981 adopted a less chiliastic language, but clearly believed that the death of 'Pharaoh' would lead, more or less miraculously, to an Islamic uprising in which the existing order would be overthrown. The conspirators in Jerusalem who planned to blow up the Dome of the Rock and the Al-Aqsa Mosque in order to rebuild the Temple were convinced that the nudge they would give to the divine eschatology would of itself be sufficient to effect a transformation, or re-Judaising, of Israeli society.

More effective, and more long-term, are those movements seeking to reconstruct the religious society 'from below', not least because they are proof against short-term political failure. Paradoxically, the messianic impulse frequently leads to impressive feats of construction: the failure of God to bring about the promised kingdom supernaturally inspires believers to create the Kingdom themselves. Under the late Rabbi Schneerson, whose followers believed him to be the promised Messiah, the Lubavitcher Hasidic order built an impressive international network of schools and social centres stretching from Brooklyn to Melbourne. If the experience of Seventh-day Adventism and other movements (including Christianity itself) built on the ruins of a Great Disappointment is anything to go by, the Rabbi's failure to become the Messiah need not jeopardise these achievements. A similar shift from messianic eschatology to church-building, in which divine intervention is deferred in favour of human action, occurs in virtually every American Protestant tradition, where the promise of Kingdom Come is covertly replaced by the more tangible, tax-deductible project of building the Kingdom Now. In the grand narrative of Islam, a comparable shift from pre-millennial pessimism to post-millennial optimism is marked by Muhammad's hijra, or migration, from Mecca to Medina: the recalcitrant Meccan polytheists were subdued, not by the supernaturally-administered punishments threatened in the Qur'an, but by the tribal empire built by the Prophet in Medina.

Shared religious impulses do not necessarily lead to the same conclusions. The prospects facing today's revivalists vary according to the very different political conditions in which they operate. In Europe, as Kepel explains, 'the re-Christianisation movements appeared in societies most of which had been living a deeply secularised existence for more than a century'. In France, the charismatic movement, which peaked in the late 1980s, never had more than 200,000 members. Even in Poland, where the Roman Catholic Church, as guardian of the national culture, was poised to replace communism as the prevailing ideological force, 'democratic aspirations proved stronger than the thirst for transcendence'. In America, uniquely, constitutional separation of church and state is guaranteed by the churches, which since the Revolution have come to recognise a common interest in denominational diversity.

In the Muslim world, what Kepel calls 'constraint by democracy' barely exists. Muslim societies have, with rare exceptions, found it difficult to maintain democratic institutions. The artificial barriers, rooted in Christian ecclesiastical history, that separated private and public realms, estates and classes, corporations and individuals, were generally absent from a religious culture that acknowledged no intercessionary authority between God and humankind. The uncompromising belief in a single transcendent deity erodes denominational boundaries; the anathematising of shirk, the sin of idolatry, militates against cultic diversity. Despite recent episodes of Hindu fanaticism, secular, pluralist India, rooted in polytheism, has held the line for democracy a lot more successfully than monotheistic Pakistan. As the Imam Ali Belhaj, a leading preacher with the Islamic Salvation Front in Algeria, never ceases to remind his congregations, there is no Qur'anic basis for the idea of demos, the people as sovereign. Sovereignty belongs to God alone, or to those proclaiming the guardianship of His government. A collapse into theocratic totalitarianism seems likely in Algeria and Egypt – if not 'from above', by a pro-Islamist coup d'état, as in Sudan, then through seepage 'from below', from what Kepel calls the 'network of mosques and pietist associations' whose tendrils have been 'spreading through civil society'.

Kepel's summary of the common features and differences underlying these movements is useful as far as it goes, but he has too little to say about the social forces involved. He notes that both American and Islamic militants are likely to be the children of urban migrants; in the Muslim world, their parents were fellahin driven by the collapse of the rural economy into the sprawling shanty towns surrounding major cities; in America, they come not from the small townships of the Deep South, as did many of their parents, but from the larger cities of the North and South (and, he might have added, the West, since Southern California, which gave birth to the original Fundamentalist movement, is still host to such key institutions as the Institute of Creation Research). Most American activists, unlike their parents, have had the benefit of a higher education, 'though not in the best universities'. A disproportionate number are qualified in the applied sciences, 'just like the Islamist militants'. Many of the followers of Rabbi Schneerson are computer programmers, or, like the Rabbi himself, electrical engineers. Few appear to have graduated in disciplines that explore ambiguities of meaning and symbolism, or analyse narratives in terms of myth. The applied, unlike the 'pure', scientist can use reason without having to adopt a posture of epistemological doubt.

An applied scientist who espouses fundamentalism therefore need experience no sense of contradiction: Herman Branover, a leading Soviet authority on magneto-hydrodynamics who became one of the Lubavitcher Rebbe's most prestigious converts, writes of the difference between 'science, which deals only with the interrelationships of phenomena, and religion, which reveals the essence and purpose of things'. Such a double perspective is easier for Jews and Muslims to sustain than for Christians, since for them behaviour, rather than belief, defines religious allegiance. Orthopraxy – in dress, food, ritual or family relationships – need not impinge on ideas about the ordering of the universe. The supernatural can be pushed aside without loss of faith or identity. Christians, stuck with a faith that demands acquiescence in a catalogue of physical impossibilities, are constrained to fight back against secularism by insisting on the historicity of events – such as the Virgin Birth, the Resurrection or the Creation in its biblical version – that run directly counter to scientific rationality.

Common to all the movements examined by Kepel is a mood of disenchantment with the Enlightenment and its failure to produce a better world. For the religious intellectuals who spearhead the 'Revenge of God', 'modernism produced by reason without God has not succeeded in creating values'. Thus Cardinal Lustiger, Archbishop of Paris, the son of a Polish Jewish convert to Christianity, describes himself as belonging to 'that generation which has plucked the fruits of Reason's pretensions to sovereignty'. The end products of what the Cardinal calls 'the arrogance of reason' were the gulags and the Holocaust: 'Reason idolises man; forgetfulness of God is the root of all social evil.' Similar sentiments reverberate through the literature of the Islamic opposition groups in Egypt and Algeria, anti-abortion activists in America and the Jewish groups who inhabit the self-imposed ghettos of Meir Shearim in Jerusalem or try to sabotage the Palestinian peace process. Kepel concludes that all such movements have arisen 'in a world that has lost the assurance born of scientific and technical progress since the Fifties. Just as the barriers of poverty, disease and in-human working conditions seemed to be coming down. Aids, pollution and the energy crisis burst upon the scene', all of them 'scourges' which 'lent themselves to presentation in apocalyptic terms'.

Disenchantment may be part of this story; but it does not provide a sociologically satisfying explanation. It places too much emphasis on the intellectual minority who articulate the new religiosity without explaining why they have become so influential. Martin Riesebrodt opts for a more limited but also more rigorous comparison between two specific movements: the original Fundamentalism of early twentieth-century America and the Shi'ite version which came to power in Iran in 1979. He identifies both as aspects of a common 'patriarchal protest movement'. Though he refrains from drawing wider conclusions, there is plenty of evidence to suggest that he is on the right track, not just for Iran and America, but also for many other current outbreaks of public religiosity.

Both movements, Riesebrodt notes correctly, embrace elements of the modernity people wrongly suppose them to despise. Fundamentalism is a 'traditionalism that has become reflexive'. Traditionalism becomes fundamentalism when its normal critique of society is transformed by religious intellectuals into a 'systematic whole' within the frame of a salvation history that both legitimises the critique and endows it with emotive force. For America's fundamentalist preachers, most of whom are pre-millennialists, social ills such as drugs, Aids, abortion and murder are confirmations that the Last Days predicted in the Scriptures are upon us. The Shi'ite militants who brought down the Shah's regime re-enacted the events of Karbala, using the eschatological return of Khomeini as Hidden Imam to reverse the defeat inflicted on the Imam Hussein, the Prophet's grandson, by the evil

Umayyads – identified with the modern Pahlavis. Though harking back to an earlier, more virtuous past, free from the supposedly corrupting effects of modernity, 'reflexive traditionalism' is highly selective in its promotional methods and choice of targets. Far from being rejected, modern technology is enlisted actively into the cause. Islamic fundamentalism, both Shi'ite and Sunni, is remarkably free from the iconophobia that was part of popular Islamic tradition before the twentieth century. All the revivalist movements deploy modern mass communications systems and the full resources of modern transportation. Those engaged in actual conflict have achieved mastery over sophisticated weapons systems – with sometimes disastrous results, as in Afghanistan, since technical proficiency has not necessitated any advance in political organisation.

Common to both the movements studied by Riesebrodt is the challenge they pose to the Weberian agenda of bureaucratisation and depersonalisation. The struggle of traditionalists in America against 'big government', 'big business' and 'big labour' was carried into the churches, where pastors were becoming 'church managers' and the 'scientific' biblical criticism emanating from the liberal-dominated seminaries was undermining hierocratic power. When theology allows scientific criteria to be applied to the province of Scripture – as in the Higher Criticism – the clergy simply become religious experts, tacitly abandoning their claim to be the exclusive purveyors of truth. In Iran, the clergy were allied to the traditional business or 'bazaari' sector, which under the Shah's regime felt increasingly threatened by the growth of a more modern, 'big business' economy symbolised by the supermarkets and Westernised suburbs of North Tehran. Like their Protestant counterparts, whose vision of small-town America was rooted in the nineteenth century, the bazaaris and their clerical allies reacted to the loss of cultural prestige by drawing up a list of targets to be demonised and 'traditional' values to be reaffirmed.

Riesebrodt sees 'Manicheism, xenophobia, religious nativism, a conspiracy mentality and a specific view of female sexuality' as being characteristic of fundamentalist ideology. American fundamentalists saw themselves as beset by Satanic forces, most of them imported: 'liberal theology, atheistic philosophy, war, as well as beer and evolutionary theory from Germany; rum from the Catholics, bolshevism from Russia'. Modern Iranians are inclined to attribute most of their society's ills to 'Westoxification' spread by the great American Satan. Sex, or more specifically, the control of female sexuality, looms large in both movements. American fundamentalists such as John Straton, writing in the 1920s, described the corrupting role of women in images strikingly similar to those to be found in the jeremiads of the Muslim militants:

> *The most sinister and menacing figure of our modern life is the cigarette-smoking, cocktail-drinking, pug-dog-nursing, half-dressed, painted woman, who frequents the theatres, giggles at the cabarets, gambles in our drawing rooms or sits around our hotels, with her dress cut 'C' in front and 'V' behind! She is a living invitation to lust.*

The revolutionary Fedayeen-i-Islam uses more dramatic, if less crudely misogynistic, language: 'Flames of passion rise from the naked bodies of immoral women and burn humanity to ashes.' More than half the provisions of a 1981 law codifying Qur'anic prescriptions governing personal rights are concerned with sexual activities, ranging from adultery and homosexuality to unrelated persons of the same sex lying naked under a blanket.

Riesebrodt sees the obsessive concern with sexuality common to the American and Iranian movements as a reaction to broader anxieties resulting from rural displacement and economic change. Fundamentalism is primarily 'a protest movement against the assault on patriarchal structural principles in the family, economy and polities'. The symptoms of patriarchal decline manifest themselves in the spheres of the family and sexual morality. But the real causes may lie in those processes Weber regarded as integral to modernity: the expansion of large-scale 'rationalised' firms, entailing formalised relationships, at the expense of small businesses governed by paternalistic relations between employers and employees. In resisting aspects of modernisation that threaten these traditional structures, the fundamentalists can indeed be called 'anti-modern', and they are buttressed by interpretations of the Abrahamic faiths that stress male dominance and female submission. But economic reality forces them to absorb many of modernity's salient features. What they cannot prevent by way of structural transformation they attempt to impose symbolically. Gender separation – undermined by modern architecture and no longer sustained by traditional domestic arrangements, since women are required in the workforce – is indicated by sartorial coding: long hair and skirts for American women, 'Christian' haircuts (short back and sides) for their menfolk; the chador or hijab for Muslim women, the pious beard and trimmed moustache for the men. The forms of religiosity mask, but do not reverse or even delay, the processes of secularisation.

If Riesebrodt had extended his analysis of American Fundamentalism beyond the 1920s to include the modern television preachers, he would have found even more material to vindicate his broadly Weberian approach. Secularism and disenchantment have crept into evangelical discourse itself, undermining its proclamation of the sacred 'Other'. By preaching the 'gospel of prosperity' and the 'theology of self-esteem', Robert Schuller provides a Christian endorsement for materialism and individualism. By constantly harping on sexual display in his *700 Club* television shows (for example, by broadcasting the late Robert Mapplethorpe's transgressive images in order to demonise them), Pat Robertson paradoxically domesticates sexuality and de-sacralises it, contrary to the fundamentalist purpose. Miracles, routinely re-enacted on his programmes, have the unintended consequence of banalising the supernatural. The same scenario, I have no doubt, is destined for the Islamic and all those other traditions where militant patriarchs are trying unsuccessfully to resist the tide of social change. In the global media market created by satellite television, where Robertson beams his messages to Africa, and Pakistani mullahs sustain their anti-Western animus by watching Madonna on MTV, fundamentalism must sooner or later lose its teeth. The enemy of God is not Satan, but rather cultural and religious choice.

Published in *London Review of Books*, 18 August 1994.

The books reviewed were:

Gilles Kepel (1993) *The Revenge of God: The Resurgence of Islam, Christianity and Judaism in the Modern World*. Cambridge, UK: Polity Press.

Martin Riesebrodt (1993) *Pious Passion: The Emergence of Modern Fundamentalism in the United States and Iran*. Berkeley, CA: University of California Press.

18
Khomeini's Rose Garden

'Two centuries of semi-colonisation sometimes seem worse than unambiguous colonisation; at least the unambiguously colonised got railways and sewers and unambiguous independence' opines de Bellaigue in this perceptive account of present-day Iran and its strangely aborted revolution. Fifteen years after the death of Khomeini, the country seethes with a corruption as deadly as any to be found in the Satanic West he denounced with his moral *jihad*. Even in the days of the Shah 'the country had never known such moral corruption. Pre-marital sex, divorce, drug addiction and prostitution had reached levels that you'd associate with a degenerate Western country'.

A fluent Farsi-speaker married to an Iranian, de Bellaigue (*The Economist* correspondent in Tehran) is well placed to interpret his adopted country to outsiders. His narrative weaves the country's recent historical background with encounters and interviews with an eclectic variety of individuals. His principle guide, the Virgil in the Ayatollah's Inferno, is the egregious Mr Zarif, a true believer and former revolutionary zealot who had 'built his sturdy little family on an absence of existential doubt'. Zarif has abandoned his revolutionary fervour (which allowed him to inform on and denounce his peers, like any Stasi-apparatchik) but clings to his religious faith, a spiritual 'essence' he believes can be made to harmonise with modernity.

If *In the Rose Garden of the Martyrs* sometimes hovers uneasily between journalistic essay and travelogue, the clarity of the writing – with the occasional lapse – and a personal sense of engagement more than make up for any confusion over genre. De Bellaigue is a patient listener who lends all his subjects a sympathetic ear. His approach is impressively different from the fastidious disdain with which V. S. Naipaul treated similar encounters in *Among the Believers* and *Beyond Belief*. As Reza Inglisi, or 'English Reza' (Reza being the Muslim name he took on his marriage, which non-anglophone Iranians find easier than 'Christopher'), he is able to converse with ordinary people and to penetrate areas that are usually inaccessible to foreigners. These include a 'house of strength' in South Tehran where weightlifting is organised according to the graduated hierarchies that prevail in the political and religious realms. When straining to lift the thick wooden weights 'it is customary to run through the names of the twelve (Shi'ite) Imams, one Imam for each lift'. The other athletes descend into a pit to accentuate their humility before God, reverentially touching the floor before dragging their fingers over their lips and foreheads.

The religiosity of South Tehran, the populist quarters where the Islamic revolution took root, where the roads and bazaars are full of strangers so that women must protect themselves by wearing the chador or risk 'swimming free in the fathomless waters of moral decay', is neatly contrasted with the wealthy suburb of Elahiyeh in North Tehran, whose teenage daughters – 'matchsticks marinated in Chanel' – adopt a less strenuous approach to self-improvement: retroussé nose jobs, illegally imported Italian shoes, dresses that rise dangerously above the knee, headscarves coyly rearranged to exhibit expensive coiffures. These women

> are courted, if the word is applicable, by boys who wear a minimalist variant on the goatee, driving Pop's sedan. A chance meeting in a coffee shop; a telephone number flung into a passing car – such are the first moves. Oral sex is, of necessity, popular. There will be a great to do if the girl doesn't bloody her wedding bed. In case of penetration, however, all is not lost. A discreet doctor can usually be found to sew up the offending hymen.

De Bellaigue deftly captures the pungent mix of sexual puritanism and social protest that animated Iran's revolutionary *kulturkamf*. His wife, a privileged North Tehranian, 'had lived for colour. It was as important to her as the sun. The Revolution had killed colour, declared it to be evil'.

The genial style of this book does not conceal the author's anger at the carnage a corrupt, incompetent and ruthless clerical government inflicted on its own people during the eight-year struggle with Iraq. Seminarians steeped in medieval theology give orders marked by extreme stupidity (such as using spades, instead of bayonets, to clear mines) in this 'gigantic army' of the faithful 'that prided itself on its ignorance of military affairs'. On the Khuzistan front, the ill-trained Basijis (revolutionary guards), like Orwell's Catalan militias, faced machine guns without artillery cover. Unlike the Spanish republicans, however, their casual attitude towards death is driven by expectations of personal immortality. Before going into battle the young Basijis anoint themselves with fragrances: 'If

you're going to meet God, there's a protocol to be followed.' The bodies
of the martyrs who die in battle do not decompose like other bodies. A
father who digs up his son after five years claims that his face has been
perfectly preserved. De Bellaigue is no sentimentalist or admirer of the
old orientalist Persia. *The Economist*'s man in Tehran administers peri-
odic reality-checks to the 'turbanned invitations to martyrdom' offered
by men who inhabit a mythological world of Muhammad's epic battles
and the immortal sacrifice his grandson, the Imam Hossein, made on the
battlefield of Karbala:

> *By encouraging the Basijis to advance across open ground and
> get massacred, Iran's military leaders violated an accepted article
> of war, the tactical concern for the lives of one's own men, on a
> scale unheard of since the Western Front.*

The Khuzistan Front was all the more shocking because this calculated
disregard for human life became the norm. In the official panegyrics,
martyrdom was glorified for its own sake, not for the attainment of military
objectives: 'The more horrific the circumstances of a man's death, the more
futile his expiry, the more acres of apartment block wall would be dedicated
to his memorial.'

Though episodic and conversational, the book is structured loosely
around the author's quest for one of these martyr/heroes, Hossein Karrazi,
a Basiji leader canonised by the revolution who taught his troops that
'One hour of holy war is better than sixty years of worship.' Seasoned in
the struggle against Kurdish separatists (whose dreams of autonomy were
reneged on by Khomeini after the revolution), Karrazi rose to a mid-
ranking command on the Iraqi front, ferrying his troops by helicopter
to save them from the devastating effects of Saddam Hussein's artillery.
Against his advice, based on his own intelligence sources, Karrazi's superiors ordered him to attack well-fortified Iraqi positions on islands in the
Shatt al-Arab: 'Within forty-eight hours the Iranians had been hurled
back across the Arab River, losing at least nine thousand dead. In Tehran,
victory was duly proclaimed.'

De Bellaigue gently exposes the fetid religiosity, public mawkish-
ness and ruthless clerical Machiavellianism that characterise the modern
Iranian state. By skilfully juxtaposing brutal facts with the clerical fantasies
and poignant human realities that flow from them, he allows his readers to
form their own judgement of this enigmatic and possibly dangerous regime.
This is an important book that deserves to be read by both defenders and
detractors of the Islamic republic. Among its many insights one senses how

the mood of apocalyptic fervour that disastrously failed the test of conventional arms may seek to vindicate itself by going nuclear, with potentially catastrophic consequences.

Published in *The Times Literary Supplement*, 28 February 2005.

The book reviewed was:

Christopher de Bellaigue (2005) *In the Rose Garden of the Martyrs: A Memoir of Iran*. London: HarperCollins.

19
Divided Iran on the Eve

Since the later 1990s the Jamkaran mosque near Qom in Iran has become one of the most visited Shi'ite shrines, rivalling Karbala and Kufa in Iraq as pilgrim destinations. Here, thousands of believers pray for intercessions to their Messiah – the Mahdi or Twelfth Imam – whose return they believe to be imminent. Written petitions are placed in the 'well of the Lord of the Age', from which many believe the Imam will emerge to bring about universal justice and peace. Six months after his surprise election to the Iranian presidency in June 2005, Mahmoud Ahmadinejad predicted that this momentous eschatological event would occur within two years. With the turmoil in neighbouring Iraq, where Shi'ites continue to be attacked by Sunni extremists, expectations for the return retain their appeal.

While the Shi'ite faithful (along with their Jewish and Christian counterparts) are still awaiting their Messiah, the Islamic Republic is investing heavily in the Jamkaran shrine, spending more than half a billion dollars on enlargements that rival those of the Grand Mosque in Mecca, with vast interior courtyards and facilities – including offices, research centres, cultural departments, slaughterhouses and soup kitchens – not to mention the farms where Jamkaran raises its meat. In a country where the religious establishment dominates state institutions, Jamkaran's burgeoning bureaucracy seems set to outstrip that of the longer-established shrine complexes of Mashhad and Qom.

While external observers perceive the struggle in Iran between conservatives and moderates in political terms, the Islamic Republic's conflicting ideological currents also find expression in the age-old rhetoric of the apocalypse, which originated in the region more than 2,000 years ago. As Abbas Amanat explains in *Apocalyptic Islam and Iranian Shi'ism*, the Jamkaran makeover was part of the campaign orchestrated by conservative clerics in Qom against the government of former President Mohammad Khatami and his reformist allies.

Unlike many academics, Amanat, a professor of history at Yale, is willing to venture into regions outside his speciality of Iranian studies, which makes his book particularly valuable, as it is informed by the knowledge – all too rare among Islamicists – that Islam is one variant in a cluster of religions rather than a subject to be treated on its own. Messianic expectations are fundamental to all the West Asian religions, articulating forces that are both dynamic and dangerous:

> *The vast number of visitors to Jamkaran demonstrates the resurgence of interest in the Mahdi among Iranians of all classes – including the affluent middle classes in the capital – and the triumph of the Islamic Republic in capitalising on symbols of public piety.*

Though these symbols, such as the Jamkaran shrine, are specific to Shi'ism, their appeal – not to mention their mobilising power – is universal. As Amanat points out, apocalyptic movements have been motors of religious change throughout history. Christian origins are inseparable from the spirit of apocalypticism that consumed the Judao-Hellenistic world in late antiquity. Muhammad's early mission cannot be explained without reference to the 'apocalyptic admonitions, the foreseen calamities, and the terror of the Day of Judgement, apparent in the early *suras* [chapters] of the Qu'ran'. Later examples – to name but a few – include Martin Luther's call for reform of the Catholic Church, and Sabbatai Zevi's claim in the seventeenth century to be the Jewish Messiah. The Mormon Church, the most successful of the new American religions, was born in the millennial frenzy that swept through the 'Burnt-Over District' of upstate New York in the 1830s. Amanat sees all these as conscious attempts to fulfil messianic visions conceived on the ancient models preserved in Zoroastrian and biblical scriptures.

In a brief but masterful compression of insights gained from readings of the works of Norman Cohn, founding father of millennial studies, and other scholars in the field, Amanat reviews the dynamics of apocalyptic histories. On the positive side, the anticipation of imminent divine judgement can be translated into a message of social justice, with individual choice replacing dogmas handed down by ancestors, tribes or communities. Historically, apocalyptic movements tend to be socially inclusive, appealing in particular to the deprived, marginalised and dispossessed. The negative side is the demonisation of perceived enemies in a world where the People of God – the saved remnant of humanity – see themselves as the sole bearers of divine wisdom or knowledge. The utopian project of realising Paradise – when the Messiah's followers choose to enact the millennial scenario in real historical time – may be as devastating as the earthquakes, fires, plagues and wars of apocalyptic imaginings.

Amanat's approach to his subject matter is sometimes daunting. It is clear that he is more comfortable writing for fellow specialists than ordinary readers, which is a pity, because his insights have implications that extend far beyond Shi'ism, showing how a particular event, such as a massacre or a crucifixion, becomes lodged in the historical memory.

In Twelver Shi'ism – the majority sect in the minority tradition of Islam – the Messiah is 12th in the line of Imams, or spiritual leaders, descended from Muhammad's cousin and son-in-law, Ali, whom the Shi'a believe was cheated of the succession after the Prophet's death in CE 632. In the Twelver version, the last of these 12 Imams 'disappeared' in 874; in the populist myth he is hiding in a cave in Samarra in Iraq awaiting his triumphant return. Shi'ite devotion centres on the fate of the third Imam, Ali's younger son, Hussain, who was massacred with his band of loyalist followers on the field of Karbala (in modern Iraq) by the forces of the Umayyad caliph Yazid in 680.

Shi'ism has for more than 13 centuries oscillated between revolutionary activism and quietist disengagement. In the early Muslim era, Ali's loyalists (his Shi'a, or partisans) instigated numerous revolts, challenging and sometimes toppling the military-tribal complexes that came to power in the wake of the Arab conquests. Many of these revolts were conducted in the name of the Mahdi (Messiah) or Qa'im (resurrector), an eschatological figure with more than a passing resemblance to the avenging Christ of the biblical Book of Revelation. The most enduring brought the Turkic Safavid dynasty to power in Iran in 1501, which made Shi'ism the state religion and created a fusion of Persian and Shi'a identities. The cult of Hussain's martyrdom, for example, evokes the theme of mourning for the murder of the Iraj – the primordial hero of Iran.

Having ridden to power on a wave of messianic expectations, the Safavids succeeded in defusing its revolutionary dynamic. In the Imam's absence, the Shi'a 'ulama – religious scholars – exercise spiritual authority on his behalf, lending them an authority and status superior to that of their Sunni counterparts. In the ensuing clergy–state equilibrium, the Hidden Imam was safely relegated to an ever-receding future, with speculations about his return dismissed as unorthodox, even heretical.

Millennial aspirations, however, are liable to escape from the grip of religious establishments, especially when current orthodoxies can be represented as a betrayal of pristine origins. As Amanat explains: 'In a millennial momentum, common to all apocalyptic trends, a crucial shift occurs from dormant aspiration to keen ambition.' In Iran this transition was overseen and manipulated by the Ayatollah Khomeini, a sophisticated theologian and consummate political operator. A vigorous opponent of the Shah's reforms, Khomeini had argued that, in the absence of the Hidden Imam, the clerics should effectively exercise power on his behalf under the aegis of a 'Guardian Jurist'. His doctrine represented a radical break with the tradition of de facto separation between religion and state that had grown up over previous centuries. The infallibility of the imam must be realised through action. As Amanat puts it:

> Khomeini in effect appropriated the function of the Imam to himself though staying short of claiming divine inspiration and infallibility ... He was not merely a 'vicegerent' of the Imam, as he theoretically claimed to be, but an imam, as he was universally addressed in the Islamic Republic, an unprecedented honorific exclusively reserved for Shi'i Imams and not assumed by any Shi'i figure since the Occultation of the Twelfth Imam in the ninth century.

By taking power so spectacularly, Khomeini shook the traditions of Twelver Shi'ism to their foundations. The culture fostered by the madrasas (religious seminaries) under the Pahlavis and their Qajar predecessors had been strong in rhetorical skills, but inward-looking theologically. Its hallmark was 'a fetishistic avoidance and frowning defiance of anything new, novel and unfamiliar' that appeared to threaten the 'ulama's power or influence. Instead of finding ways of adjusting their tradition to meet the modern world and its challenges, the Shi'ite scholars had focused obsessively on recondite issues such as the manner in which prayer may be nullified by ritual pollution. This approach served to foster a spirit of hostility to social and secular reforms enacted by the Pahlavis in areas such as land ownership, education and marriage.

A cliché of Iran's revolutionary rhetoric is that the United States is the Great Satan bent on destroying the Islamic Republic. While there is a genuine historical grievance over the CIA-sponsored 'countercoup' that overthrew the nationalist Mossadegh government in 1953, the anti-Americanism that characterised Khomeini's writings and still surfaces in Tehran street demonstrations seems closer to psychopathology than rational politics. Such frenzied antagonism, as Amanat suggests, owes more to Zoroastrian dualism than mainstream Qur'anic theology. In the Muslim scripture, Satan (shaytan) is a less than Miltonic figure. He is just one demon among others, who has the role of tempter or ethical tester.

In the Zoroastrian schema, however, eternal conflict rages between supporters of Ahura Mazda, Lord of Wisdom, and those of the evil Ahriman. The cosmic battle is unending. One of Ahriman's titles, the Demon of the

Demons, is strikingly comparable to the Great Satan. Unlike the rather docile shaytan of Qur'anic tradition, Ahriman's scope of operations and powers are immense. Amanat argues that, during the early Islamic centuries, Iranian Shi'ism absorbed the Zoroastrian view of a world divided between pure believers and polluting infidels, with bodies subject to constant danger. In the folk versions of Shi'ism that still persist, the human body is subject to all kinds of satanic onslaughts and must constantly be guarded against the enemy's insidious plots. In a patriarchal social order it is inevitable that women bear the brunt of such guardianship.

Muslims were sometimes shocked when first encountering unveiled females. Their horror was registered by a Persian visitor to Europe in 1838, who, scandalised by the way that women handled 'unclean' puppies, decided that women must be using their pets as sex toys: 'The husbands of such women are very happy and content with this arrangement ... Women are so sexually aggressive in this country that no man, no matter what his potency and skill, can hope to satisfy them.' The East–West battle over gender is brilliantly described by Janet Afary in her groundbreaking survey, *Sexual Politics in Modern Iran*. As in other patrilineal societies, the woman is the 'door of entry to the group'. Improper behaviour on her part can expose her community and family to all sorts of hidden dangers. Systems such as these exercise a double standard wherein a woman's infidelity (but not a man's) is seen to allow tangible and damaging impurities to infiltrate the family, both physically and morally. A woman's sexual and reproductive functions turned her body into a contested site of potential and real ritual contamination. The concept of *namus* (honour) and the need to control women's chastity may be related to this fear of sexual contamination.

The sexual double standard was effectively institutionalised in all the mainstream Islamic traditions: men were permitted up to four legal wives and the right of divorce by repudiation (*talaq*). However, in pre-modern Iran (prior to the 1920s), male prerogatives were enhanced by the practice of temporary marriage (*sigheh*), which was exclusive to Shi'ism, and by the availability of concubines, which persisted after the formal abolition of slavery at the end of the nineteenth century. *Sigheh* was a sexual charter for men: the ease with which it was contracted meant that consensual affairs between men (married or unmarried) and single women could hardly ever be labelled as fornication, and therefore be subject to Islamic penalties.

Gender segregation – common to most Islamic societies – contributed to the prevalence of other practices that are rarely discussed in social histories of Islam: boy concubinage and paedophilia. Though *liwat* or *lavat* (sodomy) is condemned in the Qur'an (the word alludes to the Old Testament story of Lot), homosexual relationships between older men and boys were tolerated, not least because they posed a lesser threat to the patriarchal order than unregulated heterosexual interactions.

Afary's book exposes the absurdity of claims by ideologues such as Ali Akbar Natiq-Nuri, a former Iranian minister of the interior and presidential candidate, who blame the West for 'spreading corruption and obscenity, propagating debauchery and homosexuality'. She provides plenty of evidence to show that the prohibition against *liwat* was honoured in the breach. Beardless boys, not yet being men, could be 'penetrated without losing their essential manliness, so long as they did not register pleasure in the act, which would suggest a pathology liable to continue into adulthood'. In a society where beards were *de rigueur*, the beardless European male was often thought to be an *amrad* (catamite). Institutionalised pederasty was part of a wider culture in which family security balanced or compensated for the turbulence prevailing in the public domain.

Under the Qajar dynasty, which took power in the 1790s, Iran had a rigidly hierarchical social order, with clearly defined class and ethnic boundaries, a coherent religious establishment, and above all a pattern of family obligations that fostered strong communal identities. Marriage – including child marriage – was nearly universal, with parents choosing spouses for children of both sexes.

The available records can only hint at the sexual culture that flourished in the privacy of homes: 'Reported crimes were low in a world where girls, boys, and women endured or quietly resisted incest, sexual molestation, and rape.' Yet, contrary to assumptions about the emancipatory effects of Westernisation, urban women in pre-modern Iran enjoyed a considerable amount of personal freedom. In the 1850s, the wife of Britain's ambassador observed that women of all classes

> *enjoy abundance of liberty, more so, I think, than among us.*
> *The complete envelopment of the face and person disguises them*
> *effectively from the nearest relatives, and destroying, when*
> *convenient, all distinction of rank, gives unrestrained freedom.*

Afary points to references in the indigenous literature to pimps and love-brokers, and to the secret affairs of married, divorced or widowed women. In a patriarchal order where honour was defined by women's conduct, and with sexual transgressions of respectable women being severely punished, it was the veil itself that provided opportunities for resistance.

Afary's perspective throws useful, if unfamiliar, light on the impact and consequences of the social reforms instituted by Reza Shah Pahlavi – the Cossack Brigadier who rose to supreme power in the chaotic aftermath of the First World War and the Bolshevik Revolution. The changes he imposed – European-style dress codes for men that reduced ethnic or religious distinctions, compulsory unveiling for women, and the desegregation of gender, along with measures such as raising the age of marriage to 18 and making improvements in public hygiene – were modelled on the perceived advantages enjoyed by people in the industrialised West. Mired in their medieval fortress mentality, religious leaders resisted adamantly, producing propaganda against vaccination, protesting against the installation of taps in public bathhouses, and forbidding the use of alcohol for sterilisation. The religious establishment instinctively recognised that, in enacting reforms in the realms of hygiene and dress, the state was appropriating their powers as the guardians of purity.

These reforms accelerated divisions that were cultural as well as social. A new middle class, exposed to modern education, comprising less than 10 per cent of the country's labour force, became increasingly secular in outlook and distant from the dominant religious culture, while the majority – the rural peasantry and the small traders of the urban bazaars – remained attached to the instructions of their mullahs. The outcome may be described as an era of profound psychic discomfort for a majority of Iranians going about their daily lives. Afary concludes:

> Modernity instituted a double life for pious Muslims. Outwardly, they behaved as modern citizens of the state, ignoring religious hierarchies and engaging not just in business and trade with women and non-Muslims, as they had always done, but also mingled socially, shaking hands and sharing tea or meals with them. Inwardly, many bazaaris harboured a constant sense of anxiety since they continued to believe that a pious Shi'i Muslim who ignored the proper rituals of purification after encounters with najes (polluted) individuals had 'nullified' his prayers and supplications to God and the Imams.

Initially, Khomeini's revolution upended the Pahlavi reforms, leading to a drastic reversal in women's rights. The compulsory hijab (veil) was imposed for women in public, with even slight violations bringing severe punishment (74 lashes or a year's imprisonment), though since the face was exposed, it no longer gave the advantage of anonymity. Women and men no longer enjoyed equality under the law, with evidence from a man being worth twice that of a woman. Lashing, amputation and stoning have been applied by the courts, with the latter punishment reserved for women convicted of adultery. The courts apply lighter sentences than previously for husbands, fathers and brothers accused of 'honour killings'. There are even regulations against public displays of affection.

Under Khomeini, child marriage was allowed once more, with the age of marriage being reduced from 18 to nine for girls (revised, after protests, to 13) and 15 for boys. New laws encouraged polygamy and prevented women from leaving abusive husbands. The husband's right of unilateral divorce (limited under the Shah's reforms) was reinstated. New policies encouraged temporary marriage as a 'morally sanctioned substitute for Western dating', with trial *sigheh* marriages recommended for high-school students, and sex workers being invited to enter short-term marriage contracts with returning war veterans.

In sum, Afary suggests that the sexual doctrines instituted by Khomeini vastly increased the authority of men and the state 'over women's sexual and reproductive capacities'. This was not a 'minor side effect of the [revolution]. Rather, it formed an important, though often unspoken, reason for male support or acquiescence in the face of Islamisation'. At the same time, change is moving in the opposite direction. Paradoxically, the revolution released many young women from their family ties, which is why many found it attractive or expedient to join Islamist movements. During the war with Iraq, women were encouraged to enlist in the armed forces, with Khomeini urging women to 'defend their Islamic and national honour' and to complete 'the military, partisan, and guerrilla training appropriate for a resurgent Muslim nation'. Female volunteers reported that years spent on the front, alongside their 'brother warriors', were the best in their lives.

Statistics reveal a picture that differs strikingly from the legal texts. Despite the formal reintroduction of child marriage, the mean age of first marriages for young women has continued to rise from around 19 before the revolution to 24 today – with nearly 80 per cent married after the age of 20. The revolution has maintained the momentum of the Shah's literacy campaigns, with literacy rates greater than 95 per cent for both sexes. With young women from rural families seeing education as the path to economic independence, the majority of college students are now women. 'Companionate marriage', with couples freely choosing their partners, is becoming the norm. Modern social forces are universal and, despite its reactionary rhetoric, the Islamic revolution is being carried remorselessly along by them.

Nevertheless, it takes little imagination to see how contradictory psychic currents reflecting concerns over pollution and gender may have fuelled the overthrow of the Shah in 1979. Chador-clad women were prominent in street demonstrations in Tehran, in which rituals commemorating the death of Hussain in 680 were taken from the relatively safe domain of 'sacred time' and given the urgency of Now! In his jeremiads from within Iran, later from Najaf in Iraq, and finally from his media-friendly château in a Paris suburb, Khomeini likened the Shah to the evil Yazid, a figure more akin to Ahriman than the flawed Umayyad caliph of Muslim historiography. Khomeini's fulminations, however, were more than the barks of an angry mullah. As Ray Takeyh explains in *Guardians of the Revolution*, his elegant anatomy of Iran's foreign policy since 1979, the ayatollah's special genius lay in resisting the trend whereby revolutionary energies usually become dissipated.

Inspired by his success in overthrowing the Shah, Khomeini intended a 'revolution without borders' that would impose his Islamist template on Iran's recalcitrant neighbours. The decadent princes of the Gulf, with their ostentatious lifestyles and sham 'American Islam', would be replaced by an 'authentically Islamic' popular movement, headed by Khomeini, which would re-politicise Islam. The Islamic aspiration of universal justice under the 'government of God' would finally be realised. The rhetoric was inspiring, not least because it masked age-old sectarian and national divisions, in particular the Sunni–Shi'a divide that, despite the revolution's provenance, its propaganda underplayed. Not only were neighbouring Shi'ite communities galvanised – generating dangerous tensions in Iraq, Bahrain and eastern Saudi Arabia, where Shi'as languished under harsh Sunni rule – so were Islamists in places without Shi'ite communities, including Algeria and the Hijaz in western Saudi Arabia.

The revolution's outward momentum was blocked by external factors – most notably Saddam Hussein's Iraq, which launched an unprovoked attack in 1980, leading to a war that cost as many as a million lives, two-thirds of them Iranian. Takeyh presents Khomeini as a 'relentless ideologue willing to sacrifice his nation for the sake of his religious speculations'. He waged the war against Iraq apocalyptically, with a badly equipped and appallingly led army, confident that divine support would win over better-trained and better-equipped Iraqi divisions. Having sacrificed a generation of young martyrs to repel the Iraqis, he insisted, against reason and logic, on carrying the war on to Iraqi soil. It was, he said, to be the prelude to the Muslim Armageddon, with the 'path to Jerusalem passing through Karbala'.

Takeyh argues, chillingly, that it was Saddam's use of chemical weaponry – abetted, in effect, by the US Reagan administration – that finally punctured the old man's apocalyptic zeal. Horrified by Saddam's attack on the Kurdish town of Halabja, where, as the former president Ali Akbar Hashemi Rafsanjani put it, 'people fell like autumn leaves', the regime believed that 'similar measures' would be directed at front-line cities such as Tabriz and Kermanshah. Takeyh has no doubts about the outcome.

Saddam's use of chemical weapons turned the tide of the war, and it was the trauma of this event that underpins Iran's policy of developing a nuclear capability. Enrichment within the bounds of the nuclear non-proliferation treaty may provide a level of nuclear insurance, since materials developed for such peaceful uses can theoretically be 'weaponised' within months. Iran's policy pre-dates the revolution. It was America's ally, the Shah, who initiated Iran's nuclear programme with the assistance of 'the Washington establishment, which was nurturing the shah's desire to act as the policeman of the Persian Gulf'. Takeyh points out that the Islamic revolution at first viewed the programme as 'another ploy for making Iran dependent on the West', and greatly reduced its scope. The eight-year war that spanned the 1980s altered perceptions:

> It is impossible to understand Iran's nuclear calculations without considering its war with Iraq. That conflict shaped the Islamic Republic's defense doctrine and molded its values and outlook ... The fact that Saddam had used chemical weapons against Iran with impunity demonstrated that the Western powers' hostility toward the clerical regime would always overcome their moral compunctions ... The fact that Iran had insufficient retaliatory power and could not protect its citizens from unconventional attacks was critical to its decision to end the war.

Takeyh is blunt in his condemnation of the Reagan administration's complicity in Saddam's use of chemical weapons, and especially critical of the opportunities that the Bush administration missed for improving Iran–US relations after the 9/11 attacks. The 1997 election that brought the moderate President Mohammad Khatami to power against the wishes of the clerical elite led by Ayatollah Ali Khamanei, Khomeini's successor as Supreme Leader, should have demonstrated to Washington that the regime was far from monolithic, even if some of its agencies were engaged in terrorism.

There is no question, however, that the prospects for 'one of the most intellectually vibrant democratic movements in the Middle East' were thwarted by a combination of factors. One was Khatami's personal dislike of confrontation: 'Despite his deeply held democratic convictions, [he] proved too much a man of the system' whose 'penchant for order over-whelmed his desire for change'. Another was the constitutional straitjacket that Khomeini had left behind, giving the members of the conservative-dominated Guardian Council power to block the will of a parliament whose candidates they had already vetted ideologically. But external factors, driven by US policies, were decisive.

George W. Bush's notorious 'axis of evil' speech in January 2002, linking Iran to its enemy Iraq and the maverick communist republic of North Korea, undermined many of Khatami's achievements in improving Iran's international profile, and convinced the hard-liners that the Islamic Republic would become the next target in Bush's 'war on terror'. The build-up to the US invasion of Iraq provided them with strong public support. In the local council elections of February 2003 – one month before the invasion – conservatives regained nearly all the seats they had lost in 1999, at the peak of the reformist movement. This was not a rigged poll: unlike the parliamentary and presidential races, candidates for municipal elections are not vetted for 'Islamic suitability'. The right-wing victory was sealed two years later with Ahmadinejad's election as president.

This month's [July 2009] presidential elections will reveal if the New Right, as Takeyh terms the current incumbents, retains its grip on power. Khatami withdrew from the race earlier this year, giving his support to the former prime minister, Mir Hussein Moussavi, who enjoys some conservative support and is thought by many to have a better chance of unseating Ahmadinejad. Moussavi, however, has effectively been out of politics for two decades, and may have difficulty in connecting with younger voters. Ahmedinejad, in contrast, enjoys the advantages of incumbency and is thought – unofficially – to enjoy the support of the Supreme Leader. The Guardian Council has now approved two other candidates in addition to the front-runners Moussavi and Ahmadinejad: Mehdi Karroubi, former parliamentary speaker, and Mohsen Rezai, former commander of the Revolutionary Guards, who is wanted by Interpol for alleged involvement in the July 1994 terrorist attack on a Jewish cultural centre in Buenos Aires, in which 85 people died.

It will be a setback for the Supreme Leader if Ahmadinejad does not win the first round on 12 June. Khamenei, it is true, was effectively overruled by the electorate when Khatami won the presidency in both 1997 and 2001. Since 2005, however, the New Right, as Takeyh demonstrates, has consolidated its hold over Iran's institutions, and the international situation is hardly encouraging for reformers. Despite President Obama's expressed desire for dialogue, the new right-wing government in Israel regards Iran, with its support for Hamas and Hezbollah, as the principal obstacle to peace, and is seeking to buck the international consensus by deferring – it hopes indefinitely – any 'two-state solution' to the Palestinian problem. As one analyst in Tehran put it in an interview with Radio Free Europe, 'look at the situation in Pakistan and the worsening violence in Iraq. Khamenei doesn't want to send a pigeon to confront hawks in the region in the next four years'.

Apocalyptic talk by both sides is serving to ratchet up the temperature at a time when the Obama administration is trying to steady people's nerves. Ahmadinejad's threat to 'remove Israel from the map of history' needs to be taken seriously in light of his recent announcement that Iran had successfully tested a new solid fuel missile with a range of 1,900 kilometres (about 1,200 miles). In a speech doubtless intended to boost his poll ratings, he attributed this latest technological breakthrough to divine intervention and the assistance of the Lord of the Age. Counter-threats from Israel are even more alarming, not least because, unlike Iran, it already has formidable nuclear and conventional capacities. 'You don't want a messianic apocalyptic cult controlling atomic bombs,' Israeli Prime Minister Benjamin Netanyahu said in a recent interview. 'When the wide-eyed believer gets hold of the reins of power and the weapons of mass death, then the entire world should start worrying, and that is what is happening in Iran.'

Ray Takeyh, a careful analyst, takes a much more sanguine view. It is reassuring that he has now been hired by the State Department, where his knowledge and skills will be invaluable if current diplomatic feelers are to yield positive results. He writes:

> *Iran's rulers should not be caricatured as messianic politicians seeking to implement obscure scriptural dictates for ushering in the end of the world through conflict and disorder. As with most leaders, they are interested in staying in power and will recoil from conduct that jeopardises their domain.*

With these New Safavids in power, the Hidden Imam will remain in his cave, the apocalypse safely postponed until a new generation arises, hungry for change.

Published in *The New York Review of Books*, 2 July 2009.

The books reviewed were:

Janet Afary (2009) *Sexual Politics in Modern Iran.* Cambridge, UK: Cambridge University Press.

Abbas Amanat (2009) *Apocalyptic Islam and Iranian Shi'ism.* London/New York: I.B. Tauris.

Ray Takeyh (2009) *Guardians of the Revolution: Iran and the World in the Age of the Ayatollahs.* Oxford UK/ New York: Oxford University Press.

20

The Cultures of Shi'ism

In 2004, anticipating the victory of the Shi'ite parties in the Iraqi parliamentary elections, King Abdullah of Jordan warned of a 'Shi'ite crescent' stretching from Iran into Iraq, Syria and Lebanon that would be dominated by Iran with its large majority of Shi'ites and Shi'ite clerical leadership. The idea was picked up by the Saudi foreign minister, who described the US intervention in Iraq as a 'handover of Iraq to Iran', since the USA was supporting mainly Shi'ite groups there after overthrowing Saddam's Sunni regime. President Mubarak of Egypt claimed that Shi'ites living in Arab countries were more loyal to Iran than to their own governments. In an article published in *The New York Times* in November 2006, Nayaf Obaid, national security adviser to King Abdullah of Saudi Arabia reflected on the urgent need to support Iraq's Sunni minority which had lost power after centuries of ruling over a Shi'ite majority comprising more than 65 per cent of the Iraqi population.

Shi'aphobia is nothing new for Saudi Arabia. The kingdom's legitimacy derives from the Wahhabi sect of Islam, a Sunni Muslim group that attacked Shi'ite shrines in Iraq in the nineteenth century, and today systematically discriminates against Shi'ites. We know from Wikileaks that the US government regards the Saudi monarchy as a 'critical financial support base' for al-Qaeda, the Taliban, Lashkar-e-Taiba and other terrorist groups. As well as attacking American and Indian targets, all these are violently anti-Shi'ite. We also know that the Saudi King venomously urged his US allies to cut off the 'head of the snake' by attacking Iran (*Guardian* newspaper, 12 January 2010).

In Bahrain, democratic protests by the Shi'a, who make up around 70 per cent of the population, have suffered decades of suppression by the government with the aid of Saudi troops and Sunni mercenaries from Jordan, Pakistan and the United Arab Emirates (UAE). The Saudis are terrified that the unrest will spread to the oil-bearing Eastern Province where their own Shi'a minority resides.

Syria, just a few hundred kilometres across the desert to the west, presents an even more brutal picture. Here, the protestors – many of them Sunnis, who make up three-quarters of the population – are being killed in their hundreds, even thousands, by security forces dominated by a Shi'a sectarian group – the Alawis – who have held power for more than four decades and are refusing to relinquish it. The European Union says that Iran has sent senior commanders of its Revolutionary Guards to help the Assad regime quell the unrest, a move that must add to anxieties that a sectarian conflict, comparable to Iraq's, is developing in Syria. According to human rights activists, Sunni minorities in Iran – in Khuzestan and Baluchistan provinces – have also been subject to attacks, with dozens of protestors killed.

Some of those involved in the recent Arab uprisings claim that sectarian anxieties are deliberately being stoked by authoritarian regimes to maintain their grip on power. The Assad regime is widely accused of frightening Syria's minorities – Christians, Kurds, Ismailis and wealthier Sunni clans – by raising the spectre of a take-over by Sunni fundamentalists or 'takfiris' (extreme Sunni groups who denounce others as 'infidels'). In Bahrain, the protests rapidly took on a sectarian dimension.

Many of the protesters in the Middle East deny that they have religious or sectarian agendas; they want democracy, civil rights, an end to corruption and a change of regime. As Timur Kuran pointed out in an article in *The New York Times*, 28 May, 2011, most of them do not appear to have a distinctive ideology or coherent, disciplined organisations. The exception is the highly disciplined Muslim Brotherhood, whose Freedom and Justice party stands to gain in the forthcoming Egyptian elections through the strength of its organisation and popularity of its informal welfare programmes. The Brotherhood's top-down structure, which combines features of the traditional Sufi (mystical) order based on graded levels of initiation with modern methods such as bussing supporters to polling stations, makes it a formidable contender for power in the absence of other organisations standing between the individual and the state.

The weakness of civil society organisations that characterises many Muslim societies means that power is liable to fall by default to the military or, as in the case of Syria, to a kinship group bound by tribal loyalties underpinned by a minority faith. Regimes may be 'crying wolf' when they justify repressive measures by invoking the spectre of sectarian conflict, but the experience of Iraq, where US Administrator Paul Bremer's foolish policy of dissolving both the army and the Baath party after the US invasion led to a brutal conflict involving the Shi'a majority and recently dispossessed Sunnis, has exposed the fragile foundations of national identities in the modern Middle East.

Shi'ism, as Hamid Dabashi explains in his challenging and brilliant new book, is a perfect foil for power but unimpressive as a modern state ideology. Its origins lie in the disputed succession to Muhammad, who died in 632 in his early 60s without unambiguously naming a successor. His closest kinsman, Ali – his younger first cousin and husband of his daughter Fatima, whom the Shi'a minority came to believe had been designated to succeed him, was passed over three times for the caliphate before being murdered by a disillusioned supporter after a brief and contested tenure. Ali's younger son, Husain, was killed at Karbala in 680 in an unsuccessful attempt to wrest the caliphate from the Umayyad dynasty reigning in Damascus and restore it to the Prophet's legitimate line. Though the Umayyads were replaced in a Shi'ite-inspired revolt in 750, the victors were not direct descendents of Muhammad, but of his uncle, Abbas. Like the pro-Stuart Jacobites in Britain who mounted unsuccessful rebellions against the Hanoverian monarchy in 1715 and 1745, the Shi'a were revolutionary legitimists. Believing that the cause of true Islam had been betrayed by the usurping Umayyads, and later by the Abbasids, they originally looked to their dispossessed 'pretenders', the imams of the House of Ali, to restore both true religion and legitimate government.

Shi'ite-inspired revolts were frequent during the early centuries of Islam. Unlike the Catholic–Protestant division that emerged after 15 centuries of Western Christianity, the contested legacy of Muhammad reaches back to the time of Islam's origins.

The great sociologist, Max Weber, famously distinguished between 'exemplary' prophets such as the Buddha, who showed the path to salvation by personal example, and 'ethical' prophets such as Muhammad who demanded obedience to their teachings. Dabashi, however, challenges Weber's view, arguing that the Prophet Muhammad embraces both categories, with different consequences for the two main traditions that flow from his mission. While the vast majority of Muslims assimilated his exemplary character – along with the Qur'anic teachings – into the systematised doctrines of the four main Sunni schools of Islamic law, the Shi'a 'did not want to let go of their Prophet's exemplary character and thus sought to extend his charismatic presence to their imams'. For them 'exemplary prophethood will continue to need the exemplary presence of an imam to sustain its charismatic condition'.

The differences between Sunni and Shi'a are less concerned with matters of doctrine than with ideas of spiritual authority. In the majority Sunni tradition, the legal scholars or *ulama* came to act as a rabbinical class charged with the task of interpreting the Qur'an and the ethical teachings derived from the prophet's exemplary conduct as recorded in the *hadith* reports or 'traditions'. The eventual consolidation of the Sunni tradition into four main schools of law allowed for considerable variations in interpreting these canonical texts. However, the legalistic approach of the Sunni *ulama* reproduced and extended the ethical aspects of Muhammad's mission to the Muslim majority without accommodating their devotional needs. Among the Sunnis, the articulation of the more spiritual or mystical aspects of the Prophet's legacy was the province of the Sufi or mystical orders that grew up around the 'saints' or holy men who reproduced the Prophet's charisma.

The Shi'a, by contrast, institutionalised the Prophet's charisma – at source, as it were – by investing their imams with additional sources of esoteric knowledge to which their *ulama* or religious specialists had exclusive access. Shi'ism arguably presented a more 'integrated' approach to Islam than Sunnism, though one that (like Protestantism) was oppositional to the mainstream tradition. During Islam's formative era most of the imams in the line of Muhammad were deemed to have been martyrs or victims of the Sunni caliphs, who were seen by the Shi'a as usurpers. After the Twelfth Imam in the direct line of Muhammad finally 'disappeared' in 940, authority came to be exercised by a clerical establishment – comparable to the Catholic priesthood – assumed to be in possession of the esoteric knowledge and hermeneutic skills necessary for the community's guidance. The parallels with Christianity are compelling. For the Twelvers, the disappeared or 'Hidden Imam' is a messianic figure who will return (like Christ) to bring peace and justice to a world torn by strife.

Dabashi shows how this traditional belief system, enshrined in popular culture, resurfaces in contemporary literature. The death of the Imam Husain – the prophet's grandson – at Karbala is re-enacted annually in the popular passion plays performed in every Iranian town and village. For ordinary Shi'a he is the archetypical martyr for justice and truth; for Marxist writers such as Khosrow Golsorki (1944–74) and Ahmad Shamlou (1925–2000) Husain is both Christ-like victim and revolutionary icon. For Ali Shariati (1933–75), the Islamist ideologue and leading inspiration for the 1979 Iranian Revolution, he is a 'cosmic figure whose murder weighs on the conscience of humanity'. In the Twelver tradition, the initial 'disappearance' of the last Imam in 874, a lifetime before 940, when his four chosen deputies are supposed to have lost contact with him, initiated a scholastic tradition 'in which the sanctity of the letter of law became a simulacrum of the charismatic presence of the Shi'a imams'. The crucial difference with Sunnis is not so much in the letter of the law, which the Sunni legal scholars interpret in accordance with a hierarchy of sources embracing the Qur'an, the Prophet's custom (sunna), consensus and analogical reasoning. It lies rather in the quasi-mystical authority with which the Shi'a legal scholars are invested. These do not quite constitute a church in the Christian sense, since there are no formal sacraments and the scholars are not a corporate body endowed with powers to save Muslims from sin. Their senior leaders, the ayatollahs ('signs' of God), are not organised into a top-down hierarchy, but acquire their followers – and considerable wealth – through public recognition of their learning, reinforced by the payment of religious dues. Far from being a monolith, they differ among themselves (like their Sunni counterparts) on matters of doctrine and practice. But, unlike their Sunni counterparts (whose social powers have diminished considerably since Ottoman times, with the rise of the modern state and secular education), they still dispose of formidable social capital.

Furthermore, the eschatological time-bomb wrapped in the myth of the Hidden Imam's expected return packs a formidable political charge. By and large, the tradition of Twelver Shi'ism prevails in Iran (90 per cent) and its immediate neighbours, Azerbaijan (85 per cent), Iraq (65 per cent) and Bahrain (75 per cent), with substantial minorities in Kuwait (40 per cent), Saudi Arabia (around 8 per cent), Afghanistan (30 per cent) and Pakistan (30 per cent). The Gulf rulers have good reason to be nervous. Numerous revolts throughout Islamic history were fuelled by the prospect of the Imam's expected return, or justified by reference to the Prophet's dispossessed progeny, before Khomeini's triumphant arrival in Tehran in February 1979. Though Khomeini was too canny – and religiously correct – to formally claim to be the Hidden Imam, he allowed populist expectations surrounding the Hidden Imam's return to work on his behalf.

Dabashi shows how the dialectic between the tradition's scholarly legalism and its revolutionary *élan* produces a precarious equilibrium. This was exemplified in Iraq by the 81-year-old Grant Ayatollah Ali Sistani, a scholastic jurist, on the one hand, and Seyyed Moqtada al-Sadr on the other – 'two Shi'a at opposite but complementary ends of their faith, defending their cause and sustaining the historical fate of their community in two diametrically parallel but rhetorically divergent ways'. The actual holder of power, namely the government of Nuri al-Maliki, has had to negotiate this delicate Shi'ite balance along with Iraq's Sunnis, Kurds and other minorities.

Dabashi's description applies all the more to the current situation in Iran, where President Ahmadinejad is challenging the authority of the supreme leader, Ayatollah Ali Khamenei, in an effort to boost the office of president in advance of elections in 2013. The struggle between the president, who has openly been accused by the liberal Green movement of buying the votes that brought him victory in the contested election of June 2009, and Khamenei (Khomeini's successor as supreme leader) reflect what the sociologist Sami Zubaida has neatly described as 'the contradictory duality of sovereignties' – between God and the people – embedded in the constitution of the Islamic Republic. Popular expectations surrounding the Imam and his return are central to this struggle. While Khamenei, who represents a part of the clerical 'old guard' that took power after the revolution, has gone so far as to suggest that Iran should change to a parliamentary system, without an elected president – a move that former president Rafsanjani has stated would 'be contrary to the Constitution and would weaken the people's power of choice' – Ahmadinejad has given the debate a theological twist by saying that Muslims do not need the intercession of clerics to contact the Hidden Imam. For the clerical establishment, a Return that would put them out of business must be endlessly deferred. Their attitude is similar to that of the Christian clergy, according to the 'amillennialist' vision promoted by Saint Augustine when the church reached the conclusion that Jesus would not return in the foreseeable future. For Ahmedinejad, populist expectations surrounding an imminent Return (an attitude described as 'deviant' by conservative clerics) serves to boost his presidential ambitions.

At the heart of this debate lies the problem of legitimacy, based, as Dabashi sees it, on a long tradition in which the revolutionary impulses born of historical dispossession compete with compulsive anxieties about social behaviour:

> The more volatile, unstable and impulsive the charismatic outbursts of revolutionary movements in Shi'ism have been throughout its medieval and modern history, because of its traumatic origin, the more precisely the exactitude of the Shi'i law has sought to regulate, to the minutest details, the affairs of Shi'i believers – from their rituals of bodily purity to the dramaturgical particulars of their communal gatherings, to their political suspicions of anyone's claim to legitimate authority.

Paradoxically the notion of having been wronged by the existing powers, which lies at the heart of Sh'ism, contributes to the notion that 'The veracity of the faith remains legitimate only so far as it is combative and speaks truth to power, and (conversely) almost instantly loses that legitimacy when it actually comes to power.'

A logical resolution, of course, would be a formal separation of power between religion and state, where the religious leadership 'speaks truth to power' without exercising executive authority. Such was the position of the clerical class during the regime of the Pahlavi shahs and for the most part under their Qajar predecessors. There existed what Said Amir

Arjomand has called an 'unspoken concordat' with the clerical establishment refraining from criticising the dynasty's policies. Later, even though the clerics led the famous tobacco boycott against business concessions made to foreign entrepreneurs, leading to the Constitutional Revolution of 1906–11, the majority of the *ulama* had no objection to the replacement of the Qajars by the Pahlavis in 1925. As Heinz Halm, a leading German scholar of Shi'ism, observes: 'the preservation of a monarchy in traditional form seemed most likely to offer them a guarantee that there would be no lay experiments such as those in Turkey'.

It was Khomeini who radically upset this 'de facto' concordat with his doctrine of Vilayet-e-Faqih – the 'Guardianship of the Jurisconsult' – whereby the Supreme Leader and the Guardian Council appointed by him approve parliamentary candidates and have a veto on legislation (as well as control over elements of the armed forces) in competition with the elected president. This struggle, as I see it, is the direct consequence of Zubaida's 'contradictory duality' of sovereignties. Dabashi sees it in broader terms:

> *What I believe is happening in Iran today begins with the simple fact that … the ruling Shi'ism has lost its moral legitimacy. It has lost it by simply being in power and trying in vain to remain in power by maiming and murdering its own people.*

If Dabashi had restricted himself to a political and theological analysis, his thesis would be interesting enough, but his ambitions are much wider. As he explains in his preface, part of his book charts a 'major epistemic shift' in Shi'ism, from doctrinal issues arising out of historical events to artistic manifestations of the faith, including literature and architecture:

> *At the heart of Shi'ism as a religion of protest written into the fabric of the history that it occupies, is the miasmatic manner of its inconspicuous transmutation into alternative modes of resignifying itself, of sublating itself, of speaking in a multitude of languages.*

The question that arises is how such a comprehensive vision of the faith can retain its distinctive Shi'ite labelling, since many of the features Dabashi delineates could be described, more broadly, as 'Islamic', or more specifically as distinctly Persian or Iranian. He writes eloquently about four of the masters of Persian literature – Nasir Khusraw (1004–c.1088), whom he sees as being a Shi'a revolutionary activist 'of uncommon convictions and determination'; the great mystic Jalal al-Din Rumi (1307–1273), founder of the Mehlevi order of dervishes; and the poet Sa'di (1184–1291). He sees these Persian writers as the forerunners of a literary tradition that culminates in the lyrics of the great Hafez (c.1320–89), who gave 'Anyone who was fortunate enough to be born after him an expansive universe, much as Bach, Mozart and Beethoven mapped out the topography of the emotive cosmos of European philosophers and mystics.'

These major figures, he acknowledges, transcend sectarian affiliations, just as the great composers he cites reach out beyond the Lutheran or Catholic traditions in which they were raised: 'When we remember them we scarce know or care if they are Sunni or Shi'a, nor does it matter.' In line with this approach, he argues that Shi'ism is not so much a sect or minority tradition of Islam, but a comprehensive and variegated version of the entire faith. It is 'the dream/nightmare of Islam itself as it goes about the world, a promise made yet undelivered to itself and the world'. Yet it is also the 'hidden soul of Islam, its sigh of relief from its own grievances against a world ill at ease with what it is'. This comprehensive vision of the faith can perhaps be accommodated with his earlier statement that Shi'ism is 'morally triumphant when politically defiant but morally fails when it politically succeeds' (a formulation that may also be true of Catholicism, whose direct political interventions are often disastrous, as in Franco's Spain). Yet this view of Shi'ism as a counter-cultural moral force or conscience embedded in Islam at its roots seems to contradict his historical account of Safavid Persia, which he sees as the apotheosis of Islamic civilisation, when variegated elements of Shi'ism merged triumphantly in the 'paradoxical panning out of what was now a state majority religion with an enduring minority complex'.

The Safavids, who ruled Persia and the adjoining lands between 1500 and the 1730s, made Shi'ism the state religion. According to Dabashi, they succeeded in integrating the mystical and practical dimensions of Islam on Shi'ite foundations while maintaining a philosophical approach consonant with the idea of God as the cosmic intellect or ultimate consciousness encompassing both being and essence. Dabashi sees the architectural splendour of Isfahan, the Safavid capital, as the material expression of an intellectual spirit comparable to that achieved by Western Christendom on the eve of the Enlightenment. For him, the magnificent piazza known as the Meydan-e Naqsh-e Jahan (Image of the World Square) corresponds to Immanuel Kant's vision of a vast and vital public space. It opened the way for 'reason to become public, for intellect to leave the royal courts and the sanctity of mosques alike and to enter and face the urban polity of a whole new conception of a people'.

The philosophical correlative of this great physical monument is the work of Mulla Sadra of Shiraz (1571–1640). His metaphysical ontology, building on Gnostic, mystical and rational insights of earlier Islamic thinkers, asserts the primacy of being over essence, with reality conceived as a single homogeneous continuum. Mulla Sadra's system still holds sway in Qom and other centres of Shi'ite learning. It challenges the presumption that there is a knowable reality 'out there' distinct from the knowing subject. No conceptual barrier exists between the subject and the object: the knowing subject and the known object are ontologically indistinguishable – an approach that confers validity on non-empirical happenings such as visions and revelations. As Hossein Ziai has observed, Mulla Sadra's system embraces 'the primacy of practical reason over theoretical science … "Living" sages in every era are thought to determine what "scientific" attitude the society must have, upholding and renewing the foundations using their own individual, experiential and subjective knowledge' (*New Cambridge History of Islam*, Vol. 5, p. 569).

As Dabashi sees it, Mulla Sadra's vision has contemporary relevance, as it challenges the distinction often made between 'good' Muslim philosophers and 'bad' Muslim revolutionaries:

> *Islamic intellectual history does not allow for such bifurcations, for there the most serene, sedate and sophisticated philosophers, safely tucked away at the comfortable court of kings, caliphs and conquerors, seem to have a running dialogue with rabblerousing rebels, sleepless and wounded in the remote battlefields of history.*

Tragically, in Dabashi's view, the Safavid vision of the public space as a forum for reasoned discourse succumbed to the 'hungry wolves' of Afghan invaders, imperial rivalries between Russians and Ottomans, and the colonial machinations of the French and British. Internal forces of dissolution also played their part, with raw tribalism replacing the vigorous cosmopolitan public culture the Safavids had striven to create. By the end of the eighteenth century, Shi'ite Iran had returned to forms of tribal governance, along with a restored religious scholasticism.

The triumph of nomadic tribalism under the Qajar dynasty that endured from 1795 until 1925 'necessitated a clerical class of turbaned jurists and their feudal scholasticism to shore up its precarious legitimacy'. This historic regression, according to Dabashi, was exacerbated by the doctrinal victory of the Usuli school of jurists (who use independent reasoning in their judgments) over the Akhbaris, who were more bound by precedent. On the face of it, Dabashi's view appears counter-intuitive, since the use of independent reasoning would seem to allow more room for individual initiative and public reason. But in the context of a renewed tribalism harking back to the pre-Safavid era, the victory of the Usuli jurists served to enhance clerical authority at the expense of the public and cosmopolitan aspects of Shi'ism that had been encouraged by the Safavid state. In effect, the clerical establishment made a deal with the nomadic rulers, using its authority to bolster their claims to rulership in exchange for clerical privileges. An inward-looking, xenophobic clerical establishment, obsessed with the issues of purity and pollution, became the guardians of tradition and bearers of popular identity, a process enhanced by defensive responses to Russian and Ottoman territorial encroachments, and later to the pressures arising from growing European power.

Dabashi is fascinated, not just by the intellectual and political ramifications of this process – the rise of Khomeini, the fall of the Shah and the establishment of the Islamic republic – but what might be called its manifestations in the Shi'a psyche. In exploring this landscape, he acknowledges the influence of his teacher and mentor, Philip Rieff (1922–2006), author of *The Triumph of the Therapeutic* and a major interpreter of Freud.

According to Rieff, the neurotic symptoms Freud identified in his patients were a reflection of the decline of traditional moralities: as the anchors of religion were loosened, instinctive desires became less easy to control. Freud's solution was to provide his patients with a technique that would enable individuals to manage their instinctual lives in a prudent and rational manner. The flaw in Freud's atheistic approach – according to Rieff – lay in his failure to recognise that the underpinnings of the repressive myths that inform human action lie in a supra-empirical or transcendental source of authority – namely, the sacred.

In Rieff's view, authority rooted in the sacred infuses our creativity with the guilt without which we cannot manage our instinctive impulses. Desire and limitation, eros and authority, are intimately connected. The tension between them provides the energy for all artistic endeavours. Yet if we deconstruct them by unmasking, as it were, the secret police, as therapists would have us do, our culture will lose its vigour. 'A culture without repression, if it could exist,' Rieff wrote in a passage cited by Dabashi, 'would kill itself in closing the distance between any desire and its object. Everything thought or felt would be done, on the instant … In a word, culture is repressive.'

Adopting an approach that builds on Rieff's ideas, Dabashi proceeds to analyse two works by well-known Iranian artists. In *Close-up* (1990), Abbas Kiarostami created a film about an actual person – Hossein Sabzian

– who in real life impersonated the celebrated activist turned film-maker, Mohsen Makhmalbaf. In making his film, Kiarostami has Sabzian re-enact this real episode for the camera. The film, according to Dabashi, is driven by 'the aesthetics of formalised representation': Kiarostami plays with the irony or double-mirror effect of having a real person playing himself in a fictional re-creation of an actual event. Any possible political implications are left unexplored. Dabashi sees Kiarostami's film as exemplifying the deep cultural split or bifurcation within Shi'ism between art and politics, with art disengaged from politics, and politics assuming

> *an increasingly one-sided ideological disposition, banking almost exclusively on the feudal scholasticism at its roots at the heavily expensive cost of denying, rejecting, or destroying its non-juridical heritage – from philosophical and mystical to literary, poetic, performative and visual.*

In contrast to *Close-Up*, Dabashi finds a redemptive grace and a 'singular act of visual piety' in *Tuba* (2002), a video installation by the artist Shirin Neshat. In this work, the face of a woman fades on to a perfectly matched landscape of rocky hills, and pilgrims stop at the threshold of a sacred space before transgressing, or desecrating, its boundaries. Dabashi's lengthy description traces the archaeology of Neshat's installation, from its ambiguous origin in a Qur'anic phrase, by way of its elaboration in early commentaries, to a Gnostic invocation of a female deity and vanishing paradise in the novel *Tuba and the Meaning of Night* (1988) by Shahrnush Parsipour. His commentary suggests that the psychic split afflicting Shi'ism, between the scholasticism of the ayatollahs and the aesthetic formalism he lamented in his critique of Kiarostami, may only be temporary. In a typically Rieffian passage, he writes that while a culture may fancy itself to be 'secular', 'its sacred memories are nevertheless busy thinking its ideas and populating its dreams'.

An American-Iranian well known for his hostility to Israel and America's Middle East policies, Dabashi makes no concessions. He attacks Seyyed Vali Nasser, author of the popular *Shia Revival*, for being a 'native informant', who reduces the 'multifaceted, polyvocal, worldly, transnational and cosmopolitan culture of Shi'ism' to a 'one-sided, divisive and sectarian system', a perspective that serves to 'facilitate the U.S. military domination of a strategic area', while confirming the Shi'ite religious class in their 'belligerent clericalism'. In the case of Noah Feldman, legal adviser to Paul Bremer, whom he accuses of writing sectarianism into the Iraqi Constitution, his criticism seems misplaced, particularly in view of the nuanced lengths to which Feldman has gone in arguing against 'imposed constitutionalism'.

A larger criticism of the book lies in Dabashi's failure to address Shi'ism as comprehensively as his project demands. For example, while he celebrates the Ismaili variant of Shi'ism in the work of Nasir Khusraw, he is silent on the survival of this tradition for nearly a millennium in the Pamir Mountains of Central Asia (now Tajikistan) followed by seven decades of communist rule. He is also silent on the remarkable spread of Ismailism in South Asia (mainly Sindh, Gujarat and Mumbai). With its unique language and literature, for which the Khoja Ismailis of India invented a special language and script, and its genius for translating Hindu concepts and symbols into the Islamic religious vernacular, Ismailism may be seen as a significant inheritor of the Safavid version of Shi'ism that Dabashi admires. An impressive model of an enlightenment tendency within the Islamic fold, Ismailis are engaging creatively with contemporary architectural practice, commerce, public health, women's rights, social empowerment and a range of contemporary concerns, not just in the developing world, but in Europe and North America.

I suspect that Dabashi neglects this quiet Islamic revolution because it does not fit his theme of a tragic bifurcation between artistic creativity and juridical scholasticism that afflicted Iranian Shi'ism in the post-Safavid era. As a Shi'ite minority living in the diaspora but with a strong centralised leadership, the Ismailis have preserved the integrity of their tradition while advancing public engagement with the countries in which they reside. They have achieved this by running with the flow of political power – with the British in India, East Africa and Canada; with the Portuguese in Southern Africa; with the Soviets in Central Asia; and – until the current crisis – with their former Alawi rivals in Syria. Dabashi's somewhat cliché-ridden, anti-imperialist model is based essentially on Iranian historical experience. It would have to be modified considerably if he were able to accommodate the Ismaili story of social and educational advance, business success and significant cultural achievements.

On balance, however, his swipes at academic colleagues, unfair or ill-judged as they sometimes appear, are the obverse of a generous and comprehensive vision, not just of Shi'ism, but of a reality that transcends any neat or limiting categorisation of 'Islam' as a distinct field of reference. In pursuit of this vision he combines his meditations on Islamic culture with an impressive grasp of Western thinkers (including Hegel, Nietzsche, Marx, Weber and Habermas), and above all of Freud, as refracted through the important but neglected prism of Philip Rieff. His extraordinarily rich and powerful book takes Shi'ism out of the sectarian ghettos to where it was largely confined when it became an ideological weapon of the Persian empire in its rivalry with the Sunni Ottomans. By emancipating Shi'ism from its instrumental use by the Islamic Republic of Iran, he has performed a vital cultural – and political – service to his readers.

Published in *The New York Review of Books*, 22 December 2011.

The book reviewed was:

Hamid Dabashi (2011) *Shi'ism: A Religion of Protest*. Cambridge, MA: Harvard University Press.

Part **Five**

Islam in the West

This section deals primarily with books about Muslims living in Western countries, and the problems posed both for Muslims as minorities and for the host communities, especially in Europe. These essays were written before the atrocities in Oslo and the island of Utøya in Norway committed by Anders Behring Breivik, a right-wing extremist, who killed 77 people in the course of a terrorist rampage in July 2011. It is clear, however, that Breivik – whose victims were all Norwegians, and most of them young Social Democrats at their summer camp – was influenced in part by the anti-Muslim rhetoric issuing from right-wing commentators such as Robert Spencer, Daniel Pipes and Pamela Geller in the USA, Geert Wilders in the Netherlands, Bat Ye'or (Giselle Littman) and Melanie Phillips in Britain. All these writers – most of whom have denounced the Utøya massacre in the most unequivocal terms – subscribe to variants of the thesis that Europe is sleepwalking into cultural disaster or (in the case of Phillips) enabling Islamist terrorists to gain a foothold.

The first of these articles, 'The Big Muslim Problem', exposes the critique of Christopher Caldwell, a more nuanced voice than those of Spencer, Pipes, Wilders and Phillips, but one that basically sings to the same tune. I juxtapose this with the high-minded rhetoric of Tariq Ramadan, whom I challenge for failing to address the specific charges of evasiveness and 'double talk' levelled at him by his critics. Moving across the Atlantic, I contrast Daniel Pipes' hysterical approach to the dangers posed by Muslims with the much more measured and empirically-based studies of Yvonne Haddad and other genuine scholars. The piece concludes with the perfect antidote to Islamophobia, Robert Dannin's Black Pilgrimage to Islam – a book that explains how conversion to Islam serves the legions of African-Americans who find themselves caught up in the USA's disgraceful prison system.

The remaining articles celebrate two important books published in the 1990s, by Philip Lewis and Olivier Roy. Roy is a prolific scholar, an expert on Afghanistan and Central Asia, and his critique of political Islam as an inept and incoherent ideology has never been refuted. Though my endorsement of his thesis may seem premature at a time when Islamists are making gains at the polls in Tunisia and Egypt, I am minded to stick to my guns: the fact that Islamists in Tunisia – and to a lesser degree Egypt – are looking to the Turkish model is suggestive of an evolution away from Islamism and towards institutional forms of constitutional democracy, where parties with Islamic roots find themselves locked into rule-based, organised systems of power. If this transpires (and perhaps I am being over-optimistic) the older Islamist project of a 'state ruled by God', along the lines suggested by Sayyid Qutb in his writings, may be moribund, if not yet actually dead. This part of the book also includes a retrospective look at the Rushdie Affair 20 years after the publication of The Satanic Verses *galvanised Britain's Muslims into action, and 'Made in the USA', an essay suggesting that the bizarre theology of the Nation of Islam is rather more American than Islamic.*

21
Europe's Muslim Problem

In April 1968, two weeks after the riots in US cities that followed the assassination of Martin Luther King Jr, the British Tory politician Enoch Powell (who as minister of health between 1960 and 1963 had presided over the large-scale recruitment of nursing and health staff from Britain's former colonies) predicted that a similar destiny was facing Britain. He said:

> We must be mad, literally mad, as a nation, to be permitting the annual inflow of some 50,000 dependents who are for the most part the material of the future growth of the immigrant-descended population. It is like watching a nation busily engaged in heaping up its own funeral pyre.

Quoting a phrase of Virgil's that was to resonate famously down the decades, he warned: 'I seem to see "the River Tiber foaming with much blood".'

Though the Tory party leader Edward Heath immediately fired him from his post as opposition spokesman on defence, Powell's speech had struck a powerful chord. Within ten days he had received more than 100,000 letters of support, with only 800 expressing disagreement. In London, more than 1,000 dockworkers went on strike in protest at his dismissal. Anxiety about immigration was a significant factor in the unexpected victory that restored the Conservative Party to power in 1970.

Powell, who died in 1998, has been castigated as a racist and condemned, not to say vilified, by the liberal left; but as Christopher Caldwell argues in his provocatively titled book, *Reflections on the Revolution in Europe: Immigration, Islam and the West*, his demographic predictions have proved to be remarkably accurate. In one of his speeches he shocked his audience by predicting that Britain's non-white population of barely a million would reach 4.5 million by 2002: according to the office of national statistics, the size of Britain's 'ethnic minority' population actually reached 4.6 million in 2001. His predictions for the ethnic composition of major cities such as Wolverhampton, Birmingham and Inner London were similarly on target.

Britain's Commission for Racial Equality predicted that, by 2011, Leicester would be the first major British city with a non-white majority.

This pattern is being replicated in cities throughout Western Europe. According to Caldwell, Europe is now a 'continent of migrants', with more than 10 per cent of its people living outside their countries of birth. The figure includes both non-European immigrants and citizens of countries belonging to the enlarged European Union, who are permitted to move freely within its territory. But it also includes a substantial body of immigrants – namely Muslims – who Caldwell regards as posing 'the most acute problems' because of their religion (an issue never mentioned by Powell in his speeches).

The statistics are highly variable, since many countries do not register the religion of their citizens. However, it is generally assumed that there are now upwards of 13 million Muslims, and possibly as many as 20 million (Caldwell's preferred figure), living in the European Union. The largest concentrations are in France, with more than 5 million, Germany with around 3 million, Britain with 1.6 million, Spain with a million and the Netherlands and Bulgaria with just under a million. Overall, the proportion of Muslims now residing in the European Union (including the indigenous Bulgarian Muslims) remains at 5 per cent, a proportion twice that of the 'nearly 7 million American Muslims' mentioned by President Obama in his Cairo University speech in June 2009.

Individual cities, however, have much higher concentrations. Karoly Lorant, a Hungarian economist who wrote a paper for the European Parliament, calculates that Muslims already make up 25 per cent of the population in Marseilles and Rotterdam, 20 per cent in Malmo, 15 per cent in Brussels and Birmingham, and 10 per cent in London, Paris and Copenhagen. If the French national figure of around 5 million were reproduced in the USA, it would make for 40 million American Muslims. Moreover, given that immigrant Muslims have a higher birth rate than indigenous white Europeans or other immigrant groups such as Eastern Europeans or African-Caribbeans, that population seems set to increase, regardless of the tighter controls on immigration now being imposed by governments. The US National Intelligence Council expects that by 2025 the Muslim population of Europe will have doubled.

In the first part of his book, Caldwell takes some Enoch Powell-like swipes at the policies – or lack of them – that allowed this situation to develop. In the aftermath of the Second World War, European countries overestimated the need for immigrant labour. Instead of investing in new technology, they drove down labour costs – and undermined the power of the labour unions – by importing cheap workers without regard for the social and cultural consequences. Caldwell challenges the assumptions of economists who argue that immigrants increase the national wealth. With old industries such as textiles already in decline, immigrant workers merely delayed the necessary process of restructuring. In macroeconomic terms, the wealth they generate is nugatory – approximately one three-hundredth of the advanced countries' output. In any case, much of the supposed added value contributed by immigrant businesses that appears in economic statistics is absorbed in the cost of accommodating them in their new environment, or is sent back home. In 2003, for example, Moroccans living in Europe sent home €3.6 billion ($4.1 billion) in remissions.

The picture Caldwell paints is complex, paradoxical and sometimes at variance with the anti-immigration thrust of his argument. While he dwells on the obvious points of political and cultural dystopia – the terrorist outrages in London and Madrid, the riots in the Paris *banlieues*, the growing Muslim prison populations, and the horrors of unreconstructed patriarchy in the shape of 'honour killings', systemic homophobia and the bizarre medical procedure of the 'hymen repair operation' that allows young women to recover lost virginities – he also acknowledges some of the positive contributions that immigrants are making to society. In the case of Italy, for example, he observes that the country's food and its superb urban landscape – features that lie at the heart of its attractions at the centre of European culture – are largely sustained by immigrants:

> Italy has lately received more than half a million immigrants a year from Africa and the Middle East, mostly to work in its farms, shops and restaurants. The market price of certain kinds of Italian produce, so farmers say, is in danger of falling below the cost of bringing it to market. Under conditions of globalisation, Italy's real comparative advantage may lie elsewhere than in agriculture, in some high-tech economic model that is remunerative but not particularly 'Italian' …
>
> Traditional ways of working the land may be viable only if there are immigrants there to work it. You can make similar arguments about traditional Italian restaurants, which in the present economy may be able to hold their own against soulless chains only with the help of low-paid immigrant labour. Ditto the country's lovely public parks, which have traditionally required dozens of gardeners, a level of manpower that the country's shrinking population cannot supply, except at a high price …
>
> Some natives may feel 'swamped' by the demographic change, but immigration though not ideal, may be the most practical way

> *of keeping Italy looking like Italy. As the novelist Giuseppe di Lampedusa once wrote, 'If we want everything to stay the same, everything must change.'*

Caldwell does not suggest that the paradox of foreigners 'keeping Italy looking like Italy' is necessarily unsustainable. His concern is that the majority of migrants belong to a religion that a sceptical, post-Enlightenment Europe cannot be expected to contain or resist. The level of Muslim immigration is unprecedented. Whereas in the past groups of immigrants – 'Jewish and Huguenot refugees, a few factory hands from Poland or Ireland or Italy' – were 'big enough to enrich the lands of settlement, but not so big as to threaten them', the sheer volume of Muslim immigration endangers the indigenous cultures of Europe, not least because those cultures have become precariously fragile. Political correctness, anti-racism and multiculturalism, born of guilt about colonialism and shame about the Holocaust, are eroding national cultures, while failing to produce a coherent vision of a common European identity.

No reasonable person would deny that there are problems with some of Europe's immigrant communities, or that multiculturalism challenges traditional boundaries separating citizenship from ideas centred on loyalty, identity and allegiance. For the late Sir Bernard Crick, George Orwell's biographer and a leading educator, 'Britishness' is a legal and political structure that excludes culture: 'When an immigrant says "I am British", he is not saying he wants to be English, Scottish or Welsh.' As Caldwell comments:

> *This was the EU model of belonging: you are one person for your culture and another for the law. You can be an official (legal) European, even if you are not a 'real' (cultural) European. This disaggregation of the personal personality and the legal personality sounds tolerant and liberating, but it has its downside. Rights are attached to citizenship. As soon as your citizenship becomes a legal construction, so do your rights.*

In Caldwell's view, immigrants to Europe are able to exploit their rights, not just as citizens, but also as residents, by claiming the health and welfare benefits to which natives are entitled: 'The postwar Western European welfare states provided the most generous benefits ever given to workers anywhere'; Germany's social market was the archetype of the systems replicated across Western Europe, with short working hours, seven-week holidays, full health coverage and rates for unionised workers reaching the equivalent of almost $50 an hour. While, unlike some other countries, Germany's *jus sanguinis* denied full citizenship to immigrant workers, who were mainly from Turkey and Morocco, the economic effects were ultimately the same.

The welfare burden impeded investment, stifling real risk-based entrepreneurship, epitomised by the 'small, flexible start-up companies that drove most of the innovation in recent decades', especially in the information economy. The USA, by contrast, is less indulgent: here, contrary to the myth of American openness, immigrants are pressured to conform. An immigrant may maintain his ancestral culture, but 'if it is a culture that prevents him from speaking English properly or showing up to work promptly, he will go hungry. Then he will go home'.

In Caldwell's vision, Europe's welfare states have been succouring alien intruders: as the native population grows in age and declines in proportion to immigrants, so the value they add to the 'social market' economy by working for its welfare systems is eroded by their claims on benefits. In Spain, for example, the Harvard economist Martin Feldstein has predicted that the ratio of workers to retirees, currently rated at 4.5:1, will fall to 2:1 by 2050. In Britain, the Office of National Statistics predicts a population increase of 10 million – two-thirds of them immigrants or their children – over the next quarter century, with the number of people aged 85 and over expected to double. For Caldwell, the short-term relief that immigrants bring to the welfare state is unlikely to match their longer-term claims on it:

> In the extremely short run, a baby bust such as Europe has undergone can enhance living standards, because it reduces the number of dependents per worker. But in the longer run a reckoning awaits, and the longer run has arrived.

The most egregious examples of Caldwell's aliens are Muslims, because, as he sees it, they are less susceptible to European cultural influences than are other immigrant groups such as Slavs, Sikhs, Hindus, non-Muslim Africans and African-Caribbeans. He flatly ignores evidence produced by numerous scholars, such as Aziz al-Azmeh, Tariq Modood, Philip Lewis and Jytte Klausen, that Muslim identities are shifting to meet changing circumstances, that the majority of younger British Muslims, for example, 'share many aspects of popular youth culture with their non-Muslim peers', and that their problem is not so much with the majority culture as with 'traditionally-minded parents who seek, usually unsuccessfully, to limit their access to it'.

Caldwell pours scorn on writers who emphasise the diversity of the Islamic traditions in Europe. 'For all its pleasing glibness,' he says, 'this harping on diversity is misguided.' His reading of Islam takes an essentialist perspective of a primordial religion impervious to change, as if he were oblivious of the way that essentialist views of religion have long been under sustained intellectual attack. No one remotely familiar with the work of scholars such as Aziz al-Azmeh (who ruminates on the diversities of 'Islams' and 'modernities') or the political scientist, Jytte Klausen, whose brilliant work on European Muslims investigates emerging hermeneutics and epistemologies of faith, would dismiss them, as Caldwell does, as 'glib'. Al-Azmeh and his colleagues provide plenty of support to refute 'the cliché', as al-Azmeh writes, 'of a homogenous collectivity innocent of modernity, cantankerously or morosely obsessed with prayer, fasting, veiling, medieval social and penal arrangements', while Klausen has demonstrated convincingly that European Muslims are overwhelmingly hostile to extremism, support democratic processes, accept the duties of citizenship, and are evolving distinctively local styles of Muslim identity.

Nor does Caldwell exhibit any familiarity with the rich literature describing the spread of Islam in peripheral cultures such as Sub-Saharan Africa or South Asia, where a religion originating in Arabia proved every bit as adept as Christianity in adjusting to local conditions. He has similarly failed to familiarise himself, even superficially, with the vast literature charting the encounter between Islam and modern Western society. In his review of Western attitudes towards Islam he prefers to celebrate the prejudices of writers such as Ernest Renan (in 1883) or Hilaire Belloc (in 1938) than to engage with significant Muslim thinkers such as Muhammad Iqbal, Fazlur Rahman, Mohammed Arkoun or Abdullahi an-Na'im who might challenge his essentialist assumptions. Caldwell's 'Islam' owes more to tabloid headlines than to responsible research. To borrow a phrase of Philip Lewis, it exemplifies the need for greater religious literacy in the post-9/11 era.

Nevertheless, in arguing that 'Europe became a multiethnic society in a fit of absence of mind', Caldwell makes some useful points. European societies have yet to find satisfactory ways of institutionalising Islam within their national polities. This is partly a result of the fragmentary and contested nature of Islamic spiritual authority, in which (with the partial exception of Shi'ism) no formal priesthood stands between the individual and a God who reveals Himself in texts that are subject to a wide variety of interpretations.

Umbrella bodies intended to act as interlocutors with governments, such as the Muslim Council of Britain (MCB) and the French Council for the Muslim Faith (CFCM), are rejected by many Muslims for being too political, or not political enough, or simply not representative of people who may be difficult to represent, or may not want to be represented as 'Muslims'. It is clear that, as a religion formulated during an era of political ascendancy, the mainstream traditions of Islam have yet to find comfortable moorings as minorities in the contested public spaces of a secular, pluralist West.

Two-thirds of the imams in France live on welfare, as do a similar number in Britain. The majority are foreign-born and trained, and have received little instruction in European culture or its values. A small number of them have been exposed in the press as 'preachers of hate'. The funding of European mosques and Islamic institutions from ultra-conservative countries should be a real cause for concern: in France, for example, the Union of Islamic Organisations (UIOF) – an umbrella group of doctrinaire Muslim youth organisations linked to the Muslim Brotherhood – gets a quarter of its annual budget from Saudi Arabia, the United Arab Emirates, Kuwait and other foreign donors.

The British laissez-faire model of leaving immigrant communities to manage themselves has allowed extremism to flourish in all sorts of complex ways. Missionary organisations such as the Tablighi Jamaat, known for its piety and declared abhorrence of politics, nevertheless encourage a separatist spirit in which extremism can be incubated: most of the men convicted in September 2008 for plotting to blow up transatlantic airliners using liquid explosives smuggled in soft-drink bottles had connections with the Tablighi Jamaat, as did two of the suicide bombers who murdered 52 people in the London transport system in July 2005.

Paradoxically, even marriage can be an agent of radicalisation: whereas the first generation of migrants' children pleased their parents by marrying cousins imported from Pakistan or Bangladesh (thereby swelling immigrant numbers), their children's insistence on marrying Muslim partners of their choice is leading to the creation of a Muslim identity that transcends the older patterns of 'encapsulated' settlement based on differences of region, culture, language and biradiri (extended family networks).

This novel pan-Islamic identity both feeds on and contributes to the perceived hostility of the host society: the Rushdie agitation in 1989, the row over the 'insult' to Islam conveyed by the Danish newspaper *Jyllands-Posten* in publishing a cartoon showing Muhammad with a terrorist bomb as his turban, the marches in France protesting the headscarf ban in schools, the riots of youth in Parisian suburbs, and episodes of Islamophobia reported on Al Jazeera television or in the Muslim press, all contribute to the sense of an embattled community that is also flexing its collective communitarian muscles.

Despite the legal, institutional and cultural differences of the European host cultures in which Muslim immigrants find themselves, the narrative that Caldwell extrapolates from a complicated web of data points in an alarming direction. The bottom line is that Islam is a religion of believers. Most Europeans are not only sceptical, but – as heirs to the Enlightenment – they regard religious scepticism as being essential to their outlook and identity 'as part of the essence of European-ness'. He writes:

> *A fast-shrinking population of several hundred million Europeans lives north of the Mediterranean, while a fast-growing population of several hundred million lives south of it, with a desire to take up residence in Europe that seems unshakable. What is more a certain part of it is dedicated to Europe's destruction by armed violence …*
>
> *Europe's basic problem with Islam, and with immigration more generally, is that the strongest communities in Europe are, culturally speaking, not European communities at all. This problem exists in all European countries, despite a broad variety of measures taken to solve it – multiculturalism in Holland, laïcité in France, benign neglect in Britain, constitutional punctiliousness in Germany. Clearly Europe's problem is with Islam and with immigration, and not with specific misapplications of specific means set up to manage them. Islam is a magnificent religion that has also been, at times over the centuries, a glorious and generous culture. But all cant to the contrary, it is in no sense Europe's religion and it is in no sense Europe's culture.*

Impressive though Caldwell may appear in marshalling a disparate army of sources (ranging from government statistics, social surveys and think-tank reports, to novels and newspaper stories in eight or more languages), the impression he gives is spurious and not supported by real evidence. He selects a multitude of facts or quotations that support his central premise of a 'believing' Islam pitted against a doubting or sceptical Europe. This conclusion, however, is not supported by surveys of actual religious behaviour. While the figures – and methodologies used to arrive at them – vary considerably, the conclusion to which they point is that Muslims do not differ greatly in religious behaviour from other Europeans. For example, a French study in 2001 found that only 10 per cent of Muslims were religiously observant. A study by the demographer Michèle Tribalat in the same year found that 60 per cent of French Muslim men and 70 per cent of women were 'not observant', though the great majority respected 'cultural attachments' by abstaining from eating pork or drinking alcohol and by fasting during Ramadan. Caldwell mentions none of this work.

The failures in this book are not limited to its flawed and biased research. A troubling example of Caldwell's method involves the misuse of translation in order to further his argument that, unlike other religious traditions, Islam cannot be assimilated into European culture. In an extended critique of the work of Tariq Ramadan, the charismatic and articulate advocate of a distinctive European Islam, Caldwell argues that Ramadan's project for Muslim integration into European societies is basically asymmetrical:

> *The integration of Muslims into Europe will happen on Muslim terms. Or, as Ramadan puts it, 'It will succeed when Muslims find in their tradition elements of agreement with the laws of the countries in which they are citizens, because that will resolve any questions of double allegiance.' This is an extraordinary statement: Only when Europe's ways are understood as Islam's will Muslims obey them.*

The word Ramadan uses in the original French text of this quotation is not 'tradition', but *'références'*. 'References' in this context sounds slightly odd in English, but 'tradition' is too comprehensive, tipping the semantic scale towards inassimilable Muslims. A better translation might be 'sources'. This is not splitting hairs. As Ramadan explains in *What I Believe*, in which he defends himself against charges of 'doublespeak', the idea of 'reference' is fundamental to his approach: 'Adapting one's level of speech to one's audience, or adapting the nature of one's references, is not doublespeak ... To avoid doublespeak, what matters is that the substance of the discourse does not change.'

Ramadan writes that his most distinguished defender, the philosopher Charles Taylor, exonerates him from the charge of 'doublespeak', arguing, as Ramadan puts it, that his 'discourse is clear between two highly ambiguous universes of reference'. Ramadan's aim is to 'build bridges' between these two universes. As a Muslim scholar and intellectual he applies the discipline of *ijtihad* (interpretative reasoning), an Arabic term which has the same root as *jihad* (moral striving) – a word that is often translated, too restrictively, as 'holy war'.

Ramadan presents his new book, *What I Believe*, as 'a work of clarification, a deliberately accessible presentation of the basic ideas I have been defending for more than twenty years'. The ground is broadly the same as that covered in two books of his previously reviewed in these pages. There I argued that Ramadan's belief that Islam can avoid the processes of secularisation that afflicted Christendom after the Reformation was flawed by his failure to accommodate the tragic narrative of Shi'ism and his failure to recognise that the institutionalisation of religious differences – a prerequisite for religious peace among Muslims – would ipso facto initiate a process of secularisation.

In a chapter on 'Interacting Crises', Ramadan addresses some of the issues that Caldwell raises in his book: the Muslim presence in the West, he says, should not just be seen and engaged with as a problem of religions, values and cultures, but also as a psychological one. It is not just Muslims who face challenging issues of self-identification. 'Western societies in general and Europeans in particular are experiencing a very deep, multidimensional identity crisis' flowing from the double effects of globalisation and supranationalism. Everywhere, landmarks of national identity and cultural memory are being eroded, and the presence of immigrants adds to feelings of confusion.

While ageing populations need immigrants to sustain their economies, the incomers threaten ideas of cultural homogeneity that are already endangered by globalisation and the revolution in communications. Europeans are trapped in an irreversible logic. Economic necessities are in conflict with the cultural forces around which European identities accrue. Muslims living in the West face similar predicaments. Their identity crisis generates anxiety, leading them towards attitudes of 'withdrawal and self-isolation'.

A 'Manifesto for a New "We"', with which Ramadan concludes his book, urges European Muslims to have more confidence 'in themselves, in their values, in their ability to live and to communicate with full serenity in Western societies'. There needs to be 'a revolution in trust' built on the confidence that Muslims must have in their own convictions. Their task must be 'to reappropriate their heritage and to develop toward it a positive yet critical intellectual attitude'. Contra Caldwell, he demands – without qualifications – that Muslims 'respect the laws of the countries in which they reside and to which they must be loyal'.

The tone is lofty, the language high-minded. It is the preacher, rather than the intellectual, who speaks. Ramadan does not stoop to engage directly with his critics. As he grandly writes in his introduction: 'I will not waste my time here trying to defend myself.' This is a pity. The charges of doublespeak against Ramadan are not based only on what he describes as 'double-hearings', malicious, deliberate or otherwise. The claims of his most trenchant critic, the French journalist Caroline Fourest, are specific, detailed and documented, based on the tapes of Ramadan's lectures to youthful Muslim audiences as well as his published writings.

Fourest presents Ramadan as a fundamentalist wolf in reformist clothing, a position at variance with his declared advocacy of a 'critical intellectual attitude' towards Islamic tradition. Most of her charges depend on family links Ramadan refuses to abjure – his maternal grandfather Hasan al-Banna, founder of the Muslim Brotherhood; his Islamist father Said Ramadan; and in particular his brother Hani, a more strident critic than Tariq of 'Europe's atheistic materialism', and who has publicly justified the stoning of adulteresses 'as a punishment' that is also 'a purification'. Tariq, by contrast, notoriously argued in a 2003 televised debate with Nicolas Sarkozy that the penalty of stoning should merely be subject to a 'moratorium' while scholars debated the issue.

Other troubling details that emerge from Fourest's vigilant, even obsessive, trawl through the Ramadan canon include explicit condemnations of Kant and Pascal, and fence-sitting, not to say 'double-talk', on Darwinism. A work published by the Islamist publishing house with which Ramadan is closely associated explicitly denies evolution, while his audiotapes advocate creationism as a 'complementary instruction' to the teaching of evolution in schools. Yet, when asked in a television interview whether he accepted evolutionary theory, he 'preferred to agree', rather than express his true convictions before the general public.

In one sense, Fourest's critique can be seen as reassuring: Ramadan's teachings – on sexuality, evolution and moral behaviour generally – fall into grooves already furrowed by the Christian right. Secularists may abhor any alliance between anti-Enlightenment God-fearers from among Abraham's quarrelsome children, but any such alliance may have an important advantage: it may mask or defuse religious conflicts surrounding the contested symbolic languages that afflict the contemporary world, where ancient certainties clash with what Anthony Giddens usefully calls 'the institutionalisation of doubt'.

Paradoxically, as the sociologist Steve Bruce has pointed out, alliances between clashing fundamentalisms can serve to bridge sectarian divisions. For example, in the early 1970s, when Mormons, conservative Jews and Catholics collaborated over issues such as opposition to the proposed Equal Rights Amendment for women, or abortion, they had to suppress their theological distaste for allies whose religions they regarded as false. While such alliances may have seemed threatening to liberals, and especially to women, they marked a significant step away from fundamentalist certainties, since the different parties were forced to compartmentalise their beliefs, to separate their distinctive religious outlooks and practices from 'the moral crusades which the religion has produced'. Social problems such as the 'binge drinking' and drug abuse that afflict European cities are obvious candidates for collaboration across religious boundaries. In Britain, at least one Orthodox rabbi is working alongside a local imam on such problems.

One of the strongest statements deploring the Danish cartoons came from the Vatican, along with the World Council of Churches, Archbishop Desmond Tutu and the Danish Evangelical Church. While such expressions of 'faith solidarity' may have disturbing implications for the rights of free expression cherished by Europeans, they carry the seeds of longer-term accommodations that are likely to bring the more conservative and isolated strands of Islam into the cultural mainstream. Interdenominational collaboration on any issue is a stage in the process of secularisation, pushing believers towards a recognition of religious pluralism and dethroning particular dogmas as the unique and non-negotiable sources of truth. Ramadan can afford to be more forthright about his fundamentalist views. When defensive religiosity turns into moralising, there is space for social engagement and constructive debate.

Published in *The New York Review of Books*, 17 December 2009.

The books reviewed were:

Christopher Caldwell (2009) *Reflections on the Revolution in Europe: Immigration, Islam and the West.* New York: Doubleday.

Tariq Ramadan (2009) *What I Believe.* New York: Oxford University Press.

Books quoted from:

Aziz al-Azmeh and Effie Fokas (eds) (2007) *Islam in Europe: Diversity, Identity and Influence.* Cambridge, UK: Cambridge University Press, p. 209.

Islamic Foundation (1999) *To Be a European Muslim.* Leicester, UK: The Islamic Foundation.

Caroline Fourest and Denis McShane (2008) *Brother Tariq: The Doublespeak of Tariq Ramadan*, translated by Ioana Wilder and John Atherton. Encounter Books.

Jytte Klausen (2005) *The Islamic Challenge: Politics and Religion in Western Europe.* Oxford, UK: Oxford University Press.

Tariq Ramadan (2003) *Western Muslims and the Fate of Islam.* New York: Oxford University Press.

22

The Muslim's Cell

As America and Britain prepare for war against a Muslim state, difficult questions inevitably arise about the situation facing the millions of Muslims now residing in Western countries. There are now approximately 15 million Muslims permanently resident in Western Europe and North America. During the previous Gulf War, when world opinion and most of the Arab–Muslim world were broadly united in condemning Iraq's invasion of Kuwait – when even Hamas, the Palestinian Islam movement, tacitly backed the US coalition in contrast to Yasser Arafat's support for Saddam Hussein – Egyptians, Syrians, Pakistanis and Saudis fought alongside the Americans. Yet a substantial body of Muslim opinion in Britain and other Western countries still saw Operation Desert Storm as an attack by infidels against a part of the Muslim umma. As the anthropologist, Pnina Werbner, observed, in 1991 the 'Muslim street backed Saddam Hussein, from Karachi to Manchester', creating a 'counter-narrative' or 'resistive reading' which reversed the image of Saddam Hussein as a vicious, tyrannical villain, casting him instead in the role of hero. During the current crisis, when public opinion in Europe and the Arab world is much more divided about the wisdom of attacking Iraq, with anti-American feeling throughout the Muslim world fanned by the George W. Bush administration's apparently unconditional support for Israel, and when far from being seen to threaten its neighbours at present (if not at some hypothetical time in the future) the Iraqi government has lost effective control over two-thirds of its territory, domestic Muslim opinion in the West seems even more likely to side with Saddam. In the event of another war, the alienation and disaffection of Muslims in the West may become a factor to be reckoned with. Though very few commentators appear to have recognised this, it seems likely that France and Germany's reticence in supporting America is connected to the relative size of their domestic Muslim constituencies. With 4 million Muslims, half of whom are citizens, France has more than twice the number of Muslim voters than Britain. In Germany in 1990, before unification made its full impact, Muslim Turks comprised 34 per cent of the country's manufacturing force.

Since most of the material in the three books under review dates from before 11 September 2001 (9/11), the subsequent 'war on terrorism' and its conflation by the hawks Washington and Whitehall with the campaign against Iraq, none deals directly with this second round of the Gulf crisis and its problematic ramifications. Nevertheless, all three provide insights into the course of events that may flow from it, both internationally and domestically.

Reprinted in the aftermath of 9/11, Daniel Pipes' collection of essays exhibits a certain triumphalism. As Judith Miller, the former Middle East correspondent of *The New York Times*, commented, the intemperate, polemical tone of Pipes' writing may be forgiven, since long before the Islamist attack on New York and Washington he had been warning of the dangers of Islamism and was often ridiculed for his pains by Muslim apologists. Miller correctly suggests that it is often Pipes' tone rather than the substance of his writing that raises the hackles of colleagues who have adopted a much more measured approach towards analysing the Islamist phenomenon. Having surveyed much of the same territory (both of us published books on the Rushdie affair), I find myself in agreement with many of Pipes' judgements.

In line with the current Bush administration, which after an unfortunate reference to a 'crusade' against evil has carefully sought to reassure Muslims in America and worldwide that America's 'war against terror' is not directed at them, Pipes distinguishes between traditional, or moderate, Islam 'which seeks to teach humans how to live in accordance with God's will' and militant Islam or Islamism 'which aspires to create a new order'. He shares with many contemporary scholars the view that Islamist fundamentalism is distinctly modern: 'Though anchored in religious creed, militant Islam is a radical utopian movement closer in spirit to other such movements such as communism and fascism than to traditional religion.' He stresses the movement's vicious anti-Semitism (which combines religious Judaeophobia with Nazi ideas imported from Europe) as well as its totalitarian and anti-democratic character. He quotes the notorious statement of Ali Belhadj, the leader of the Algerian Islamic Salvation Front (FIS) before the military intervention that prevented the FIS from winning at the polls, initiating Algeria's costly and bloody civil war: 'When we are in power there will be no more elections because God will be ruling.'

The problem with Pipes' perspective is not so much that it is flawed, but rather that it is not balanced by data that would add depth and complexity to his arguments. The boundary he draws between Islamists and moderates or traditionalists is far too crude. 'The notion of good and bad Islamists has no basis in fact,' he declares, quoting Osmane Bencherif, a former Algerian ambassador to the US. 'It is misguided to distinguish between moderate and extremists Islamists. The goal of all is the same: to construct a pure Islamic state, which is bound to be a theocracy and totalitarian.'

While it is true that Islamism, in common with other fundamentalist movements, contains many unacknowledged borrowings from the secular Jacobin tradition, these borrowings have attached themselves to 'traditionalist' Islam through a seamless web of connections. To take one, obvious, example: the al-Qaeda organisation generally assumed to be responsible for the 9/11 attacks on US embassies in East Africa, the USS *Cole* and other atrocities, may have been spearheaded by modern Islamist ideologues, such as Mohamed Atta, the Egyptian architect who flew American Airlines flight No. 11 into the World Trade Center; but al-Qaeda was protected in Afghanistan by the Taliban, whose theology is rooted in the reforming traditionalism of the Indian Deobandi School. The Taliban's principal sponsors were the fundamentalist governments of Saudi Arabia and the United Arab Emirates, facilitated locally by Pakistan intelligence. Because of its dual provenance, bin Laden's propaganda appeals to a wide spectrum of Muslim constituencies. Basing his pitch initially in the sense of outrage that many traditionally-minded Muslims feel about the presence of 'infidel' US troops in the Arabian peninsula, he has broadened his message to embrace all the major sources of current Muslim discontent, including Palestine, Chechnya and Kashmir, along with the more general anxieties voiced by many 'moderate' Muslims about the corrupting effects of Western consumer capitalism and changing gender relations. Though Pipes is correct in arguing that there has been a politicisation or 'ideologisation' of religion in Islam (as in Protestant fundamentalism, orthodox Judaism, Hinduism and even Buddhism in parts of the world) it is difficult, if not impossible, to disentangle the use from the abuse of religion in the field of ideas. All religions contain a repertory of myths, symbols and values that can be adapted to suit particular circumstances. The utopian myths promulgated by the Islamists are not just add-ons or borrowings from occidental ideologies: they are better understood as hybrids or graftings, where contemporary modes of political action ('armed struggle' redefined as '*jihad*', or the anarchist's slogan 'propaganda of the deed' Islamicised as 'a fury for God') are authenticated by reference to traditional sources – the famous 'sword verses' of the Qur'an, the Prophet's own battles, or the eschatological traditions in the collection of Ibn Kathir that are currently doing the rounds, in English, among Muslim students on American campuses.

If the challenge of political analysis is to distinguish between benign and harmful ideas in the realm of action, Pipes signally fails in his task. As Mamoun Nandy explains in his essay in *Muslims in the West*, the undifferentiated image of the Islamists promoted by Pipes and other media commentators, including many whose views are close to those of the 'hawks' in the current US administration, distorts reality by failing to distinguish between different types of political activity. Islamist groups such as Hamas or the Islamist Associations in Egypt have engaged in terrorist violence, but they are also involved in a range of activities, including social, humanitarian and educational work which might even bring social stability by compensating for the failures and corruption of the Palestine National Authority and the Egyptian government. Isolating the 'extremists' is not the straightforward task suggested by the Israeli and US governments. Nandy argues:

> This simplified, confrontational version of reality draws strength from the simplified, confrontational images found in American discourse. By lumping Islamists together in one group and perpetuating an aggregate image of the West's Middle Eastern enemies, US foreign policy bolsters the ideological credit of those who claim to defend all Arab or all Muslim interests in the face of a unified foreign threat.

This generates responses similar to the counter-narrative Werbner noted in the case of the Mancunian Muslims she studied in 1991.

In contrast to Pipes, who rails against the 'political correctness' which, he claims rather bizarrely, privileges Muslim-Americans in contrast to members of other faith communities, the scholars in Haddad's collection strive to find a balanced view of the situation facing Muslims in the West. Estimates of the numbers in North America vary widely, from the 5 to 8 million claimed by the American Muslim Council to much more modest figures claimed by scholars. One scholar, Karen Leonard, claims that Islam is poised to displace Judaism as 'second to Christianity in the number of its adherents'. But the impact of this statement depends on how one defines 'adherent'. A 1987 study by Yvonne Haddad and Adair Lumis estimated mosque attendance by Muslim-Americans at between 10 and 20 per cent, far below the 40 per cent church attendance estimated for the Christian population. At the top end of the spectrum the picture is one of prosperity and growing public recognition, with Muslim prayers offered in Congress and the recent appointment of America's first Muslim ambassador (to the admittedly rather modest post of Fiji). The 1990 census placed immigrants from South Asia well ahead of other groups in terms of income and educational attainments, with the highest proportion of newcomers working in management and the professions. Though Muslims from India, Pakistan and Bangladesh may not outweigh the numbers of Hindu and Sikh immigrants, the general ethos is such as to make South

Asians seem a 'particularly privileged group' with a reputation for being 'model immigrants', making them 'conspicuous and powerful in Muslim American discourse and politics'. Often classified as 'white' rather than Asian-Americans or Muslim-Americans, they fare better than immigrants from Arab countries, who are more likely to be victims of prejudice.

Even before the attacks of 9/11 produced massive round-ups and detentions of young men of 'Middle Eastern' appearance, Muslims from Arab lands were faring much less well than their South Asian co-religionists. They are more likely to see themselves as victims of media prejudice (with numerous Hollywood blockbusters depicting Arabs and Iranians as terrorists); while Arab students on university campuses find themselves in conflict with Jewish students over US support for Israel. 'Arabic-speaking American Muslims ... are more heavily invested in diasporic politics' than their South Asian confrères, especially those originating in India, for whom Pakistan 'did not quite become a homeland'. Furthest down the social scale are the African-American Muslims, who find in Islam a way of nurturing their African roots and developing a separate, non-Christian identity, which has set them at odds with Muslim immigrants from Asia. Though many followed Malcolm X and Wallace (now Warith al-Din) Muhammad in embracing orthodox Sunnism, deserting the separatist and racially driven apocalypticism of the Nation of Islam (NOI) founded by Wallace's father, the charismatic 'Prophet' Elijah Muhammad, African-American Muslims still tend to give *'asabiyya* (group solidarity) precedence over membership of the umma, the universal Muslim community.

Robert Dannin's fascinating study, *Black Pilgrimage to Islam*, relates a number of individual conversions with a view to explaining how African-Americans would want to 'fashion themselves into a double minority by converting to Islam'. After exploring numerous facets of the African-American experience with insight and subtlety, based mainly on interviews and direct observation, he concludes that the rituals of Islam and its heroic narrative themes serve to resolve the 'historical tensions of African-American society by concluding that liberation from racial domination and spiritual redemption are one and the same'. As painstakingly respectful of his subject as Pipes is dismissively offhand, Dannin's account brings to life a side of American life rarely accessible to outsiders.

His chapter on prisons in the state of New York is especially illuminating. With Muslims – most of whom are converts – representing more than 16 per cent of the total prison population of 70,000, and an impressive 32 per cent of all African-Americans incarcerated by the state (excluding the large population of municipal prisons), the appearance of Islam as an alternative religion and culture in the prisons is quite remarkable.

'Prison is a bizarre and violent "university" for those who reach maturity behind bars', in which the brutality and corruption of the streets in the downtown ghettos are vastly magnified. Far from teaching the skills that will enable an inmate to lead a law-abiding life after his release, prison effectively destroys his sense of personal integrity by methods that include 'physical brutality, psychological manipulation and frequent homosexual rape'. Conversion to Islam allows the prisoner to use his right to freedom of worship to 'circumscribe an autonomous zone whose perimeter cannot officially be contested'. The new Muslim's Islamic identity and membership of the worldwide umma means a 'fresh start, symbolised by a new name, modifications of his physical appearance and an emphasis on prayer'. The prison mosque becomes an alternative focus of authority. The Muslim's cell 'can be recognised by the absence of photographic images and the other-wise ubiquitous centerfold pin-ups of naked women'. The Islamic regime's strict opposition to homosexuality acts as a 'counter-disciplinary resist-ance' to the dominant hierarchies of prison life, where 'sexual possession, domination and submission represent forms of "hard currency"'. Muslim prisoners persist in resisting the ubiquitous body searches ostensibly used to find drugs, but are actually employed to humiliate inmates. They claim, plausibly enough, that since their religion forbids alcohol and narcotics, there is no reason to probe their orifices. The Islamic prison regime extends into the outside world. Inside the prison, the

> Shari'a *(Islamic law) becomes an autonomous self-correcting process administered by and for Muslims ... So widespread is the fierce reputation of the incarcerated Muslim that the most ruthless urban drug dealers carefully avoid harming any Muslim man, woman or child lest they face extreme prejudice during their inevitable prison terms.*

Dannin's study provides few indications that the black Muslim organisa-tions inside US prisons, with their superior leadership and discipline, will acquire a political direction in the event of conflict between the US government and a Muslim state. Indeed, the authorities had every reason to encourage the Islamic prison missions as a force for stability and reha-bilitation. During the prison rising in Attica in 1971, the Muslims acted as mediators, protecting the guards who had been taken as hostages. Post 9/11, however, there are ominous signs of change. As the *Wall Street Journal* reported on 7 February 2003, at least one black Muslim prison chaplain with links to Saudi Arabia has been preaching that bin Laden is a hero, that the atrocity of 9/11 was inflicted by God, and that the victims of the atrocity 'deserved what they got'. Given the growing religious influence of Saudi-funded Wahhabi Islam in both Asian-American and African-American mosques throughout the United States (as well as in many other parts of the world), it is only too likely that there are other state-funded imams who share his views. The Islamist movement has been fuelled by petrodollars from its inception in the 1970s. The fact that the Saudi leadership is now one of its targets does nothing to diminish the force of its appeal to Muslims who feel themselves to be victims of Western policies, or their co-religionists living in the West who empathise with them. If the hawks in Washington persist in singling out Iraq for attack while other violators of the international order, such as Israel or North Korea, are treated diplomatically, America, like Britain, will find itself with a sizeable, disaffected minority in its midst. Fears about 'asylum-seekers' fuelled by the tabloid press miss the point. The 'war against terror' already has a domestic dimension, one that seems bound to loom larger as the war unfolds.

Published in *The Times Literary Supplement*, 28 February 2003.

The books reviewed were:

Robert Dannin (2002) *Black Pilgrimage to Islam*. New York: Oxford University Press.

Yvonne Yazbeck Haddad (ed.) (2002) *Muslims in the West: From Sojourners to Citizens*. New York: Oxford University Press.

Daniel Pipes (2002) *Militant Islam Reaches America*. New York: W. W. Norton.

23

The Shrinking Sphere

Are the Muslims of Bradford, 'Britain's Islamabad', incurably militant? There have been troubles in other cities with Asian Muslim populations, but the Muslims of Bradford have shown a consistent pattern of refusing to 'take insults lying down'. They first demonstrated their militancy during the Honeyford affair in 1984–5, when the head teacher of the Drummond Middle School, 90 per cent of whose pupils came from Muslim families, was forced into early retirement after publishing anti-Pakistani remarks in *The Salisbury Review*. The city became notorious in December 1988 for the public burning of Salman Rushdie's *The Satanic Verses*. Though not the first group of Muslims to demonstrate their sense of outrage in this fashion (the first burning actually took place in Bolton), it was the Bradfordians who knew how to grab the headlines, by alerting the media and selling them videos of the event.

The recent Bradford riots, said to have caused more than a million pounds' worth of damage, have been blamed on insensitive policing. The Police Complaints Authority is currently investigating 15 complaints, including one of alleged assault on a young mother carrying a baby. The wider causes to which the riots are attributed include a familiar litany of problems: high unemployment among a growing, unqualified, youth population; racial discrimination and harassment; drug dealing and prostitution. All these problems afflict Asian populations in other cities and do not usually lead to rioting. It may be, however, that the tolerance of Bradford Muslims had been stretched beyond breaking point by the issue of prostitution. Lumb Lane, a notorious red-light area in the Manningham district, has seen a growing confrontation between the pimps and prostitutes who used to own the streets and the Asian families in the area. Just when the police, aided by groups of local vigilantes clad in baggy jeans, trainers and bomber jackets, felt they had reclaimed the streets from prostitutes and kerb crawlers, an ITV drama series called *Band of Gold* was broadcast, bringing in hordes of new customers from as far away as Germany. The same psycho-social ingredients – transgressive sexuality, community honour and religion – that exploded during the Rushdie affair seem to have been present. The rage may not have been religious in any strict sense of the term: the young British-Asian men from Kashmir or Sylhet who vented their anger are not necessarily the same people who regularly attend the city's mosques. During the anti-Rushdie demonstrations in London's Hyde Park in 1989 I noticed that those who carried the most blood-curdling slogans seemed the least familiar with the forms of prayer and most reluctant to participate in communal worship. But in Britain, as in the rest of the world, the word Muslim (like the word Jew) can convey secular identity as well as religious faith. Tariq Modood, an astute commentator on British-Muslim affairs, states that, where 'racism and cultural contempt are mixed with Islamophobia', a reactive assertiveness crystallises into what he terms 'Muslim pride' – an assertiveness that 'may at times owe as little to religion as political blackness does to the idea of Africa'.

Philip Lewis, a resident of Bradford with firsthand knowledge of its complex and often divided Muslim communities, did not anticipate the latest round of troubles to afflict the city. Rather, he offers a cautiously optimistic view of accommodation and change. He cites with approval the anthropologist Pnina Werbner's contention that 'stress on cultural independence' can constitute 'a protection from stigma and external domination … The one-way deterministic approach which defines immigrants as victims is unable to account for the dialectic process which interaction between the immigrant group and the state generates'. Despite the evidence of militancy, Lewis succeeds in dismantling 'the myth of an undifferentiated "fundamentalist" Islam'. 'Fundamentalism,' he argues, 'is a useless word for either description or analysis. Its pejorative overtones of religious fascism obscure the diversity of traditions within Islam', ignoring in particular 'the vitality, popularity and persistence of Islamic mysticism' in Britain. In Bradford, it was the largely non-political and mystically-inclined Barelwi sect (thought to control at least half of Britain's 1,000 mosques) which took the lead in the anti-Rushdie agitation, setting the agenda for the most forceful expression of Muslim feeling ever witnessed in Britain. Lewis shows how the Bradford Council of Mosques, a model of co-operation between different Muslim sects established on the initiative of Bradford City Council, tried to orchestrate the campaign against Rushdie and Penguin (his publishers) until the issue was hijacked by the Ayatollah Khomeini for very different purposes. His account, though without any new insights, is fair and judicious, locating the source of scandal not in the abstract domain of Muslim 'fanaticism' but in the specific concerns of a group of South Asian Muslims who saw the book as an attack on the honour of the Prophet Muhammad, their most revered religious symbol.

Though Lewis writes with considerable sympathy about a community – or rather, a series of communities – beset by conflicting economic and social pressures, he does not evade the conceptual and theological difficulties facing a religion whose triumphalist character was forged under conditions of conquest and global dominion. One symptom of the way Islam is 'programmed for victory' at source, as it were, is the law of apostasy by which men such as Rushdie may be condemned to death for leaving the faith into which they were born. Lewis cites several statements by Muslim preachers and editors which reveal that religious imperial ambitions still hold sway, even in Britain, where Muslims are a relatively small minority. It seems clear that most of the *ulama* (religious scholars) in Britain are unequal to the task of formulating a theology appropriate to societies in which individuals are offered freedom of religious choice. Yet, as Lewis points out, this is the situation that now faces approximately a quarter of the world's Muslims, who live in predominantly non-Muslim societies: 'Religious freedom for the individual, as enjoyed by the West, is not seen as a positive good but rather an unfortunate necessity to be borne.'

There are some indications that the situation may be changing, and that significant Muslim organisations are moving in the direction of voluntarism. While the puritanical Deobandi sect – the second-largest group of British Muslims – has yet to renounce the essentially political aim of having Muslim law accepted by Parliament, their principal offshoot, the Tablighi Jamaat, is explicitly pious and non-political. It is also one of the world's fastest-growing Muslim sects, with a presence in more than 90 countries, from Malaysia to Canada. Even within Muslim majority countries it avoids the argument that Islam must supply the framework for political life. A similar trend towards the separation of religion and politics is observable even in the formerly militant Jamaat-i-Islami, the South Asian counterpart to the Muslim Brotherhood in Egypt, which has recently toned down its message in an effort to recruit converts in the West.

As in Bradford, so globally: the Islamic militancy that dominates the headlines proves, on closer inspection, to offer a less formidable challenge to a secular, hedonistic West than appeared to be the case 16 years ago. The Iranian Revolution, hailed in 1979 as an Islamist victory, has failed to break out of the Shi'ite sectarian enclave in which it occurred. The failure of Shi'ites to rise up against Saddam Hussein between 1980 and 1988, despite his murder of their leaders, proved that in Iraq at least, national allegiances were stronger than sectarian or religious ones. The overwhelming majority of Iraqi Shi'ites fought loyally for Iraq during the first Gulf War. However much pressure it might have been subjected to, this majority (and Arab Shi'ites make up about 60 per cent of the Iraqi population) has shown no interest in a war against the Iraqi state. The same inference must be drawn from Iran's failure to intervene after Operation Desert Storm, when Saddam Hussein attacked the holy Shi'ite cities of Najaf and Karbala. The interests of the Iranian state took precedence over religious solidarity or the protection of the holiest shrines of the Shi'a.

Iran is exceptional in having Shi'ism as the state religion. As representatives of the Hidden Imam who, like Jesus, is expected to return one day to restore justice and peace to a world torn by conflict, the Shi'ite *ulama* constituted a separate estate comparable to the Christian clergy, with responsibility for dispensing individual moral guidance and upholding the Shari'a (religious law). They benefited directly from religious taxes, and as trustees of religious endowments they administered large tracts of land – which from the 1960s brought them into conflict with the Shah over the latter's ambitious land reforms. When the Shah's regime collapsed, the *ulama*, with their independent network of mosques, schools and properties, were able to take power under the radical banner of Khomeini, who broke with tradition by insisting on the active guardianship of the *ulama* during the absence of the Hidden Imam. As mujtahids (independent interpreters of the Qur'an and other holy texts) the Shi'ite *ulama* incorporated a good deal of modern thinking into their understanding of the religious tradition – enough to make it possible for many of them to occupy positions of influence or power in a modern state.

The situation in Sunni countries such as Algeria is more problematic, as no contemporary Islamist leader possesses authority comparable to Khomeini's. The traditional Sunni *ulama*, who for centuries had been subordinate to state power, had seen their role as guardians of the religious law restricted to the areas of family law and personal status. The task of bringing Islamic precepts into line with modern realities has largely been undertaken by thinkers and leaders from outside the ranks of the *ulama*. Intellectuals and activists such as the Indo-Pakistani Sayyid Abul Ala Maududi (d. 1979) and the Egyptian Sayyid Qutb (executed by Nasser in 1966) were mostly laymen without official ranking in the religious hierarchy. The radical movements they espoused (the Jamaat-i-Islami in South Asia and the Muslim Brotherhood in Egypt) contained a mixture of modernist and traditional elements.

However, as these movements have gained ground with mass support from the newly urbanised poor (the mustadhafin or 'wretched ones' from whom Khomeini drew his support in Iran), the message has gone down-market, with more naïve and literal versions of the faith coming to the fore. For example, whereas in the past members of the Muslim Brotherhood adopted the typically modernist position that the Qur'anic penalties for theft (including amputation) should not be enforced until the perfect Islamic state had been instituted, where no one could be driven to crime by need, the more traditionally-minded are demanding the restoration of these penalties, regardless of the circumstances. Where modernists are ecumenically-minded, upholding Islam's historical commitment to the religious liberties of the 'peoples of the book' (Jews and Christians, and by extension members of other scriptural faiths), traditionalist groups use the pretext of the struggle (*jihad*) against the 'infidel West' to attack foreigners, Shi'ites or local Christians. The division between the Islamists and more traditional elements, or 'neo-fundamentalists', as Olivier Roy calls them, is drawn most sharply on the highly emotive question of the status and rights of women. Where the Islamists argue that the Qur'an endowed women with full civil and religious rights, and that women should participate in social and political life so long as sexual segregation is maintained, neo-fundamentalists insist that woman's place is the home. In Iran, chador-clad women were highly visible in the street demonstrations that brought down the Shah; in the Algerian crisis, despite initial female participation in anti-government demonstrations, they have been conspicuous by their absence. FIS leaders are against women's right to work – a right Khomeini conceded in 1979 (though he had opposed it in 1963). Where the Islamists, by no means all of them Shi'ites, nevertheless look to Iran for their model, neo-fundamentalists, despite their attacks on the petrodollar princes with their pro-Western foreign policies, are more attuned to the Saudi model, where women are socially invisible outside the home. Disagreement between the more progressive Shi'ite Mujahidin groups backed by Iran and neo-fundamentalists supported by Saudi Arabia over the right of women to vote was a major cause of the breakdown of the 1990 peace agreements in Afghanistan. Issues of personal status (wives, family, divorce) continue to be the main area of contention between Islamists and neo-fundamentalists in Egypt, Pakistan and other predominantly Sunni countries, with the latter demanding adherence to the letter of the Shari'a but not the social and educational improvements demanded by the former.

The absence of a modernising hierarchy capable of enacting reforms makes it probable that the Algerian neo-fundamentalists will eventually win out, despite recent claims by Islamist opposition leaders that they are committed to religious tolerance and human rights. Unlike the Islamists, who try to embrace modernity on their own cultural terms, the neo-fundamentalists are rabidly opposed to everything that fails to conform to their received notions of Islam. A foretaste of FIS victory occurred in Algeria in 1990, when a large number of municipalities came under neo-fundamentalist control. Not only was alcohol banned but also rai (a blend of traditional music and rock); subsidies for athletics were abolished; night-clubs were closed; and decrees were introduced making 'Islamic attire' obligatory. The victory of traditionalism at the micro-level, Olivier Roy predicts, is already being reflected in the Muslim world at large. In the very different context of Afghanistan, a country riven by ethnic and tribal divisions, the triumph of the Islamic Mujahidin over the Russians led, not to an Islamic state, but to a return to a traditional, if reconfigured, segmen-tation and to power struggles that are more ethnic than ideological. The combined effects of the war and the Iranian Revolution are leading to an increase in sectarian conflicts, notably in Pakistan, where Sunni militants are now preaching the *jihad* against Shi'ite infidels. Despite the Islamist rhetoric from Algeria, where the war between the Islamists and the govern-ment has already cost some 40,000 lives, the overall picture is not of a concerted, or even coherent, challenge to the West, and the corrupt and 'infidel' regimes it allegedly supports, but of a Muslim world in danger of being torn apart by local and regional feuds and rivalries, all conducted in the name of Islam.

Roy's analysis of the conflicting Islamic currents is impressive in both its range and grasp of detail. This is an important book and deserves the widest possible readership. Since its original publication in French in 1992, events from Pakistan to Algeria have vindicated Roy's analysis of the social and ideological forces at work in the Muslim world. The failure to which the title refers, like the failure of communism, is connected to the inadequacy of virtue as a political principle. One need not deny the moral idealism of the Islamists (despite the atrocities the extremists have committed in Algeria and elsewhere) to recognise the poverty of their political philosophy. The great weakness of modern Islamic political thought, in Roy's view, is the closed or virtuous circle in which it is trapped. Virtue as a political principle was tried in France in 1789: Islamist political principles may fall short of totalitarian terror, but they lead nowhere. Political institutions function only as a result of the virtue of those who run them; but virtue can become widespread only if society is already 'Islamic'.

Rather than offering a radically new political vision for a Muslim world beset by tyrannical, corrupt and incompetent regimes, Islamism is proving incapable of unifying the Muslim world, or even changing the regional balance of power. The result, as Roy sees it, is little more than a bid for political power justified in Islamic terms. Despite a formal commitment to the solidarity of the Islamic umma (worldwide community) and even, in some cases, to a restored universal caliphate, the Muslim national state remains the only plausible object of political ambitions: 'From Casablanca to Tashkent, the Islamists have moulded themselves into the framework of existing states, adopting their modes of exercising power, their strategic demands, their nationalism.' While the Islamists are committed to the elimination of corruption, Roy argues that, on acceding to power, they will face exactly the same alternatives that face the present regimes, as well as most other Third-World governments: a tired and corrupt state socialism offset by a black market, or a liberal neo-conservatism constrained to follow the prescriptions of the International Monetary Fund, with occasional pious gestures in the direction of 'Islamic banks'. The 'restoration of the Shari'a' simply means that Islamisation will target personal law and penal law, as has happened in Pakistan.

This is not, however, a totalitarian onslaught comparable to attacks on intellectuals in Nazi Germany or the former Soviet bloc. Under the Islamist rubric, the family remains sacrosanct. Because the Shari'a protects the family – the only institution to which it grants real autonomy – the culture of Muslims under neo-fundamentalist rule will become passive, privatised and consumerist. The practical effects of Islamisation entail not a confrontation with the West, but rather a cultural retreat into the mosque and private family space. It is impossible to censor satellite dishes, videos, faxes, email or access to the internet – except in small, highly urbanised areas. By attempting to silence indigenous artists such as Tasleema Nasreen, Naguib Mahfouz or Yousuf Chahine, the Islamists are successfully attacking the public culture of the countries in which they operate. If the Islamists come to power, Muslims under Islamist rule will become passive consumers of, rather than active participants in, the emerging global culture. Despite recent bans on satellite dishes and attacks on the technicians who install them (many of whom have had their throats cut in Algeria), the militants will never be able to stop the flow of this consumption. Herein, Roy predicts, lies a savage irony: having terrorised the Muslim artists and intellectuals on whom local cultures depend, for challenging their narrow versions of Islam, the militants have cleared the way for the thing they most profess to hate: the Americanisation of their culture in its most vulnerable position – in the bosom of the Muslim family.

Given Western dominance over international communications systems, there is a challenge and an opportunity here. The Muslim diaspora in Europe and the United States is bound to become an increasingly powerful force within the Muslim lands, not least because of the intellectual freedoms it enjoys and the greater ability it has for getting its message across. Significant modernist thinkers such as Mohammed Arkoun, currently residing in France, or the British-Muslim philosopher, Shabbir Akhtar, who came to prominence as a defender of 'fundamentalism' during the Rushdie affair but has since modified his views, may have only a marginal impact at present. But if Olivier Roy's analysis is correct, their influence is likely to grow as the failure of political Islam to deliver on its promises leads to disillusionment and decline. With globalisation eroding the classic distinction between *Dar al-Islam* (the sphere of submission) and *Dar al-Harb* (the sphere of war), the coming decades are likely to see a retreat from direct political action and a renewed emphasis on the voluntary, personal and private aspects of the faith.

For all the efforts of political Islam to conquer the state, on the basis of new collectivist ideologies constructed on the ruins of Marxism and using some of its materials, the processes of historical and technological change point remorselessly towards increasing individualism and personal choice – primary agents of secular modernity. Conflicts as different as those of Palestine, Kashmir and Algeria may continue to be articulated in Islamic terms, but the long-term prospects for Islam point to inevitable depoliticisation. Muslim souls are likely to find the path of inner exploration more rewarding than revolutionary politics. Sadly, much blood remains to be spilt along the way.

Published in *London Review of Books*, 6 July 1995.

The books reviewed were:

Philip Lewis (1994) *Islamic Britain: Religion, Politics and Identity among British Muslims.* London: I.B.Tauris.
Olivier Roy (1994) *The Failure of Political Islam*, translated by Carol Volk. London: I.B.Tauris.

24

The Satanic Verses Revisited

On 26 September 1988, Salman Rushdie published his long-awaited fourth novel, *The Satanic Verses*. Five years in the making, it was widely expected to top the bestseller lists. Rushdie's title was provocative: 'the Satanic Verses' refers to an episode in the life of the Prophet Muhammad, recorded by some of his chroniclers, but not those considered to be the most reliable, when Satan is said to have interpolated some verses into the Qur'an, a book that most believing Muslims consider to be the unmediated word of God. The verses extolled three female deities worshipped by the pagans of Mecca and were subsequently removed, but the episode could be used to cast doubt on the divine authenticity of the Qur'an (although not by some early commentators, who had no problem with the story). The Satanic Verses episode is only a small part of an extremely complex novel that explores the psychological impact of migration and the conflicting cultural forces to which migrants find themselves exposed. A playful, transgressive work in the magical realism genre pioneered by Jorge Luis Borges and Gabriel García Márquez, it contains a bewildering cast of characters who satirise, sometimes brilliantly, the cosmopolitan milieus of London and Bombay, with their mixtures of argot and street language and, in the case of London, seedy immigrant ghettos. The alienations and humiliations of the migrants' world, with its disintegrating and reconstituted identities, are treated with the flat burlesque of a cartoon. The characters seem two-dimensional, and critics have faulted Rushdie for being condescending or even offensive in his attitude towards Indians and West Indians.

The novel's strength lies in its exuberant surface qualities – its intense visuality, its way with syntax and its astonishing lexical range. The shifting of names and characters who dissolve and re-emerge in different guises is matched by a stylistic ingenuity that is sometimes breathtaking, and occasionally wearing, as when sentences lasting a page or more teeter on the brink of collapse.

The novel parodies the ingredients of Indo-British-Muslim identity, mixing fact with fiction, history with myth. It ridicules some of the brittle shibboleths surrounding Muslim beliefs and identities: not just the integrity of the Qur'an, but, more dangerously, the sexuality of Muhammad and the honour of his wives. In the dreams of Gibreel, one of the novel's two protagonists, Islam's most central rite, the Meccan pilgrimage, and the Prophet Muhammad are subject to merciless lampoon. In a brothel called 'The Curtain' (the primary meaning of hijab, or veil) prostitutes play the part of the Prophet's wives, the most popular being 15-year-old Ayesha (the name of Muhammad's youngest wife). Their clients circulate around a Fountain of Love 'much as the pilgrims rotated for other reasons around the ancient Black Stone' in Mecca. The anti-mosque satirises attitudes to women legitimised by Muhammad's numerous marriages. The poet Baal presides in the brothel as a kind of anti-prophet. Whether or not Baal symbolises his creator, his role in the novel is uncannily prescient:

> A poet's work is to name the unnameable, to point at frauds,
> to take sides, start arguments, shape the world and stop it from
> going to sleep. And if rivers of blood flow from the cuts his verse
> inflict, then they will nourish him.

At least 60 people might have been killed in the agitation that followed the book's publication – 19 in India and Pakistan, two in Belgium, and 37 in Sivas, Turkey, in an arson attack by Islamists on a hotel where the book's Turkish translator, the novelist Aziz Nesin, and other writers were meeting. Rushdie's own fate seems to have been prefigured in the novel: after Baal is discovered in the brothel, the Prophet Mahound (the name Rushdie borrowed from crusading demonologists) issues a fatwa sentencing him to beheading. On 16 February 1989, nearly five months after the book's publication, Rushdie and his then wife Marianne Higgins were obliged to 'go underground' for their own protection after Iran's supreme leader, Ayatollah Khomeini, issued a fatwa declaring Salman Rushdie an apostate from Islam:

> I would like to inform all the intrepid Muslims in the world that
> the author of the book entitled The Satanic Verses, which has
> been compiled, printed and published in opposition to Islam, the
> prophet and the Qur'an, as well as those publishers who were
> aware of its contents, have been declared madhur al dam [those
> whose blood must be shed]. I call on all zealous Muslims to
> execute them quickly, whenever they find them, so that no one
> will dare to insult what Muslims hold sacred. Whoever is killed in
> this path will be regarded as a martyr.

A *fatwa* is a responsum or legal opinion in answer to a question put to a legal authority. In his capacity as a mujtahid – an interpreter of the law – Khomeini had the authority to issue such a ruling, but it should only have concerned Shi'ites who recognised the Ayatollah's spiritual authority, and it would have been open to them and others to consult a different authority who could have produced a different verdict. The *fatwa* was a naked political act: by enjoining 'all intrepid Muslims' to execute Rushdie, Khomeini was proclaiming his leadership over the whole *umma* (Islamic community), Sunnis as well as Shi'ites. Moreover, this *fatwa*, directed at a British citizen living outside any Islamic jurisdiction, was supplied with teeth. Immediately after Khomeini's pronouncement, the Fifth of June Foundation, one of the many Islamic charitable trusts set up after the revolution in 1979, offered a reward of 20 million tumans to any Iranian who would 'punish the mercenary for his arrogance'. Non-Iranians would get the equivalent of US$3 million.

The *fatwa* had not come out of the blue. In the months since the book's publication there had been a mounting campaign originating in the Indian subcontinent. Even before the novel's publication, its title and Rushdie's pre-publication interviews began stirring controversy in Muslim circles in India, where the author of *Midnight's Children* and *Shame* was an established celebrity. The prime minister, Rajiv Gandhi, in an effort to woo the Muslim vote in forthcoming elections, decided to ban the book, a decision repeated in most Muslim majority countries, as well as in South Africa. Rushdie's response, in a scathing open letter, prompted a number of Muslim politicians to defend their 'offended' electorate, even before anyone had read the book.

The close family and communal ties between the subcontinent and Britain made it inevitable that British Muslims would respond to the book as soon as it appeared in print. The protest came from a variety of different quarters. One was the Islamic Foundation in Leicester, an organisation with close ties to the Jamaat-i Islami, the Islamist party founded by Sayyid Abul Ala Maududi (1906–79), one of the leading ideologues of the Islamist movement. Maududi, who was strongly influenced by the totalitarian movements of the 1930s and 1940s, argued that the purpose of Islam is to set up a state on the basis of its own ideology and programme. He believed that the whole world should convert to Islam, that women should remain in purdah, and that debate in his 'theodemocracy' should be restricted to the interpretation of laws deemed to have been revealed by God for all people and times. The Maududists have affinities with the Saudi Wahhabis, from whom they receive considerable support.

After the publication of *The Satanic Verses*, the Islamic Foundation sent a circular to all Muslim organisations, mosques and Islamic figures in Britain, a carefully crafted document whose exact wording would be repeated in several other formal protests:

> *This work, thinly disguised as a piece of literature, not only grossly distorts the Islamic history in general, but also betrays in the worst possible colours the very characters of the prophet Ibrahim and the prophet Mohammed (peace be upon them) ... The work also disfigures the characters of the prophet's companions ... and the prophet's holy wives: and describes the Islamic creed and rituals in the most foul language.*

The circular was accompanied by extracts from the book that Muslims would find most offensive. A very different campaign was spearheaded by the Bradford Council of Mosques, an umbrella organisation representing several popular strands of Indo-Pakistani Islam in a city that has one of Britain's larger Muslim populations. As was the case with the Maududists, the first intimations of the book had come from India: a circular printed in Urdu and English contained extracts from two articles from journals published in New Delhi and Surat. The tone, however, was very different from the Islamic Foundation circular. It treated Rushdie's novel as if it were dangerous to handle, a defective product to be recalled by its manufacturer. It briefly summarised the supposed blasphemies contained in the novel, without repeating them – because to do so would, logically speaking, repeat Rushdie's offence. The letter from the council's chairman, Sher Azam, to Prime Minister Margaret Thatcher, written in imperfect English, conveyed a tone of outrage, of genuine hurt:

> *Honourable Madam*
>
> *The Muslims of Bradford and all over the world are shocked to hear about the Novel called 'SATANIC VERSES' in which the writer Salman Rushdi [sic] has attacked our beloved prophet Mohammed PBUH and his wives using such dirty language which no any Muslim can tolerate ... As citizens of this great country, we have expressed our very ill feelings about such harmful novel and its publishers and state the novel should be banned immediately.*

Unaware that the British government had no legal powers to ban the novel, on 14 January 1989 the Council of Mosques organised the spectacular auto da fé that brought their city – and their protests – to the world's attention, by publicly burning the book. Although no reporters from the national press attended, the amateur video the Council shot and circulated to television stations made bulletins all over the world. The image – which Westerners viewed through spectacles darkened by memories of book-burning by the Inquisition and the Third Reich – fuelled further anti-Rushdie protests.

It was a demonstration organised by the Maududist party, the Jamaati-Islami, in Islamabad early in February, in which five people were killed and more than 100 injured, that brought the anti-Rushdie movement to Khomeini's attention. The pretext for the demonstration was somewhat thin: since Pakistan had already banned the book, the demonstrators attacked the US Embassy, the ostensible reason being the forthcoming publication of the novel's US edition on 15 February.

Prior to the *fatwa*, Tehran's literary press had been hostile, but not in any way menacing. The novel had not been formally banned: there was no law to prevent readers from bringing copies through customs. However, with the Maududists making the running in Pakistan, the radicals in Tehran (who were competing with the pragmatists for the dying Khomeini's attention) could not be seen to be lagging in the defence of Islam. By seeming to challenge the Prophet's honour, Rushdie's novel had set off an auction in militancy.

In retrospect, the affair of *The Satanic Verses* marks a watershed in the globalisation of Islam and the contradictory currents that flow from it. In Britain, the anti-Rushdie protest proved a catalyst in the process of creating a British-Muslim identity. It brought together a number of disparate Muslim traditions – Shi'a and Sunnis, Maududists, Momens, Deobandis, Barelvis, Tablighis and other groups that had previously had few connections with each other – to create a common platform.

A vital ingredient in the mix was the mystically inclined Barelvi tendency, who belong at the opposite end of the political-religious spectrum from the Maududists and their Saudi supporters. Unlike the Wahhabis, who believe that devotional reverence towards Muhammad or any other human risks the sin of idolatry, Barelvis almost worship Muhammad, who is seen as a semi-divine being blessed with powers of intercession. Like other South Asian Muslims, Barelvis are fairly recent converts from Hinduism, and retain some Hindu devotional attitudes.

The strength of feeling against Rushdie was dramatised by demonstrations in London in which thousands of Muslims were bussed in from northern and midland cities. The slogans – 'Rushdie is a devil!', 'Rushdie is a son of Satan!', 'Kill the bastard!', '*Jihad* on agnostics!' – were more menacing than any previously seen on Britain's streets. The demonstrators – the vast majority of them male – included elderly men with curly grey beards, wearing turbans and baggy trousers, and clean-shaven youths sporting Western jeans and bandanas: the protest bridged the cultural gap between generations.

The horrified response of the host community – expressed in government statements, newspaper editorials and discussions in television studios, served to consolidate Muslim feeling. As Gilles Kepel, a leading commentator on modern Islam, observed: 'The more the outside world heaped opprobrium on Muslims, the more the Muslim community closed ranks. It was a vicious circle.'

Yet there may have been a more positive outcome of the protests that moved, paradoxically, in the direction of the domestication of Islam in Britain. The UK Action Committee on Islamic Affairs, set up to 'guide the Muslim community in their efforts to express their anger and hurt through democratic means, and to ensure that their protest stayed within the framework of the law' has evolved – through its founder and leading activist, Iqbal (now Sir Iqbal) Sacranie – into the Muslim Council of Britain (MCB), an umbrella body covering more than 400 affiliated Muslim organisations. While the MCB has been criticised for its Maududist leanings, and its claims to represent all British Muslims are hotly disputed, its role as an interlocutor for a substantial body of Muslim opinion *vis-à-vis* the British government has pushed it in a pragmatic direction that may conflict with its original instincts. In 1989, Sacranie was saying of Rushdie: 'Death, perhaps, is a bit too easy for him.' Two decades later, the MCB's official spokesman, Inayat Bunglawala, told the *Financial Times*: 'Looking back, it seems we were foolish trying to get the book banned. We were demanding that others be prevented from reading it, which I now think is preposterous. When you go down that road it is dangerous.' Internationally, common sense also broke through the clouds. In September 1998, after months of tortuous negotiations, Britain and Iran restored the full diplomatic relations that had been ruptured by the Rushdie affair. Kamal Kharazi, the Iranian foreign minister, declared that his government 'has no intention, nor is it going to take any action whatsoever, to threaten the life of the author of *The Satanic Verses* or anybody associated with his work; nor will it encourage or assist anybody to do so'. After a decade of living in safe houses protected by Special Branch police, Rushdie emerged from hiding. Sensibly, he chose to live in New York. In 2007 – two years after Sacranie – he was offered, and accepted, a knighthood for his services to literature.

The final outcome of the Rushdie affair in Britain may seem encouraging, but the broader picture is sombre. In the age of the internet, the relationship between a European host society and an embattled, underprivileged Muslim minority – the original context of the protest – has been overtaken by the vaster context where similar issues arise and instantly become global. Even before the attacks on New York and Washington in September 2001, and the West's ill-judged interventions in Iraq and Afghanistan raised political temperatures, the Ayatollah's warning against insulting 'what Muslims hold sacred' was being heeded. After the trauma and expense suffered by Rushdie's publishers, Viking Penguin in London, whose offices in Kensington were in a virtual state of siege for several months, publishers have been chary of taking on titles considered risky, regardless of their literary merits. In 1998, David Caute's *Fatima's Scarf*, a brilliant and witty political novel that satirises the Rushdie affair, was turned down by more than 20 publishers. The author bravely decided to publish it himself. An entirely insult-free and non-satirical effort of my own, *Islam: A Very Short Introduction,* had to be modified after the publishers (Oxford University Press) were flooded with emails objecting to a picture of Muhammad receiving a revelation from the Angel Gabriel. The picture – from a twelfth-century manuscript in the Edinburgh University Library – had been reproduced many times before, but on this occasion health and safety issues were invoked, as warehouse staff expressed anxieties about handling the book. The objectors included a medical doctor working in the National Health Service.

In November 2004, the Dutch film-maker, Theo van Gogh, was murdered in Amsterdam by Mohammed Bouyeri, a 'born-again' Muslim of Moroccan origin. Van Gogh had made a controversial film with the Somali-born MP and feminist, Ayaan Hirsi Ali, which showed verses from the Qur'an playing over a woman's body. A note attached to van Gogh's body informed Ali that she would be next. In court, where he was sentenced to life imprisonment without parole, Bouyeri addressed van Gogh's mother: 'I don't feel your pain. I don't have any sympathy for you. I can't feel for you because I think you're a non-believer.'

Perhaps the most striking example of Khomeini's legacy in the wake of the Rushdie affair is the case of the 'Mohammed cartoons' published by the Danish newspaper *Jyllands-Posten* in September 2005. As in the Rushdie case, a controversy concerning cultural relations between Muslim immigrants and the host community in a northern European country sparked a global movement of protest, ranging from peaceful demonstrations to diplomatic sanctions and consumer boycotts, and in some cases open violence against targets symbolising 'Western' power. Furious Muslim citizens of countries as far apart as Lebanon, Sudan and Indonesia attacked Danish embassies, with threats extended to all citizens of countries belonging to the European Union. Editors in France and Jordan who published the cartoons – to inform their readers or out of journalistic solidarity with *Jyllands-Posten* – were fired.

No British newspapers published the cartoons – though they were instantly accessible on the internet. The most egregious of them depicted Muhammad – with bushy eyebrows and an aggressive expression – wearing a black turban in the shape of a bomb with a lighted fuse. The front of the bomb-turban has a cartouche inscribed with the Arabic letters of the Islamic confession of faith – 'There is no god but God, Muhammad is the Messenger of God'. By comparison, the other cartoons seemed rather puerile. In one of them, four suicide bombers with exaggeratedly big noses stand on clouds symbolising heaven. They are greeted by Mohammed, who appears to be barring the gates of paradise with the phrase 'Stop, stop! We ran out of virgins.'

It is not difficult to see how ordinary Muslims – and not just radicals – would find these images offensive. In particular, the bomb cartoon cleverly encapsulates Western anxieties about 'Islam' in the aftermath of 9/11 and the Madrid and London bombings. By associating the figure of Muhammad directly with terrorism, it implies that all Muslims are potentially dangerous. The point is driven home by the cartouche on the bomb-turban: the kalima – or confession of faith – is a formula to which all believing Muslims subscribe. More conservative Muslims, both on the Maududist–Wahhabi and mystical–Barelvi ends of the religious spectrum, would take additional offence at the very idea of drawing the Prophet Muhammad. In the larger scheme of Islamic cultural history, however, the taboo against depicting the Prophet (or indeed, other human beings and animals) has tended to be honoured in the breach. While images of living creatures, from the Prophet down to animals, never appear in places of worship or in public buildings, there is a rich repertoire of medieval pictures in books and manuscripts depicting him, sometimes unveiled, but often veiled because of his special holiness. Traditionally, Shi'a have been less iconophobic than Sunnis in allowing pictures of the Prophet and his family for devotional purposes.

Recently, two French scholars, Pierre and Micheline Centilivres, were fascinated to discover that an image of Muhammad circulating in present-day Tehran, depicting him as a young man with a bare shoulder, had been plagiarised from a photograph of a young Tunisian taken by the German orientalist photographer Rudolf Franz Lehnert (1878–1948) in 1905 or 1906. The idea that depicting the Prophet is offensive to all Muslims is of recent provenance, and reflects the influence of the Wahhabi–Saudi petro-dollars and the fundamentalist tendencies they help to sustain.

Khomeini's *fatwa* against Rushdie was a warning, but also a challenge. In the aftermath of the *fatwa* – and in particular after 9/11 – publishers (with a few exceptions) have been chary about offending the religious sensitivities of all Muslims, not just fundamentalists. Muslim minorities in Europe, many of whom face difficult social circumstances, with high unemployment and poor education opportunities, may respond to religious satire as an attack on themselves as people. A sense of collective victimhood has been exacerbated by the 'war on terror' and the shocking evidence of abuse emerging from Abu Ghraib and Guantanamo Bay. In the febrile atmosphere generated by the 'war on terror', attacks on prominent figures deemed to have 'insulted' the Prophet of Islam may appear cathartic, as acts of revenge. However, there is a paradox here, because there is no way that transgressive ideas can be silenced. The authors, translators, film-makers and publishers who offend Muslim sensitivities make easier targets than the anonymous websites and blogs where transgressive ideas and images may appear with impunity. In the virtual world, where everything goes, from pornography to advocacy for the 'gay *jihad*', self-censorship by other media must prove unsustainable.

Published as 'Naming the Unnameable' in *Index on Censorship*, November 2008.

25
Made in the USA

There may be as many as 8 million Muslims in the United States, and if the numbers continue to rise at the present rate Islam will soon surpass Judaism as the largest non-Christian religion, dwarfing such mainstream denominations as the Episcopal Church and the United Church of Christ. The majority of the Muslims are immigrants and guest students from more than 60 countries. However, a sizeable and growing presence – about 3 million – are African-Americans. Of several black Muslim groups, the most prominent is the Nation Of Islam (NOI), an organisation described by the FBI as 'violently anti-white, anti-Christian, anti-integration and anti-United States'. Founded by Elijah Muhammad in the 1930s, the NOI split under the leadership of Elijah's son Wallace Muhammad (who has now Islamicised his name to Warith-ud-Din Muhammad). Following the example of Malcolm X, who broke with Elijah Muhammad and joined the Islamic mainstream before his assassination in 1965, Wallace took the Nation in the direction of Sunni orthodoxy, converting its temples into mosques, liquidating its businesses and eventually dissolving its organisation, urging members to worship at their local mosques. In 1992, having supported the US-led coalition in the Gulf, Muhammad became the first Muslim imam to be invited to offer prayers in the US Senate.

The reborn NOI, which has stuck with Elijah Muhammad's separatist principles, claims that Elijah Muhammad – like the Twelfth Imam of the Shi'a – is still alive and is guiding the movement spiritually. Its current leader is a former musician, Louis Farrakhan. Notorious for his anti-Semitism and the racist language he uses against whites, Farrakhan is one of the most hated men in (white) America. He is duly idolised by the black underclass, especially the youth of the ghettoes and hip-hop rap groups such as Public Enemy and NWA (Niggaz With Attitude).

In the no-go areas of Washington, Detroit, Los Angeles and other cities, it is the Nation Of Islam, not the police, that gets results. The NOI has brokered peace agreements between rival gangs, Farrakhan being the only national leader for whom the young gangsters have any respect. In many inner city areas the NOI's 'Islamic patrols', manned by unarmed vigilantes wearing business suits and bow ties, are now a familiar and increasingly popular sight, and having driven away the dealers and pimps have brought calm and safety to the streets. The NOI Security Agency has 'dope-busting' contracts in several cities, while its guards provide security for respectable corporations such as Federal Express. Such contracts have created consternation among Jewish groups concerned about virulently anti-Semitic statements made by Farrakhan and his henchmen.

Of the two books under review, Gardell's masterful study provides by far the most detail, being the first comprehensive scholarly treatment of Farrakhan and the NOI. Gardell's research is meticulous and thorough. Not only has he trawled through hundreds of FBI files made available through the Public Information Act; he has also had the advantage of extensive interviews with Mr Farrakhan and other NOI leaders. Kepel only deals with the NOI in the first third of his book, which looks at Islamic communities in Britain and France as well as the United States. Nevertheless, his overall view of the NOI is broadly consistent with Gardell's much more detailed analysis.

The broad contours of the story of the Nation Of Islam are widely known through the immensely popular *The Autobiography of Malcolm X* and Spike Lee's film version of the book. Less well known is the bizarre and eclectic theology from which Malcom X eventually distanced himself, and which Farrakhan has revived and enriched. God is a man, not a spirit, and of a condition to which humans may aspire by recognising and realising the black god within themselves. He has given the devil embodied in the white man a temporary dispensation to rule the world, allowing all the evils that afflict his chosen people – colonialism, slavery, racial oppression and poverty – to flourish. That period is about to end with the approach of Armageddon, when the black Nation will be redeemed, and Babylon utterly destroyed:

> *The extermination will be absolutely complete, destroying all stock markets, skyscrapers, transportation nets, harbors, cities and hamlets. Every trace and deed, including the languages, knowledge, and thoughts of the devil, will be eradicated in the global atomic-chemical fire, as described in 2 Peter 3:10. The heavens shall pass away with great noise and the elements shall melt with fervent heat, the earth also and the works that are therein shall be burned up.*

God is supervising these events from an artificial planet known as the 'Mother Ship' or 'Mother Wheel'. UFOs or 'baby planes' from this planet are regularly sent to earth with Divine instructions. In one such encounter, Farrakhan meets the Honourable Elijah Muhammad, the occulted Messiah, who confirms his authority as Leader. A scroll containing the sacred scriptures has been placed in the back of Farrakhan's brain to be revealed in its entirety in the fullness of time. While awaiting deliverance, the faithful must purify themselves, eschewing meat, junk food, alcohol, drugs and sexual promiscuity – all of them devil's weapons aimed specifically at enslaving African-Americans. The mid-term objective, the Nation's 'interim programme', is an independent black state on American or African soil, acquired through reparations paid by American and African governments for the crimes of slavery. The state will be ruled in accordance with strict 'Islamic' law: the death penalty will be mandatory for adultery, rape, incest and inter-racial sex.

Similar ingredients, mixed and cooked somewhat differently, can be found in other American religions, including Seventh-day Adventists, Jehovah's Witnesses, Christian Science and especially Mormonism. A small criticism to be made of Gardell's book is that he could have devoted more attention to the way the NOI recycles themes already widely present in American religious culture. While placing the NOI well outside the boundaries of mainstream Islam, the NOI's doctrine combines elements of the pre-millenial dispensationalist eschatology common to most Baptist churches, black and white, gnosticism, kabbalism, Zionism, identity Christianity, Scientology, Arminianism, the deification of man as taught by the Mormons, the positive thinking of Norman Vincent Peale and the science fantasy theology of L. Ron Hubbard – all of them packaged in colourful mythological wrappings adapted from Jewish, Christian and Islamic traditions. Gardell speculates interestingly that Elijah Muhammad's original mentor (the movement's Jesus to his Paul), a street pedlar from Detroit named W. D. Fard or Ford who disappeared in 1924 leaving Elijah in charge, may have been a Druze from Syria. Detroit had many street pedlars of Syrian origin at that time. Gardell finds traces of the Ismaili neo-platonist system (also adopted by the Druzes) in the NOI's gnostic teachings, along with echoes of the Native American Smohalla religion. The whole package, however, bears one unambiguous label: 'Made in the USA.'

As with Mormonism and other bizarre belief-systems, the sceptical outsider will always have difficulty in accepting that intelligent people can take such beliefs seriously while operating successfully in the 'real' world. However, the parallels with Mormonism, one of the world's most rapidly growing religions, reveals how successfully religious heterodoxy can sustain group identity while buttressing a style of 'this-worldly asceticism' conducive to capitalism along classic Weberian lines. Gardell's study shows how the Nation Of Islam, like the nineteenth-century Mormons, prepares for the end of the world, breaking with the majoritarian society it considers doomed by flaunting its transgressive beliefs.

The Mormons defied the world by practising polygamy in the mid-Victorian American West. The NOI challenges liberal values by turning them on their head, preaching anti-white racism and anti-Semitism. The latter, while reflecting the real experiences of some African-Americans in inner city areas, whose encounters with Jewish landlords or shopkeepers have often been less than happy, also addresses what the NOI sees as a scandalous anomaly. The 6 million white victims of the Holocaust (for which America bears, if anything, only the most vestigial responsibility) attract far more public attention than the notorious 'middle passage' across the Atlantic, when, according to Farrakhan, 100 million Africans died. 'America you owe us something,' Farrakhan shouts, 'and we don't want you to dole it out in welfare checks.' Just as Germany paid Israel compensation, so the US government should now pay its debt to its black citizens: 'Now, let's add up what they owe us. If a hundred million of us lost our lives in the middle passage, add it up! Three hundred years working millions of slaves for nothing. Add it up!'

Reparations or no, there are plenty of indications that the NOI is already moving along the path from marginality to respectability previously trodden by Mormons, Adventists and others. In addition to the dope-busting contracts, the theology is being spiritualised, with demonic whiteness explained as an attitude of mind (and hence changeable) rather than an unalterable attribute of persons. The Million Man March on Washington organised by Farrakhan in 1995 may not have produced very much in terms of concrete results: but it certainly proved the NOI's capacity for organisation and its ability to work within the system.

In *Allah in the West*, Gilles Kepel identifies several common threads linking the activities of Farrakhan and the NOI in America, the Muslim agitation in Britain against Salman Rushdie's novel *The Satanic Verses* and the 'affairs of the scarf' in France, when the refusal by head teachers to allow Muslim pupils to wear the Islamic hijab or 'veil' in school opened up divisions in society not seen 'since the Dreyfus affair'. His perceptive analysis grapples with a central paradox: the assertion of Islam within Western societies that are generally moving in the opposite direction, towards greater individual choice, in which inherited identities are fading away. Why, he asks, do the Muslim activists in all three countries *choose to identify with Islam in open societies where individuals have much more freedom in their allegiance than in the 'traditional' societies of the Muslim world, where the predominance of the inherited culture remains a determining influence on social identity?*

In the United States, Kepel sees the NOI project as an exercise in community building by creating a positive identity for African-Americans. Much of the theology is a straight inversion of white cultural prejudices against blacks. The anti-Semitism has a similar purpose: Jews must be denied the high moral ground of victimhood. In the NOI's pseudo-scholarly study, *The Secret Relationship between Blacks and Jews*, published in 1991, Jewish participation in the slave trade is stressed obsessively, by repetition, while Muslim participation is consistently ignored. Slavery replaces the Holocaust as 'the ultimate genocide in the history of humanity'; Jewish victimhood is contaminated, as it were, by Jewish participation in the slave trade and therefore in the perpetration of genocide, with the tacit conviction that culpability is heritable. As Gardel warns us, the demonisation of Jews must not be taken in isolation from the larger demonisation of whites. A new reconstructed Muslim identity, decontextualised and 'pure', helps to build community:

Communalism is based on strong personal attachment to a reconstructed identity and necessarily resists the reflexive process of comparison between diverse human experiences. Outside the community of the self-proclaimed 'pure' there can only be barbarism. No other communities can claim ethical justification for their status.

In similar fashion, British Muslims defended the honour of their Prophet against the perceived assaults in Salman Rushdie's novel. At stake here, however, was not a reconstructed or reinvented Muslim identity but rather the inherited Islamic identity the British-Muslim majority brought with them from the Indian subcontinent – an identity already forged by the communalist policies fostered by the Raj.

Rushdie's work was bound to upset the religious leaders who had managed to establish control over the populations of Muslim origin in Britain. By undermining the very basis of an Islamic community identity, it threatened their cultural, social and political domination of their flock. But the language used by Rushdie in relation to Islam and the Prophet aroused the anger of a much wider Muslim population:

> By using ironic names for figures held in reverence by pious Muslims, especially the Prophet ... and his entourage, and placing these characters in obscene or morally degrading circumstances, Rushdie alienated a great number of ordinary Muslims outside the inner circle of mullahs and Islamic association leaders. Paradoxically the controversy surrounding the book brought together those who felt that their closest beliefs had been attacked, reinforcing many Muslims' sense of community and making them even more receptive to the mullahs and Islamic leaders.

The 'affair of the scarf' in France played a similar role to the Rushdie affair in Britain. If the occasion seems more trivial to Anglo-Saxons, this is because France's centralising traditions offer much less scope for communalism than the United States or Britain: 'Unlike the US and Britain, the state in France exerts strong pressure on society to prevent the formation of religion-based communities which would weaken the link between the Republic and its citizens.'

The demand in 1989 by three Muslim pupils in the Paris suburb of Creil to wear the hijab in school was seen as a challenge to the jealously guarded principle of laïcité or secularity. Though the Council of State eventually upheld the girls' right to 'display their religious beliefs within educational establishments' the debate engendered by the affair was used by numerous Muslim associations to outbid the Muslim 'establishment' represented by the Paris Mosque, which has close connections with the Algerian government. The concessions won by the three girls in Creil, far from satisfying Muslim communalists, led to further demands, with the rights of pupils in their capacities as French citizens gaining ground over the rights of their immigrant Muslim parents. The veil itself became wrapped in paradox: donning what was seen by most French people as a symbol of female submission became an act of auto-emancipation. Schèrazade of Grenoble, who escalated Muslim demands on the system by refusing to remove her head-covering even for physical education, became both heroine and pariah: 'France is my freedom, so is my veil!' In conclusion, Kepel sees France adopting a position closer to that of Britain with regard to its Muslim population, with notions of citizenship losing their meaning for increasing numbers of young people from immigrant families, 'victims of social disintegration and labour-market exclusion, yet officially citizens of a country where most of them were born'. The policy of 'assimilation' by individuals having manifestly failed is giving way before demands for 'integration' as communities. Whilst communalism in France is unlikely to go so far as it has in Britain or the

United States, Kepel concludes that the whole question of citizenship needs to be re-examined in its light.

The merit of Kepel's essay is that it asks the right questions, all of them difficult. Its cardinal weakness is that it concentrates exclusively on the flashpoints and militancies that catch the headlines, and neglecting the countervailing trends that point in the opposite direction. Many Muslims in the West are voting for assimilation with their feet, in bars or hair-dressing salons, or just in private homes, eschewing militancy, and avoiding social visibility. Communalism depends on the perception of an external threat. Without the flames of prejudice, perceived or actual, it must wither.

Published in *The Times Literary Supplement*, 30 May 1997.

The books reviewed were:

Mattias Gardell (1996) *Countdown to Armageddon: Louis Farrakhan and the Nation of Islam.* London: Hurst.

Gilles Kepel (1997) *Allah in the West: Islamic Movements in America and Europe*, translated by Susan Milner. Oxford, UK: Polity Press. (Originally published as *A l'Ouest d'Allah.* Paris: Éditions du Seuil, 1994.)

Part **Six**

Beyond Islam

This final selection of reviews and articles strays a little outside the theme of encounters with Islam through the work of several writers. The first item is an unpublished review of William Dalrymple's From the Holy Mountain, A Journey in the Shadow of Byzantium. Fifteen years on, the main theme of his thoroughly engaging narrative – the disappearance of Christianity from the lands of its origin – is as topical, and poignant, as ever. The fears of Christians and other minority communities in Syria that they will suffer if the minority Alawite-based regime finally crumbles, are by no means groundless. Since the departure of the Mubarak regime in the spring of 2011, Egypt has seen a significant rise in attacks on the Coptic minority, while the US-led invasion of Iraq and subsequent struggles between Shi'a, Sunnis and Kurds has seen the virtual disappearance of that country's ancient Christian communities. Islamic spokesmen often state that their religion is one of tolerance, but the actual record speaks differently.

The second item is an obituary of Edward Said, written for The Guardian a few days after his death in 2003. It incorporates elements of my review of his memoir – Out of Place (1999) – and earlier pieces, as well as accounts of his wider political and cultural activities, including his highly commendable partnership with Daniel Barenboim in creating the remarkable and hugely successful West-Eastern Divan Orchestra. Though familiar with his writings, I only met this remarkably talented intellectual, who came from a Christian Palestinian family and who died after a long and heroic struggle against a rare form of cancer, on a single occasion, at a literary gathering in London. It was not a comfortable encounter: he reprimanded me for a recent piece I had written in favour of the Oslo accords between the Israelis and Palestinians. For him, Oslo was the Palestinian Versailles – an abject capitulation to Israeli–American pressure. Ten years on, with the rampant increase in illegal Israeli settlements on Palestinian land, the construction of special roads for the settlers, the proliferation of check-points and an eight-metre-high concrete wall that cuts through Palestinian farms and suburbs, it is hard to quarrel with his verdict.

The final item – an appropriate tailpiece perhaps – reproduces a 'blog' I wrote for The New York Review of Books, which unexpectedly won an award from the Foreign Press Association. As I am not a regular blogger, I count this beginner's luck – like the proverbial monster pike caught by a novice, to the annoyance of seasoned anglers. It concerns a mundane but distressing topic: the lack of toilets in India, and how this diminishes the life-chances of the female half of its people, and how this is being addressed by an Islamically based charity – the Aga Khan Foundation – in a Muslim quarter of Delhi. In a country with an enviable rate of economic growth, as compared with most of Europe, the lack of toilets is a scandal that deserves to be exposed.

26
A Holy (O)mission

In CE 578, John Moschos, an elderly Byzantine monk, and his pupil Sophronius set out on a journey around the Eastern Mediterranean in search of spiritual wisdom. After visiting the major religious centres of the empire, Moschos returned to Constantinople where he wrote a book called *The Spiritual Meadow* before succumbing to exhaustion and illness. A collection of sayings, anecdotes and holy stories in the tradition of the *Apophthegmata Patrum* or 'Sayings of the Desert Fathers', *The Spiritual Meadow* is also a travel book. As William Dalrymple, one of the most accomplished exemplars of the genre, observes: 'Moschos did what the modern travel writer still does: he wandered the world in search of strange stories and remarkable travellers' tales. Indeed, his book can legitimately be read as the great masterpiece of Byzantine travel writing.'

Inspired by *The Spiritual Meadow*, Dalrymple retraces Moschos' route, from the monastic republic of Mount Athos to the Great Oasis of Al-Kharga in Southern Egypt. In the manner of his predecessor, he records spiritual marvels, miracles, conversations and anecdotes. In the remoter places he visits, he encounters the mutual respect and tolerance that once bound Muslims and Christians together under a common sacred canopy. At the abbey of Mar Gabriel in Eastern Turkey, built by the Emperor Anastasius in 512, Syrian Christians who still use the language of Christ in their liturgy prostrate themselves in the Muslim manner when praying – living proof of the way in which Islam grafted itself on to much older Middle Eastern religious traditions. The saint's relics – 'holes in the curtain wall separating the human from the divine' – are still venerated by members of both faiths. In the now abandoned city of Cyrrhus in northern Syria, once the site of a great cathedral, he finds that the medieval Muslim saint buried in a much older Byzantine tomb is now identified with the unfortunate Uriah, husband of Bathsheba. Members of both religions worship there, receiving blessings and miracles from the saint; and those who fail to honour him, regardless of confession, find their purposes supernaturally thwarted. Dalrymple rightly regards such holy places where popular religious syncretism survives as vital oases of tolerance in an increasingly polarised region:

> *The practice emphasises an important truth about the close affinity of the two great religions easily forgotten as the Eastern Christians – the last surviving bridge between Islam and Western Christianity – emigrate in reaction to the increasing hostility of the Islamic establishment.*

Dalrymple does his best to project himself back into this enchanted world common to Byzantium and early Islam, when men acquired celebrity through spectacular spiritual feats. Pausing under the pillar of St Simeon Stylites the Younger, who sat on his mountain top while the church was constructed around him, he reflects on the difficulty of reaching back across the centuries:

> *At the base of a stylite's pillar one is confronted with the awkward truth that what has most moved past generations can today sometimes be only tentatively glimpsed with the eye of faith, while remaining quite inexplicable and absurd when seen under the harsh distorting microscope of sceptical Western rationality.*

What really moves in this narrative, however, is not the futility of trying to grasp the numinous quality of a world that has been lost, but the much more recent catastrophes that occurred in the aftermath of its collapse. Just as the Holocaust in Europe happened after the Enlightenment, when religious hostility against Jews was buttressed by German, Polish, Romanian and other nationalisms, so the greatest disaster to have befallen Eastern Christianity occurred at the end of the Ottoman period, when pluralistic Islamic allegiances were crumbling before an emerging Turkish identity. The ghosts of the Armenians follow Dalrymple throughout Turkey, Syria and Palestine. In Diyarbakir province, where the government now fights Kurdish insurgents, with 500 unsolved murders in the city blamed on the secret police, more than half a million Armenians and Syrian Orthodox Christians (Suriani) were butchered in 1915, 'clubbed to death like rabbits'. Thousands more were driven into the Syrian desert, to die of starvation or thirst. These crimes remain unacknowledged by the modern Turkish state, and hence unpropitiated. This denial of the past is systematic, deliberate and ideologically driven. A scholar who dares to recall (in a footnote in the Turkish edition of the *Encyclopaedia Britannica*) that Cilicia was once a Christian kingdom is arrested and charged with 'making propaganda with intent to destroy or weaken national feelings'; in Eastern Anatolia, Armenian churches – some of them important monuments – continue to disappear. The names of Armenian villages have all been changed. Once the churches have gone, there will be no evidence that the Armenians ever existed.

In Urfa, the site of ancient Edessa, once a flourishing centre of Eastern Christianity, Dalrymple finds the old Armenian cathedral is being converted into a mosque:

> 'Are there any Armenians left in Urfa?' [he asks one of a pair of workmen]
>
> 'No' he answered, smiling broadly and laughing. His friend made a throat-cutting gesture with his trowel.
>
> 'They've all gone,' said the first man, smiling.
>
> 'Where to?'
>
> The two looked at each other: 'Israel,' said the first man, after a pause. He was grinning from ear to ear.
>
> 'I thought Israel was for Jews,' I said.
>
> 'Jews, Armenians,' he replied, shrugging his shoulders. 'Same thing.'

Encounters such as these are all the more chilling, as Dalrymple's writing is usually so genial and apparently effortless. His erudition is lightly worn. His knack of conjuring reflections out of tombs and buildings is refreshingly free from self-consciousness or high-mindedness. The cold, neo-classical faces of saints and apostles staring down from the broken apses and shattered naves of a hundred abandoned churches give him 'very little idea of what the early Byzantine peasant or shopkeeper looked like … what he longed for, what he loved and what he hated'. But he is happy to indulge in speculation, finding in a group of early Christian sarcophagi the thinly-veiled relics of pagan antiquity, asking himself if the people inside had still led

> a version of the old life of the late classical landowner: their youth spent in the law school at Beirut or the School of Libanius in Antioch; a period as a provincial official posted to Hippo or Harran; of perhaps a spell in the army on the Rhine frontier, peering into the cold battlements of Cologne or Trier to catch a glimpse of a Gothic raider padding across the ice into Roman territory.

He finds the Egyptian mummy portraits in Alexandria 'astonishingly familiar', with colours and technique resembling Frans Hals or Cézanne, still conveying with

> *penetrating immediacy the character of the different sitters: the fop and the courtesan, the anxious mother and the tough man of business, the bored army officer and the fat nouveau-riche matron, hung with gold, dripping with make-up … Even today behind glass in a museum, the portraits are so astonishingly life-like that they can still make you gasp as you find yourself staring eyeball to eyeball with a soldier who had fought at Actium, or a society lady who may have known Cleopatra. There is something deeply hypnotic about the silent stare of these sad, uncertain Graeco-Roman faces, most of whom appear to have died in their early thirties. Their fleeting expressions are frozen, startled, as if suddenly surprised by death itself; their huge eyes stare out, as if revealing the nakedness of the departed soul.*

An urbane, Catholic Scot who grew up on the shores of the Firth of Forth, Dalrymple engages in some plausible speculations about the transmission of Christianity from the Middle East to Ireland and Scotland. Fascinated by the similarity between the stories of the desert fathers in the Middle East and those of the Celtic monks of his childhood, he runs to ground some compelling iconographic correspondences suggestive of Byzantine influences on early Christian art in the British Isles. At the Monastery of St Antony in Egypt, birthplace of Christian monasticism, he is shown an icon of St Paul and St Antony breaking bread: the image (convincingly demonstrated in photographs) is almost identical with that of a seventh-century Pictish carving from St Vigeans, near Dundee.

Though comfortable with antiquity, Dalrymple is aesthetically tuned to the present. When descending the twisting mountain road into Beirut he notes that the shrapnel marks decorating the buildings resemble abstracts by Kandinsky – 'a perfect peppering of dots and dashes'. He registers the bizarre ghastliness of that city's post-modern apocalypse, where Khomeini fights for space with Calvin Klein:

> *It was like a morality tale, spiralling downwards through one of the world's greatest monuments to human frailty, a huge cortex of greed and envy, resentment and intolerance, hatred and materialism, a five-mile-long slalom of shell-holes and designer labels, heavy artillery and glossy boutiques. Like a modern updating*

of a Byzantine Apocalypse, it was the confusion that was most
hell-like: Ayatollah Khomeini, hands raised in blessing, shared
a billboard with a bottle of American after-shave; below, huge
American cars – Thunderbirds, Chevrolets, Corvettes – roared
past building sites where monstrous machines, thickly carapaced
like metal-clad cockroaches, moved earth, demolished ruins, dug
holes. Occasionally there was an explosion and a small mush-
room-cloud of dust as a doomed tower block crashed to the earth,
nudged by one of the grunting metal beetles below.

The strength of this book, however, lies less in the quality of its descriptions than its thematic agenda. Dalrymple set out to visit and record the dwindling Christian communities of the Middle East just as Moschos had done 14 centuries before during the high summer of Byzantine civilisation, before they were overwhelmed by the Islamic tide. Guaranteed survival under Islamic empires, which recognised them as dhimmis, or protected communities, many of the Christians prospered anew under the colonial hegemony through access to modern education and the business opportunities provided by contacts with Western co-religionists. The resurgence of political Islam throughout the region is now placing these gains in jeopardy, and Christians are leaving the area in droves for countries where they feel safer and where their skills are appreciated. There are now only 14 million Christians left among a non-Christian population of 180 million, and their numbers are shrinking fast. Since the early 1990s, at least 2 million have left the Middle East to make new lives for themselves in Europe, Australia and America.

The causes of this massive decline, as Dalrymple found, are complex and by no means exclusively attributable to the resurgence of political Islam. In Turkey, the Syrian Orthodox Christians he met were caught between rival Kurdish and Turkish nationalisms, and here it was their ethnicity as much as their religion that counted against them. In Lebanon, the once-dominant Maronite Christians had virtually self-destructed. Feuding between rival Maronite clans, the Franjiehs and Gemayals, tore the community apart along with the whole country. The Maronites 'reaped a bitter harvest of their own sowing'. They emerged from the war with their reputation for 'ruthlessness, brutality and political incompetence enormously enhanced', while by the war's final stages, more than a third of a million of them – over a quarter of the entire Christian community of Lebanon – had left the area for good. It would be wrong to see the Lebanese civil war primarily in terms of a Christian–Muslim conflict: Greek Orthodox and Armenians were attacked by the Maronite Phalangist militias, along with other Maronites.

Of the countries visited by Dalrymple, Syria, the ultimate victor in this war, has by far the best record of dealing with its Christian citizens. Lebanon apart, it is the only country in the region where Christians can claim to live on equal terms with Muslims – an impression confirmed by Dalrymple's experience of crossing the border, where 'icons of Christ and images of his mother fill almost every shop and decorate every other car window – an extraordinary display after the furtive secrecy of Christianity in Turkey'. The population of Aleppo, the main city of refuge for persecuted Turkish Christians, is now between one-fifth and one-third Christian. Syria 'may still be a one-party police state, but it is a police state that leaves its citizens alone so long as they keep out of politics'. Only in Syria did Dalrymple find the Christian population looking 'happy and confident', but even here their future looked uncertain, with most of them expecting a major backlash when the Alawite minority regime of Al-Assad collapses. Unfortunately, Dalrymple omits to mention the human cost of Syria's religious tolerance: between 10,000 and 20,000 people were killed after the Muslim Brotherhood's abortive uprising in the city of Hama in 1981, most of them by troops commanded by Rifaat al-Assad, the president's playboy brother, *pour encourager les autres*. One of the paradoxes he might have addressed is that, in the Muslim world, religious tolerance and democracy may actually be incompatible, as the example of Turkey demonstrates. The more responsive a government is to the feelings of its Muslim majority, the less likely it is to grant minorities equal status as citizens.

The legacy of Islamic supremacism runs deep. However, of the countries Dalrymple visited, it was only in Egypt that Christians were confronted directly with the power of resurgent Islam in the shape of sectarian attacks. Armed with permission from the president, Dalrymple managed to penetrate the roadblocks to visit Asyut, the southern city of mixed Christian–Muslim population closed to foreign reporters since a massacre of Copts by Islamic militants in 1992. He discovered that the feuding in the city originated in a dispute over property. Hitmen from the Islamist Gema'a al-Islamiya had become embroiled in an argument between a Muslim and a Copt over the sale of a house. Everywhere, the priests and monks he spoke to reflected the general sense of insecurity experienced by the Coptic minority. The government was allowing Muslim terrorists literally to get away with murder. Some of these attacks followed demands for protection money, which the Copts refused to pay. Though Dalrymple omits to mention this, payment of the jizya, the poll tax demanded exclusively from non-Muslims, is part of the Islamist agenda, a symbol of past Islamic hegemony that the Islamists are trying to revive. Dalrymple's Christian interlocutors consistently underplayed the significance of these attacks: 'Like the Suriani in

Turkey, the Copts are very reluctant to talk about their worries; hundreds of years of living as a minority under Muslim rule has taught them to keep their heads down.'

Some of the monks even claimed to have found spiritual consolation in the persecution. 'God is most easily discernible in times of trouble,' explained one. 'When your troubles cease, then you leave God. But in difficult times men go to God for help.' His faith seemed to have been borne out by the revival of monasticism occurring in recent years. The Monastery of St Antony was bursting with monks and novices, many of them equipped with survival skills such as expertise in irrigation and chicken-farming as well as degrees in theology.

It is, above all, in Israel–Palestine – the Christian Holy Land – that this picture of general Christian decline becomes really bleak. Squeezed between the Jewish take-over of Jerusalem and its surroundings, and the rising pressures of Hamas in the occupied areas (the book was written before the Oslo accords began to be implemented), the Palestinian Christians, who may be descended from the very first Christians of all, are abandoning the Holy Land for ever. As in Turkey, archaeological vandalism is rife, with the ruins of two Byzantine monasteries in Jerusalem recently built over to make car parks, with precious mosaics destroyed for ever.

At Ariel, outside Ramallah, Jewish settlers have built a replica of an American town complete with shopping arcades, sports centres and supermarkets. Ron, the mayor, who talks fast in flawless American, has no problems with Arabs. 'I'm no racist,' he insists. 'I have an Arab cleaning lady – that's right – *an Arab cleaning lady*. She is alone with my babies. I can't say everyone would trust an Arab like that.' Dalrymple comments:

> No Palestinian either Christian or Muslim ever needed to bother applying to live in Ariel: its houses were available only to Jewish settlers. When local Palestinian labourers at the settlement were forced to wear large badges reading 'Foreign Worker' some liberal Israeli commentators went so far as to draw comparisons with the race laws of Nazi Germany. The badges were later removed.

The Christians who used to make up a third of the Arab population of Palestine are now reduced to less than a quarter of 1 per cent. In the Old City of Jerusalem, where in 1922 Christians constituted 52 per cent of the population, they are now reduced to 2.5 per cent. If the present decline continues there will soon be none left at all. The most important shrines in the Christian world will be left as museum pieces or, as the Archbishop of Canterbury warned recently, a 'theme park' preserved only for tourists.

Despite this impending extinction, some priests take a remarkably sanguine view, relying on God to put things right. At Mar Saba on the West Bank, Dalrymple shared a glass of ouzo with Father Theophanes, the monastery's tall, gaunt Guest Master, who regaled him with direful descriptions of the coming apocalypse:

> Fire – fire that will never end, terrible, terrible fire – will come from the throne of Christ, just like it does on the icons. The saints – those who are to be saved, in other words the Orthodox Church – will fly in the air to meet Christ. But sinners and all non-Orthodox will be separated from the Elect. The damned will be pushed and prodded by devils down through the fire, down from the Valley of Josephat, past here – in fact, exactly the route those Israeli hikers took today – down, down to the Mouth of Hell ... near the Dead Sea.

Most Palestinian Christians are much less confident of salvation and the inevitable retribution in store for Muslims, Jews, non-Orthodox Christians and others, and continue to abandon the Holy Land for richer pastures in the West. Most of them are well-educated professionals and better placed than their Muslim compatriots to find homes and jobs abroad.

Surprisingly, the demise of Christianity in the land of its origin appears to have met with very little comment or protest among churches in the West, especially in the United States, a much more actively Christian society than Europe's. Dalrymple refrains from speculating about the possible reasons for this deafening silence, but a clue appears in his interview with Father Theophanes, who bizarrely sees in supermarket barcodes a sign of the coming Anti-Christ. In his fascinating study, *When Time Shall Be No More: Prophesy Belief in Modern American Culture* (Cambridge, MA: Belknap Press of Harvard University Press, 1992), an American scholar, Paul Boyer, describes how many American Protestants, convinced that the 'end-times' are upon us, believe that the number 666 and its various permutations, the 'number of the Beast', are already being encoded into the magnetic strips of credit cards and supermarket barcodes. A book on the subject published in America in 1981 sold more than half a million copies. I suspect that copies of this or similar texts may be circulating in Orthodox monasteries: where else would Father Theophanes have learnt about the apocalyptic character of supermarket barcodes? As Boyer points out, the American pre-millennialists subscribing to such beliefs (who number at least 8 million) consider the restoration of the kingdom of Israel to be a vital part of God's plan for humanity. The foundation of the Jewish state in 1948 was the first act in an eschatological drama that will culminate with Armageddon and the Millennium, the thousand-year reign of Christ on earth. Sharing Father Theophanes's confidence in their own salvation, American fundamentalists give Israel their wholehearted support and the Israelis (while privately laughing behind their backs) reciprocate, awarding honours to fundamentalists such as Gerry Falwell and generally extending the warmest hospitality to visiting Christians of this persuasion. A film version of Hal Lindsay's *Late Great Planet Earth*, the book of which has sold more than 30 million copies to date, included an interview with the late President of Israel, Chaim Herzog. This relationship of mutual support between Protestant millenarians and Zionists is not without future complications: according to the pre-millennialist scenario, a portion of Jewry – the 'righteous Jews' – will convert to Christianity and be 'raptured' up to Christ along with Theophanes and his fellow monks. The remainder will perish horribly in rivers of blood, with the rest of the unsaved portion of humanity. Compared with a destiny of this magnitude, the future of a few thousand Palestinian Christians must seem a trivial sideshow.

Commissioned by the *London Review of Books* (1997), but rejected for publication.

The book reviewed was:

William Dalrymple (1997) *From the Holy Mountain: A Journey in the Shadow of Byzantium.* London: HarperCollins.

27
Edward Said, 1935–2003

Edward Said, who has died aged 67, was one of the leading literary critics of the last quarter of the twentieth century. As professor of English and comparative literature at Columbia University, New York, he was widely regarded as the outstanding representative of the post-structuralist left in America. Above all, he was the most articulate and visible advocate of the Palestinian cause in the United States, where it earned him many enemies.

The broadness of Said's approach to literature and his other great love, classical music, eludes easy categorisation. His most influential book, *Orientalism* (1978), is credited with helping to change the direction of several disciplines by exposing an unholy alliance between the enlightenment and colonialism. As a humanist with a thoroughly secular outlook, his critique on the great tradition of the Western Enlightenment seemed to many to be self-contradictory, deploying a humanistic discourse to attack the high cultural traditions of humanism, giving comfort to fundamentalists who regarded any criticism of their tradition or texts as being off-limits, while calling into question the integrity of critical research into culturally sensitive areas such as Islam.

Whatever its flaws, however, Orientalism appeared at an opportune time, enabling upwardly mobile academics from non-Western countries (many of whom came from families who had benefited from colonialism) to take advantage of the mood of political correctness it helped to engender, by associating themselves with 'narratives of oppression', creating successful careers out of transmitting, interpreting and debating representations of the non-Western 'other'.

Said's influence, however, was far from being confined to the worlds of academic and scholarly discourse. An intellectual superstar in America, he distinguished himself as an opera critic, pianist, television celebrity, politician, media expert, popular essayist and public lecturer.

Latterly, he was one of the most trenchant critics of the Oslo peace process and the Palestinian leadership of Yasser Arafat. He was dubbed 'professor of terror' by the right-wing American magazine *Commentary*; in

1999, when he was struggling with leukaemia, the same magazine accused him of falsifying his status as a Palestinian refugee to enhance his advocacy of the Palestinian cause, and of falsely claiming to have been at school in Jerusalem before completing his education in the United States.

The hostility Said encountered from pro-Israeli circles in New York was predictable, given his trenchant attacks on Israeli violations of the human rights of Palestinians and his outspoken condemnations of US policies in the Middle East. From the other side of the conflict, however, he encountered opposition from Palestinians, who accused him of sacrificing Palestinian rights by making unwarranted concessions to Zionism.

As early as 1977, when few Palestinians were prepared to concede that Jews had historic claims to Palestine, he said: 'I don't deny their claims, but their claim always entails Palestinian dispossession.' More than any other Palestinian writer, he qualified his anti-colonial critique of Israel, explaining its complex entanglements and the problematic character of its origins in the persecution of European Jews, and the overwhelming impact of the Zionist idea on the European conscience.

Said recognised that Israel's exemption from the normal criteria by which nations are measured owed everything to the Holocaust. But while recognising its unique significance, he did not see why its legacy of trauma and horror should be exploited to deprive the Palestinians, a people who were 'absolutely dissociable from what has been an entirely European complicity', of their rights.

He wrote in *The Politics of Dispossession* (1994):

> *The question to be asked is how long can the history of anti-semitism and the Holocaust be used as a fence to exempt Israel from arguments and sanctions against it for its behaviour towards the Palestinians, arguments and sanctions that were used against other repressive governments, such as South Africa? How long are we going to deny that the cries of the people of Gaza ... are directly connected to the policies of the Israeli government and not to the cries of the victims of Nazism?*

He insisted that the task of Israel's critics was not to reproduce for Palestine a mirror-image of a Zionist ideology of diaspora and return, but rather to elaborate a secular vision of democracy as applicable to both Arabs and Jews. Elected to the Palestine National Council (PNC) in 1977 as an independent intellectual, Said avoided taking part in the factional struggles, while using his authority to make strategic interventions. Rejecting the policy of armed struggle as impermissible – because of the legacy of the

Holocaust and the special conditions of the Jewish people – he was an early advocate of the two-state solution, implicitly recognising Israel's right to exist. This policy was adopted at the PNC meeting in Algiers in 1988.

In adapting the English version of the Arabic draft text, Said used his influence to rephrase the Arabic; though his modifications were insufficient to satisfy the Reagan administration, which dictated the crucial words that appeared in Arafat's speech to a special session of the UN General Assembly (convened in Geneva because the US State Department refused to grant Arafat a visa to attend the UN in New York), there can be little doubt that Said's tireless representations in the American media, explaining that the declaration amounted to a 'historic compromise' on the part of the Palestinians towards the Jewish state, opened the way for the US–PLO dialogue that would lead to the Madrid conference and the Oslo peace process.

As the peace process gained momentum, however, Said adopted an increasingly critical stance and in 1991 resigned from the PNC. The Oslo declaration, he argued, was weighted unfairly towards Israel; the scenario, pre-visioning an Israeli withdrawal from Gaza and Jericho in advance of the other territories and agreement on the final status of Jerusalem, amounted to 'an instrument of Palestinian surrender, a Palestinian Versailles'.

To the end, he remained a thorn in the side of the Palestinian authorities. The best-known and most distinguished Palestinian exile became the subject of censorship by the representatives of his own people, one of the standard-bearers of the liberal conscience in the increasingly illiberal climate of intolerance and corruption surrounding President Arafat and his regime.

Said was born in Jerusalem into a prosperous Palestinian family. His father, Wadie, a Christian, had emigrated to the USA before the First World War. He volunteered for service in France and returned to the Middle East as a respectable Protestant businessman – with American citizenship – before making an arranged marriage to the daughter of a Baptist minister from Nazareth.

In *Out of Place* (1999), the memoir of his childhood and youth, Said described his father, who called himself William to emphasise his adopted American identity, as overbearing and uncommunicative. His Victorian strictness instilled in Said 'a deep sense of generalised fear', which he spent most of his life trying to overcome. To his father, Said owed the drivenness that brought him his remarkable achievements:

> I have no concept of leisure or relaxation and, more particularly, no sense of cumulative achievement. Every day for me is like the

beginning of a new term at school, with a vast and empty summer behind it, and an uncertain tomorrow before it.

Wadie Said revealed little about himself or the source of his money, but certainly Edward and his sisters never wanted for anything, travelling with battalions of servants, summering (after 1947) in the cultivated comfort of Dhour el Shweir in Lebanon, and enjoying sumptuous dinners on transatlantic liners. Said described his mother, whom he evidently adored, as brilliant and manipulative, neurotically difficult to please, always giving the impression that 'she had judged you and found you wanting' – yet instilling in him a love of literature and music.

Said's first name, improbably inspired by the Prince of Wales, was the creation of his parents, whom he would come to see as 'self -creations' out of an eclectic blend of elements and aspirations: American lore culled from magazines and his father's memories, missionary influences, incomplete and hence eccentric schooling and British colonial attitudes. Arabic was forbidden at home, except when speaking to servants; even the waiters at Groppis, the fashionable Cairo cafe, were addressed in bad French.

According to Said, his un-Arab Christian name induced a split in his adolescent sense of identity, between 'Edward', his outer self, and the 'loose, irresponsible, fantasy-ridden metamorphoses of my private inner life'. Bright but rebellious, he described himself as having been a leading troublemaker at Cairo's Victoria College, the British-style public school whose snooty captain, Michael Shalhoub, would later achieve celebrity as film star Omar Sharif.

Sent at his father's insistence to Mount Hermon, a private school in Massachusetts, he blossomed academically, but lacked the right attitude to be acknowledged as an outstanding student. He responded positively to the American approach to essay-writing, which he found more imaginative and stimulating than the buttoned-up British approach in Cairo.

The contrast between his burgeoning academic distinction and the absence of formal recognition clearly marked him deeply. He would claim that it was this experience, as much as the work of his more widely acknowledged intellectual mentors, including R. P. Blackmur, Antonio Gramsci, Theodor Adorno, Raymond Williams and Michel Foucault, that influenced his anti-authoritarian outlook.

Said's engagement with Palestine drew on deep emotional roots, particularly his affection for his Aunt Nabiha, his father's sister, who, after 1948, devoted her life to working with Palestinian refugees in Cairo, though she never discussed the political aspects of the dispute in Said's presence. Until his 30s, Edward was too preoccupied with his studies, progressing smoothly through Princeton University and Harvard graduate school, developing his critical methodologies and indulging his passion for music, especially the piano, at which he achieved an almost professional level of competence, to take much interest in the politics of his homeland.

It was the trauma of the Arab defeat in 1967, which unleashed a second wave of refugees (many of them already refugees from the 1948 exodus), that shocked him out of what he would come to see as his earlier complacency, and reconnecting him with his former self.

Said's writings on English literature, such as *Culture and Imperialism* (1993), and Western classical music drew heavily on his sense of being an outsider. Like Joseph Conrad, the subject of his Ph.D. thesis and first published book, he retained an 'extraordinarily persistent residual sense of his own exilic marginality', which enabled him to deploy a kind of double-vision in his readings of the English novel, discerning the invisible colonial plantations that guarantee the domestic tranquillity of Mansfield Park, or finding in Conrad's self-consciously circular narrative forms the sense of the potentiality of the challenges to Western hegemony that would erupt during the post-colonial era.

Where African writers such as Chinhua Achebe dismissed Conrad as a racist, suggesting that, whatever his gifts as a writer, his political attitudes must make him despicable to any African, Said saw such reasoning as amounting to spiritual, intellectual and aesthetic amputation. Contrary to the assumption sometimes made about him, he did not consider that the hidden political agendas and attitudes of cultural supremacy, which he regarded as informing the canons of Western culture from Dante to Flaubert, necessarily diminished their artistic integrity or cultural power.

His achievement may have been to enhance artistic comprehension by drawing attention to unstated political dimensions in the knowledge that art must always escape enlistment for partisan ends. In a brilliant essay on 'Die Meistersinger' that grapples with Wagner's anti-Semitism, he quoted, with approval, Pierre Boulez's remark that 'Wagner's music, by its very existence, refuses to bear the ideological message that it is intended to convey'.

A similar statement could be made about Said's work as a critic. The anti-colonial perspective that animates his work does not result in ideological consistency. Rather, it challenges conventional assumptions about art, music and literature, opening up new avenues of inquiry and questioning the criteria by which knowledge is organised and husbanded. Like his hero, Theodor Adorno, Said was 'the quintessential intellectual, hating all systems, whether on our side or theirs, with equal distaste'.

Versatile and subtle, he was better at elucidating distinctions than formulating systems. A Christian humanist with a healthy respect for Islam, he was a member of the academic elite; yet he inveighed against academic professionalism, venturing into territories well outside his area of speciality, insisting always that the true intellectual's role must be that of the amateur, because it is only the amateur who is moved neither by the rewards nor the requirements of a career, and who is therefore capable of a disinterested engagement with ideas and values.

The unusual complexity of his background – privileged yet marginal, wealthy yet powerless – allowed him to empathise with dispossessed people, especially the victims of Zionism and its Western supporters, while enjoying in the fullest measure the cultural riches of New York, a city that rang louder than any other with Jewish achievement and success.

In his final years, Said's health grew ever more fragile and, while passionately concerned with the unfolding Palestinian disaster in the wake of 9/11 and the Anglo-American invasion of Iraq, he took a conscious decision to withdraw from political controversy and channel his energies into music. The West-Eastern Divan Orchestra he founded with the Israeli citizen Daniel Barenboim in 1999 grew out of the friendship he forged with the musician, who shares his belief that art – and, in particular, the music of Wagner – transcends political ideology. With Said's assistance, Barenboim gave master classes for Palestinian students in the occupied West Bank, which infuriated the Israeli right.

The orchestra received a tumultuous reception at the BBC Proms last month. It may prove a fitting legacy for an intellectual whose work illuminated our crisis-ridden world by embracing its contradictions and celebrating its complexities.

Published in *The Guardian*, 26 September 2003.

28

Rupees for Relief

Walking above the village of Mehrauli, on Delhi's southern perimeter, we pass a woman with a half-empty bottle of water – one of several we have already met since daybreak. It's her cleaning bottle. Dressed immaculately in a brightly coloured sari, she emerges from behind a prickly bush on a tract of waste ground. If she were a man, we might not have merited such discretion. India is about the only country in the world where you actually see human adults defecating. When travelling by road or rail you can be struck by the image of men squatting openly, impervious to the public gaze. The UN estimates that 638 million people – or 55 per cent of the Indian population – still defecate out of doors. The practice is clearly born of necessity in a crowded country where the development of public amenities has conspicuously failed to keep pace with economic and demographic growth.

Conspicuous defecation, however, is restricted to males. Female modesty – enjoined by Hinduism, Islam and Sikhism alongside age-old patriarchal codes – dictates that women may relieve themselves only after dark, or in the most secluded reaches of the forest, thus exposing them to violence or even snake bites. Women of the poorest classes notoriously suffer from a range of urinary and bowel disorders born of taboos about pollution and other social constraints applied to the most basic and banal of bodily functions.

My companion and I are looking for the walls of Lal Kot – one of the oldest of Delhi's numerous cities, built by the Rajputs in the mid-eleventh century, before the first Muslim invasion. The three-kilometre-long walls enclose a space that has been largely abandoned to jungle. The cladding of irregular quartzite blocks was cut so accurately that no mortar was needed to hold them together. Set on a high ridge overlooking the present-day city, Lal Kot is a magnificent outpost of a forgotten civilisation – a worthy precursor to the great Delhi sultanate that flourished during the centuries of Islamic rule, as well as to its grandiose successor, New Delhi, designed by Edwin Lutyens and Herbert Baker and completed in 1929, barely two decades before Britain was forced to abandon its Indian empire.

Lal Kot is far from the tourist trail. To reach it you have to cross a large rubbish dump, and negotiate the odoriferous detritus – what used to be known as night soil – left by Mehrauli's less-favoured human residents. They sleep rough in old tombs or flimsy, home-made shacks erected near the open sewers that intersect the area's magnificent architectural monuments. In the absence of municipal services, refuse disposal is performed by long-haired pigs, which eat up every kind of organic matter, including human and canine waste. (As Moses and Muhammad taught their followers, ham and bacon are best avoided in southern latitudes.)

The lack of sanitation is emblematic of India's failure as an emerging economic giant to include the majority of its population in its achievements. India is now home to the fourth-largest number of dollar billionaires. According to Tim Sebastian, the former BBC journalist who chairs a forum in Doha, Qatar, for debate about social and political issues in the Middle East, some 60 million people – who make up the world's most populous and most powerful middle class – now enjoy living standards higher than those in Britain and France. Yet the vast majority are excluded from India's version of the American dream. As a former government minister, Mani Shankar Ayar, told Sebastian:

> We have a tiny elite that is obsessed with itself. If democracy doesn't deliver for the rest – we could be heading for violence. We're seeing a failure to bring 900 million people inside the system of entitlements. Without entitlements, you pick up the gun.

A third of the country's districts are now facing rural insurgencies spearheaded by the Maoist Naxalites. Is it not just a matter of time before violence spreads to major conurbations such as Delhi, home to 20 million people, many of them living on less than a dollar a day?

A visit to one of Delhi's poorest quarters provides a glimmer of hope. The Nizamuddin district takes its name from the shrine of a holy man – Shaikh Nizamuddin Auliya (1238–1325) – renowned for his religious inclusiveness, his commitment to the poor, his disdain for the rulers, and a love for music and dance that set him apart from his more austere Muslim contemporaries. The shrine attracts visitors from all over the Muslim world, as well as non-Muslim devotees. It typifies the spiritual syncretism one finds in India, where the tombs of holy persons attract followers from all religions. Until recently, this run-down area groaned with the weight of rural migrants and pilgrims hoping to benefit spiritually from the Shaikh's baraka (blessedness), or materially by taking odd jobs serving other pilgrims.

With no serviceable toilets available for pilgrims, the ground beneath the pillars of the overhead metro railway that is now under construction (causing a huge disruption to Delhi's burgeoning traffic) has become an open latrine, a magnet for flies and disease. Now the Aga Khan Foundation, in partnership with other NGOs and agencies, is rehabilitating the area in a major initiative with the municipal corporation of Delhi. Measures include the organised collection of refuse, the provision of public toilets managed by the community, where users are charged a small fee to cover cleaning and supervision, and the re-housing of squatters who had constructed precarious additions to the fourteenth-century *baoli*, or stepwell – the water is reached by descending flights of steps – which is now being dredged and reconstituted using the latest radar technology.

The local government school in Nizamuddin has received a comprehensive makeover funded by the Aga Khan Foundation in collaboration with one of India's oldest charities, the Sir Ratan Tata Trust. In addition to bright new classrooms, well designed for children, a vital outcome of the project, the headmaster suggests, is the renovated toilet block, with separate cubicles for girls and boys.

In Delhi – as in rural Gujarat, where similar conditions prevail – school drop-out rates have been highest among girls. Purely cultural factors – such as the demands of mothers for domestic help – are partly responsible. But teachers and aid workers see the lack of toilets as the primary reason girls have not been attending school, since there is no private place where they can relieve themselves. A programme for building school toilets in Gujarat that I looked at several years ago has yielded not just improvements in family health and hygiene, but also a marked increase in female school attendance. Fifteen of the girls who took part in the programme – whereby the children themselves cleaned the toilets – were going on to higher education.

Since the introduction of the new toilets in Nizamuddin, female drop-out rates have declined dramatically: girls now make up 55 per cent of the pupils. Living in London, one takes the humble lavatory for granted. A fortnight in Delhi reveals its potential for kick-starting a social revolution.

Index